T0324087

THE THEOLOGY OF LIBERALISM

The Theology of Liberalism

Political Philosophy and the Justice of God

ERIC NELSON

THE BELKNAP PRESS OF HARVARD UNIVERSITY PRESS
Cambridge, Massachusetts & London, England
2019

Second printing

Library of Congress Cataloging-in-Publication Data
Names: Nelson, Eric, 1977– author.
Title: The theology of liberalism : political philosophy and the justice of
   God / Eric Nelson.
Description: Cambridge, Massachusetts : The Belknap Press of Harvard
   University Press, 2019. | Includes bibliographical references and index.
Identifiers: LCCN 2019012524 | ISBN 9780674240940 (hardcover : alk.
   paper)
Subjects: LCSH: Liberalism—Religious aspects.—Christianity. | Liberalism. |
   Religion and politics. | Pelagianism.
Classification: LCC BR1615 .N45 2019 | DDC 261.7—dc23 LC record
   available at https://lccn.loc.gov/2019012524

For Andrew Stern, in friendship

Contents

Preface

In Act III of *King Lear,* the wretched king finds himself marooned on the heath, confronting "the tyranny of the open night." His loyal subject Kent entreats him to seek shelter from the storm, but Lear resists. Instead, he confronts the tempest and allows the experience of his own vulnerability to excite a new kind of empathy for the least fortunate:

> Poor naked wretches, whereso'er you are,
> That bide the pelting of this pitiless storm,
> How shall your houseless heads and unfed sides,
> Your loop'd and window'd raggedness, defend you
> From seasons such as these? O, I have ta'en
> Too little care of this![1]

This moment of recognition and self-reproach then provokes an extraordinary exclamation:

> Take physic, pomp,
> Expose thyself to feel what wretches feel,

That thou mayst shake the superflux to them
And show the heavens more just.[2]

The first three lines of the passage are relatively straightforward. Lear is bidding himself, apostrophized as "pomp," to undergo a kind of therapy. If he
subjects himself to the living conditions experienced by the most wretched,
he will be inspired (or so he thinks) to "shake the superflux to them"—to
divest himself of his unnecessary wealth and assign it instead to those in
need. The last line of Lear's outburst, however, is striking and unexpected.
By shaking the superflux to these wretches, he insists that he will "show the
heavens more just."

It is a claim worth dwelling on. Lear is suggesting that the inequality of
fortunes enjoyed by human beings—the chasm that separates "pomp" from
"wretches"—impeaches the justice of God. The fact that some have super-
fluities and luxuries while others must endure "houseless heads" and "unfed
sides" strikes him suddenly as incompatible with the hypothesis that a just
God could have elected to create the world in which these inequalities obtain. He feels that he must rectify this injustice by correcting the initial,
faulty distribution, and supposes that by doing so he will somehow save the
honor of heaven.

This book is about the long shadow cast by Lear's intuition over contemporary political philosophy. For the past fifty years or so, liberal political theorists in the Anglophone world have taken it as axiomatic that the
unequal distribution of advantage among human beings—not merely of
social position, but also of natural endowments—is, in John Rawls's famous phrase, "arbitrary from a moral point of view," or inconsistent with
the principles of justice or fairness. Not only is the mere fact of the unequal
distribution unjust or unfair, they have claimed, but its injustice or unfairness must be seen to diminish our degree of moral responsibility for the
actions we take. Each individual's allotment of natural and social advantage, on this account, determines in important ways the choices that he or
she will make and therefore renders traditional notions of merit or desert
highly suspect. For some of these theorists, indeed, the way in which we
play the cards we are dealt is itself simply a *function* of those cards, and inequalities deriving from our choices and effort are taken to be as morally
arbitrary as those attributable to our talents and aptitudes. Contemporary
liberals disagree with Lear only insofar as they tend to believe that the

distribution of goods among human beings is incompatible with the justice
of a God who doesn't exist.

My central claim in what follows will be that these liberal political philosophers have been unwittingly taking up positions in the theodicy
debate—that is, the debate over whether the justice of God is impeached by
the nature of the created world. Moreover, their approach to the set of questions raised by this debate represents the sharpest possible break with the
earlier liberal tradition. Those we anachronistically regard as liberal or pro-
toliberal philosophers in the early-modern period arrived at their political
commitments precisely because they rejected the notion of moral arbitrariness. Their animating conviction was instead the theological position
known as Pelagianism, which inferred the possibility of human freedom
and merit from the justice of God. The first two chapters of the book offer
a reconstruction of this earlier "liberal" position, while the third demonstrates that Rawls's approach to political philosophy derived from his self-
conscious repudiation of the Pelagian theological tradition. The remaining
chapters explore the ways in which the theodicy debate, rightly understood,
exposes deep incoherencies in the various strands of liberal political philosophy that have emerged in Rawls's wake. I argue that all of these fail in
different ways to offer a plausible grounding for their egalitarian commitments. In conclusion, I propose a different way forward for liberal political
philosophy.

My project is somewhat unusual, in that it attempts to bridge two customary intellectual divides. The first is that between those who write the
history of political thought and those who practice what is now called normative political theory. Indeed, the whole of this book reflects a deep dis-
satisfaction with that division of labor. It is of course the case that historical
scholarship and philosophical argument require different aptitudes and
forms of training, and no one is likely to be equally proficient in both. I
certainly am not. But the costs of the mutual outsourcing engaged in by
these two fields of study have been unacceptably high. Put simply: getting
the history right will often enable us to do better philosophy. And what follows represents my attempt to argue that the phenomenon of contemporary
liberalism offers us a case in point. Once we see that early-modern "liberalism" simply was Pelagianism, we will be in a better position to understand the nature and implications of the Rawlsian challenge; and once we
appreciate the degree to which contemporary liberals are implicitly taking

up positions in the theodicy debate, we can use philosophical insights gained from the latter to expose errors and faulty assumptions made by the former. Liberalism, I believe, took a fateful wrong turn in the 1970s. If we have failed to register this fact, it is because we have been unable to identify the course it was initially on.

The second divide with which this book implicitly takes issue is the long-standing one between political theory and theology. Much of my previous work has aimed to challenge standard accounts of secularization in early-modern political thought, and this project is continuous with those earlier efforts to some degree.[3] But here I wish to go further. My claim in this context is not simply that religious claims and premises played a central role in earlier political discourses, but rather that even to distinguish sharply between theology and political philosophy in most of Western intellectual history is to commit anachronism. Given the metaethical assumptions that most premodern theorists shared, the boundaries between these two disciplines were so porous as to be effectively nonexistent. And even in today's secular age, it turns out to be surprisingly difficult to do one without simultaneously doing the other. The late Patrick Riley once wrote to me that "theology is political philosophy raised to a higher power." I regard this as at once the cleverest and most profound statement I have ever read about the subjects that I study. By the end of this book, I hope you will agree.

THE THEOLOGY OF LIBERALISM

CHAPTER ONE

Pelagian Origins

> Nothing impossible has been commanded by the God of justice and majesty.
>
> —Pelagius, *Letter to Demetrias*[1]

THERE IS NO SUCH THING AS early-modern liberalism. The concept is anachronistic for the obvious reason that "liberalism" is a nineteenth-century term, coined to denote a specific political program in post-Revolutionary France. But some anachronisms are indispensable, and this, I believe, is one of them. We who are heirs to the liberal tradition in modern political and moral philosophy have urgent reasons to understand the character of our inheritance, and, accordingly, to identify its pedigree. The search for the origins of what, in the nineteenth century, became distinctively liberal ideas leads ineluctably back to the seventeenth and eighteenth centuries—to a series of theorists who did not regard themselves as "liberals," but who jointly developed an intellectual program that would come to define the liberal persuasion in the modern Atlantic world. In what follows, I ask: what essentially was that intellectual program? And I want to propose an answer to this question. Liberalism, or the cluster of commitments defended by those we tend to identify as "protoliberals"—from Milton and Locke to Rousseau and Kant—was, at bottom, the theological position known as Pelagianism. Taking this claim seriously can, I hope, give us a clearer understanding of the deep structure of liberal political ideas, as well as a new appreciation of what is so striking and problematic about what has become of Anglophone liberal political philosophy in the last five decades or so.

The Pelagian controversy, from its beginnings in the fourth century, can best be seen as the product of two great and enduring dialectics. The first of these is the dilemma most famously posed in Plato's *Euthyphro*: are deeds holy because the gods love them, or do the gods love them because they are holy?[2] Put more abstractly, are moral principles discovered, or are they made? Do they exist necessarily and objectively, as Plato insisted, or must they be seen as the product of some agent's will—either a god's or our own? This question posed a dilemma because both answers to it seemed to undermine traditional conceptions of the divinity. If moral principles exist separate and apart from God's will, then they might seem to vitiate his omnipotence and threaten to render him superfluous, at least in the realm of morality. The laws of nature would then be just what they are, as Grotius famously insisted, even if there were no God.[3] On the other hand, if we take the voluntarist path and define goodness or rightness as whatever God arbitrarily wills, then God begins to look like a tyrant whose commands are simply to be obeyed because we wish to avoid punishment. We can no longer offer as an independent reason for following God's laws that they are good or just, for goodness and justice are now defined as whatever God's laws happen to tell us to do. To ask "but are the laws *themselves* good or just?" is, on this view, to speak nonsense.

Most early-modern philosophers found the voluntarist answer to the *Euthyphro* dilemma unacceptable, and so embraced the Platonic, rationalist answer. But rationalism immediately yielded a dilemma of its own. If justice is a value separate and apart from God's will, and if God is omnipotent and perfectly good, it follows that his every act and choice should be consistent with the principle of justice.[4] Yet the world in which we live seems to contain a great deal of evil and undeserved suffering—and Christian doctrine insists that a large proportion of the human race will be damned to an eternity of punishment. How can these facts be reconciled with God's justice? It was Leibniz in 1710 who coined the term "theodicy" to describe this problem, but it had by then been exercising Christian theologians for fifteen centuries.

The dilemma goes as follows. If we wish to acquit God of the charge of injustice, the most natural strategy is to insist upon the reality of human freedom. If it is always in our power to choose not to sin, then God can be said to act justly when he punishes our sins. But, as Leibniz observed, God's *punitive* justice is only one of two branches of the theodicy problem.[5] If we are free, then surely a sinner "may be deemed guilty and open to punishment" in a future life by a just God. But we would still need to account for the evils and suffering in this world, which appear "contrary to the goodness, the holiness and the justice of God, since God co-operates in evil as well physical as moral."[6] How is all of this suffering compatible with the hypothesis that a perfectly good and just God elected to create the world? Here again, freedom promised to supply an answer. If the human capacity for morality—that is, our ability freely to choose the right—is transcendently good and valuable, and if the existence of creatures who possess this capacity requires a set of physical realities that jointly produce suffering as a necessary by-product, then God's justice in creation can likewise be vindicated.

This set of views is what I understand by Pelagianism, named for the fourth-century British ascetic who first defended something like it.[7] A Pelagian, in short, is a rationalist who insists on the metaphysical freedom of human beings in order to address the theodicy problem. But this Pelagian insistence on human freedom seemed to pose grave dangers to orthodox Christian doctrine. If human beings are fully able to choose not to sin, and thereby to merit God's favor, then why did Jesus have to come to earth to be crucified? Why the Incarnation and the Atonement? As Augustine canonically complained, to argue that man "could have become just by the law of nature and free will . . . amounts to rendering the cross of Christ void."[8] Those exercised by the theodicy problem may believe they are "serving the cause of God by defending nature," but, Augustine counters, "in declaring this nature to be sound" they reject "the mercy of the physician. . . . We should not so praise the creator that we are compelled to say, or rather [are] convicted of saying, that there is no need for the savior."[9]

To defend the Christian mystery, Augustine was therefore driven to formulate his mature doctrine of original sin, according to which human nature is depraved and incapable of meriting election by obeying the law. We depend utterly on God's grace, which comes irresistibly to those he has predestined for salvation by means of faith in the Atonement: "This and nothing else is the predestination of the saints, namely, the foreknowledge and the preparation of God's favors, by which those who are delivered are most certainly delivered."[10] If we ask "why God delivers this person rather than that one," the response is simply, "How incomprehensible are his judgments, and how unsearchable his ways."[11] Yet, while this Augustinian rejoinder to Pelagius may have promised to shore up Christian orthodoxy, it seemed to its critics to aggravate the initial theodicy problem quite badly. For how can God justly punish us for our sins if we *cannot but sin*—if not sinning is simply beyond our power? To reply that our incapacity, or unfreedom, is *itself* a just punishment for Adam's sin appears to make matters even worse. Why should we have been so momentously punished by a just God for someone else's sin? Surely such caprice would be the act rather of a tyrant.[12]

This, then, is the theodicy dialectic. The Pelagian defense of the transcendent value of human freedom promised to vindicate God's justice, but only at the expense of Christian orthodoxy. Pelagians would deny the doctrine of original sin and attribute human evil, not to our depraved nature, but rather to the corrosive force of social convention (Rousseau's second *Discourse* is, in this sense, the ultimate Pelagian text). They would likewise be attracted to a series of other heresies, including anti-Trinitarianism, Arianism, Socinianism, and mortalism (with its accompanying rejection of the doctrine of hell). The Augustinian rejoinder, conversely, seemed to rescue the Atonement, the Trinity, and the doctrine of hell at the expense of theodicy. There were no easy choices. Early-modern philosophers and theologians had to decide which horn of the dilemma was less painful to sit on.

At this stage it is worth pausing to identify an interpretive difficulty. "Pelagian" was a term of abuse in the seventeenth and eighteenth centuries, much like "atheist," "Erastian," and "democrat." Virtually no one used these terms to identify him or herself. And yet there undoubtedly were early-modern Pelagians, just as there were atheists, Erastians, and even a democrat or two. The challenge for historians is therefore as daunting as it is inescapable: we need to be able to identify genuinely Pelagian views where they are not advertised, but we must be careful to avoid attributing such views, as early-modern Calvinists incessantly did, to relatively orthodox Christians with whom they simply disagreed. In general, I reserve the label "Pelagian" for those who either deny the doctrine of original sin outright, or accept it in principle while denying that it brought about any effective change in the ability of human beings to avoid sin. We do no violence to the thought of these individuals, I claim, by placing them in a Pelagian theological tradition.

I

My first task is to demonstrate that those we identify in retrospect as "protoliberals" arrived at their political commitments because they all, to varying degrees, took the Pelagian side of the theodicy debate. Liberalism, in other words, began life as a theodicy. It is clear, first of all, that each of these theorists unambiguously endorsed the Platonist or rationalist answer to the *Euthyphro* dilemma. That is, they all believed that moral principles have objective, eternal validity and ought to govern the conduct of all rational beings, including God. They were all therefore deeply exercised by the theodicy problem. This, I take it, is obviously true of Milton, whose masterwork aimed entirely "to justify the ways of God to men" and whose God is constrained by the requirements of justice to demand satisfaction for Adam's sin ("Die he or justice must; unless for him / Some other able, and as willing, pay / The rigid satisfaction, death for death").[13] But it is equally true of the other figures I mentioned at the outset. Locke clearly insists in *The Reasonableness of Christianity* that Christian doctrine must be consistent with the free-standing "Justice and Goodness of God" and the "Eternal Law of Right."[14] This law, he explains, "is Holy, Just, and Good; Of which no one Precept or Rule is abrogated or repealed; nor indeed can be; whilst God is an Holy, Just, and Righteous God, and Man a Rational Creature. The Duties of that Law, arising from the Constitution of his very Nature, are of Eternal Obligation; nor can it be taken away or dispensed with, without changing the Nature of Things, overturning the measures of Right and Wrong, and thereby introducing and authorizing Irregularity, Confusion, and Disorder in the World."[15]

Leibniz—who tried hard to hold the line against Pelagianism, but proved nonetheless to be a crucial conduit for Pelagian ideas—was, if anything, even more emphatic on this point. He posed the *Euthyphro* question with great clarity in his 1702 *Meditation on the Common Concept of Justice:* "It is agreed that whatever God wills is good and just. But there remains the question whether it is good and just because God wills it or whether God wills it because it is good and just: in other words, whether justice and goodness are arbitrary or whether they belong to the necessary and eternal truths about the nature of things, as do numbers and proportions."[16] "The former opinion," he explains, "has been followed by some philosophers and by Roman and Reformed theologians," but is in fact completely unacceptable. Such a view "would destroy the justice of God. For why praise him because he acts according to justice, if the notion of justice, in his case, adds nothing to that of action? And to say *stat pro ratione voluntas*, my will takes the place of reason, is properly the motto of a tyrant."[17] Leibniz adds in the *Theodicy* itself that "it would be as if the most wicked spirit, the Prince of evil genii, the evil principle of the Manichaeans, were the sole master of the universe. . . . What means would there be of distinguishing the true God from the false God of Zoroaster if all things depended upon the caprice of an arbitrary power and there were neither rule nor consideration for anything whatever?"[18] One must hold instead with Plato that "goodness and justice have grounds independent of will and of force."[19]

Rousseau straightforwardly defended this aspect of Leibniz's system in his reply to Voltaire after the Lisbon earthquake of 1755: "If God exists, he is perfect; if he is perfect, he is wise, powerful, and just."[20] "If the puzzle of the origin of evil forced you to diminish one of God's perfections," Rousseau challenges his opponent, "why would you want to justify his power at the expense of his goodness? If one has to choose between two errors, I prefer the first."[21] Kant, as Michael Rosen has shown, likewise endorsed the Platonic / rationalist answer to the *Euthyphro* question so many times in his oeuvre that one could fill a good-sized book by simply quoting the various passages.[22] But let this statement from his *Lectures on the Philosophical Doctrine of Religion* stand in for many:

> But *moral theology* is something wholly different from *theological morality,* namely, a morality in which the concept of obligation presupposes the concept of God. Such a theological morality has no principle, or if it does have one, this is nothing but the fact that the will of God has been revealed or discovered. Morality, however, must not be grounded on theology, but must have itself the principle which is to be the ground of our good conduct. Afterward it can be combined with theology, and then our morality will obtain more incentives and a morally moving power. In theological morality the concept of God must determine our duties; but this is just the opposite; for here one pictures in one's concept of God all sorts of terrible and frightening attributes. Now of course this can generate fear in us and hence move us to follow moral laws from coercion or so as to avoid punishment, which,

however, does not provide any interest in the object. For we no longer see how abominable our actions are, but abstain from them only from fear of punishment. Natural morality must be so constituted that it can be thought independently of any concept of God, and obtain zealous reverence from us solely on account of its own inner dignity and excellence.[23]

"The cognition of God," Kant adds later in the text, "must therefore complete morality, but it must not first determine whether something is morally good or a duty for me! This I must judge from the nature of things in accordance with possible systems of ends; and I must be just as certain of it as I am that a triangle has three angles."[24] This is pure Platonism.

For each of these theorists, then, the rationalist question of God's justice was meaningful and urgent. They were therefore required to seek a theodicy, and they agreed wholeheartedly on where it was to be found: human freedom alone could vindicate God's justice, both punitive and creative. In relation to punishment, the case was quite clear. Milton's God declares in *Paradise Lost* that man has only himself to blame for his sins: "ingrate, he had of me / All he could have; I made him just and right, / Sufficient to have stood, though free to fall."[25] In the *De doctrina christiana,* Milton makes his rationale for this claim explicit: "if, because of God's decree, man could not help but fall . . . then God's restoration of fallen man was a matter of justice not grace."[26] That is, if we were not created free and "sufficient to have stood," then God would have owed us election as a matter of justice, despite Adam's sin, since it is unjust per se to punish an agent who, by nature, could not have avoided committing the sin in question. Milton's own understanding of the fall is more Arminian than that of his later disciples, insofar as he accepts that Adam's sin did have the effect of enslaving the will of his descendants—or at least would have done, had God not immediately elected to "renew" man's "lapsed powers, though forfeit," so that "Upheld by me, yet once more he shall stand / On even ground against his mortal foe."[27] But the end result is essentially the same: no man is ever punished by God for a sin that he did not freely choose to commit, and which he could not perfectly well have avoided.

Locke, for his part, went a good deal further. He opens *The Reasonableness of Christianity* by rejecting out of hand the view of "some Men" who "would have all *Adam*'s Posterity doomed to Eternal Infinite Punishment, for the Transgression of *Adam,* whom Millions had never heard of, and no one had authorized to transact for him, or be his Representative."[28] Such a view, Locke insists is "little consistent with the Justice or Goodness of the Great and Infinite God." Human beings, on his account, experienced death as a result of the Fall, but their nature was in no way altered or depraved.[29] They remained free to live in "sincere Obedience to the Law of Christ."[30] True, no human being can keep this law perfectly, "void of slips and falls," but those who obey it "to the utmost of their power" will be justified through their faith in Jesus as the Messiah.[31] "Though he come short of Perfect Obedience to the Law of Works," God is willing to "Justifie or make Just those who by their Works are not so: Which he doth by counting their Faith for Righteousness, *i.e.* for a compleat performance of the Law."[32] This act of forbearance on God's part is not, however, an act of grace, but a requirement of natural law:

> The Law is the eternal, immutable Standard of Right. And a part of that Law is, that a man should forgive, not only his Children, but his Enemies, upon their Repentance, asking Pardon, and Amendment. And therefore he could not doubt that the Author of this Law, and God of Patience and Consolation, who is rich in Mercy, would forgive his frail Off-spring, if they acknowledged their Faults, disapproved the Iniquity of their Transgressions, beg'd his Pardon, and resolved in earnest for the future to conform their Actions to this Rule, which they owned to be Just and Right. This way of Reconciliation, this hope of Atonement, the Light of Nature revealed to them. And the Revelation of the Gospel having said nothing to the contrary, leaves them to stand and fall to their own Father and Master, whose Goodness and Mercy is over all his Works.[33]

Leibniz took much the same view, despite his efforts to distance himself from the Pelagian heresy.[34] "Freedom is deemed necessary," he announces in the *Theodicy,* "in order that man may be deemed guilty and open to punishment."[35] The word "deemed" *(jugée)* is worth dwelling upon in this context. By using it, Leibniz makes explicit a vitally important point of logic that had been only implicit in Milton's presentation of the Pelagian case, and which Locke had only endorsed in private correspondence: the metaphysical freedom of human beings is not something that can be demonstrated on the basis of evidence, but is rather an *inference* from God's justice.[36] We ask, in essence: "what would have to be true of our nature in order for it to be just for God to punish us when we sin?" And we conclude, in answer to this question, that we must be free. As Leibniz puts it at the end of the text (paraphrasing Lorenzo Valla), because God is just, "it *follows* [*il s'ensuit*] that his decrees and his operation do not destroy our freedom."[37] The argument goes like this: (1) God exists, (2) He is perfectly just, (3) He punishes human beings for their sins, (4) it is unjust to punish an agent for sins that are not freely committed, therefore (5) human beings must be free.

Rousseau's Savoyard Vicar follows suit in *Émile,* insisting that "man is at once active and free" and "he acts of his own accord; what he does freely is no part of the system marked out by Providence and it cannot be imputed to Providence. . . . Providence has made him free that he may choose the good and refuse the evil. It has made him capable of this choice if he uses rightly the faculties bestowed upon him."[38] Kant is yet more emphatic. He writes in *Religion within the Boundaries of Mere Reason* that "surely of all the explanations of the spread and propagation of . . . evil through all members and generations of our race, the most inept is that which describes it as descending to us as an inheritance from our first parents; for one can say of moral evil precisely what the poet said of the good: *genus et proavos, et quoae non fecimus ipsi, vix ex nostra puto.*"[39] On the contrary, "in the search for the rational origin of evil actions, every such action must be regarded as though the individual had fallen into it directly from a state of innocence. For whatever his previous deportment may have been, whatever natural causes may have been influencing him, and whether these causes were to be found within him or outside him, his action is yet free and determined by none of these causes; hence it can and must always be judged as an original use of his will."[40] The sinner "should have refrained from that action, whatever his temporal circumstances and entanglements; for through no cause in the world can he cease to be a freely acting being. . . . However evil a man has been up to the very moment of an impending free act (so that evil has actually become custom or second nature) it was not only his duty to have been better [in the past], it is now still his duty to better himself. To do so must be within his power."[41] Again, because man has the duty to better himself, and because God will justly punish him if he fails to do so, it must be "within his power" to better himself. "Ought implies can" is the Pelagian battle cry!

Kant likewise agrees with Leibniz that human freedom is an inference from God's justice and our consciousness of the moral law:

We can quickly be convinced that the concept of the freedom of the power of choice does not precede in us the consciousness of the moral law but is only inferred [*geschlossen werde*] from the determinability of our power of choice through this law as unconditional command. We have only to ask whether we are certainly and immediately conscious of a faculty enabling us to overcome, by firm resolve, every incentive to transgression, however great. . . . Everybody must admit that *he does not.*[42]

Indeed, Kant is clear that we have no epistemic access to evidence of any kind that would demonstrate our freedom.[43] On the contrary, it is a transcendental fact about human reason that it can (and must) be able, in retrospect, to embed any given action in an explanatory causal chain—otherwise the action in question would appear random: "According to the principle of causality we can assign to a being, regarded as having been brought forth, no inner ground for his actions other than that which the producing cause has placed there, by which, then, (and so by an external cause) his every act would be determined, and such a being would therefore not be free."[44] Rather, we infer from the reality of "the legislation which is divine and holy, and therefore concerns free beings only" that humans are "free beings who are determined not through their dependence upon nature by virtue of their creation but through a purely moral necessitation possible according to laws of freedom." Our freedom may not suffice to allow us to follow the law perfectly, but Kant agrees with Locke (and Milton) that God, being loving, will count our best efforts as a "perfected whole," so that "notwithstanding his permanent deficiency, a human being can still expect to be *generally* [*überhaupt*] well-pleasing to God, at whatever point in time his existence be cut short."[45]

So much for the first theodicy problem—that having to do with God's punitive justice. I now want to suggest that freedom was equally important in this tradition of thought as a response to the second theodicy problem: namely, that God seems to have chosen to create a world full of evil and undeserved suffering. The argument here is that morality, or the human ability to choose freely to do the right, is of transcendent value, such that it outweighs the badness of the suffering that, in Rousseau's words, is "inevitable in any world of which man is a part."[46] This transcendent value is described with striking uniformity in the Pelagian language of athletic or epic heroism. Milton's use of such language is, of course, the most famous. He writes in *Areopagitica* that

He that can apprehend and consider vice with all her baits and seeming pleasures, and yet abstain, and yet distinguish, and yet prefer that which is truly

better, he is the true warfaring Christian. I cannot praise a fugitive and clois-
tered virtue, unexercised and unbreathed, that never sallies out and sees her
adversary but slinks out of the race, where that immortal garland is to be
run for, not without dust and heat. Assuredly we bring not innocence into
the world, we bring impurity much rather; that which purifies us is trial, and
trial is by what is contrary. That virtue therefore which is but a youngling in
the contemplation of evil, and knows not the utmost that vice promises to
her followers, and rejects it, is but a blank virtue, not a pure; her whiteness is
but an excremental whiteness. Which was the reason why our sage and serious poet Spenser, whom I dare be known to think a better teacher than
Scotus or Aquinas, describing true temperance under the person of Guion,
brings him in with his palmer through the cave of Mammon, and the bower
of earthly bliss, that he might see and know, and yet abstain.[47]

"The knowledge and survey of vice," Milton insists, "is in this world . . . necessary to the constituting of human virtue."[48] The distinctive excellence of
human beings is our ability to withstand temptation and choose the good.
But this excellence cannot be instantiated in agents who are immune from
temptation or ignorant of its charms. Our moral heroism is one of over-
coming. "We ourselves esteem not of that obedience, or love, or gift, which
is of force: God therefore left [man] free, set before him a provoking object,
ever almost in his eyes; herein consisted his merit, herein the right of his
reward, the praise of his abstinence."[49] Of course, freedom requires the possibility of sin, and along with it a great deal of human error and suffering.
But the bargain is worthwhile: "were I the chooser, a dream of well-doing
should be preferred before many times as much the forcible hindrance of
evil-doing. For God sure esteems the growth and completing of one virtuous
person more than the restraint of ten vicious."[50]

If Milton's words are familiar, these nearly identical ones from Rousseau's
Émile—in which Milton is apostrophized as "divine"[51]—are rather less so:

To complain that God does not prevent us from doing wrong is to complain
because he has made man of so excellent a nature, that he has endowed his
actions with that morality by which they are ennobled, that he has made
virtue man's birthright. Supreme happiness consists in self-content: that we
may gain this self-content we are placed upon this earth and endowed with
freedom, we are tempted by our passions and restrained by conscience. What
more could divine power itself have done on our behalf? Could it have made

our nature a contradiction, and have given the prize of well-doing to one who was incapable of evil? To prevent a man from wickedness, should Providence have restricted him to instinct and made him a fool? Not so, O God of my soul, I will never reproach thee that thou hast created me in thine own image, that I may be free and good and happy like my Maker![52]

Rousseau's Vicar returns to the agonistic language of the "prize of well-doing" later in his remarks. "One might judge from the complaints of impatient men," he observes, "that God owes them the reward before they have deserved it, that he is bound to pay for virtue in advance. Oh! let us first be good and then we shall be happy. Let us not claim the prize before we have won it, nor demand our wages before we have finished our work. 'It is not in the lists that we crown the victors in the sacred games,' says Plutarch, 'it is when they have finished their course.'"[53] To live a human life is, on this view, to find oneself in the "sacred games," competing heroically for a crown of laurels. What has transcendent value is the free conquest of vice; not the reward itself, but the being worthy of it.

Kant agrees wholeheartedly (recall that he was so entranced with *Émile* when he first read it that, for the one and only time in his adult life, he is said to have forgotten to take his daily walk). As he writes in *Religion within the Boundaries,* "that which alone can make a world the object of divine decree and the end of creation is *Humanity* (rational being in general as pertaining to the world) *in its full moral perfection,* from which happiness follows in the will of the Highest Being directly as from its supreme condition."[54] "The combat which every morally well-disposed man must sustain in this life, under the leadership of the good principle, against the attacks of the evil principle, can procure him, however much he exerts himself, no greater advantage than freedom from the sovereignty of evil. To become free, 'to be freed from bondage under the law of sin, to live for righteousness'—this is the highest prize he can win [*der höchste Gewinn, den er erringen kann*]. He continues to be exposed, none the less, to the assaults of the evil principle; and in order to assert his freedom, which is perpetually being attacked, he must ever remain armed for the fray."[55] At this point, Kant raises a concern: "But is there not also perhaps a dizzying illusion of virtue [*einen . . . schwindligen Tugendwahn*], soaring above the bounds of human capacity, which might be reckoned, along with the cringing religious illusion, in the general class of self-deceptions?"[56] Does this heroic image of human self-overcoming not smack, in other words, of an intolerable pride? His answer is unambiguous:

> No! The disposition of virtue occupies itself with something real which of itself is well-pleasing to God and conforms to what is best for the world. True, an illusion of self-sufficiency may attach itself thereto, an illusion of regarding oneself as measuring up to the idea of one's holy duty; but this is merely contingent. To ascribe the highest worth to that disposition is not an illusion, like faith in the devotional exercises of the church, but is a direct contribution which promotes the highest good of the world.[57]

Or again:

> In the purity of this concept of virtue, in the awakening of consciousness to a capacity which otherwise we would never surmise (a capacity of becoming able to master the greatest obstacles within ourselves), in the dignity of humanity which man must respect in his own person and human destiny, toward which he strives, if he is to attain it—in all this there is something which so exalts the soul, and so leads it to the very Deity, who is worthy of adoration only because of His holiness and as Legislator for virtue, that man, even when he is still far from allowing to this concept the power of influencing his maxims, is yet not unwillingly sustained by it.[58]

Kant assigns equal prominence to this grand theme in his *Lectures*. "What incentive, if one may so express it," he asks, "could move God to create a world?"[59] His answer: "The true perfection of the world-whole has to lie in the use *rational creatures* make of their reason and freedom." "Virtue," he announces, "consists precisely in *self-overcoming*."[60] "Among the many creatures, the human being is the only one who has to work for his perfections and for the goodness of his character, producing them from within himself."

> God therefore gave him talents and capacities, but left it up to the human being how he would employ them. He created the human being free, but gave him also animal instincts; he gave the human being senses to be moderated and overcome through the education of his understanding. Thus created, the human being was certainly perfect both in his nature and regarding his predispositions. But regarding their education he was still uncultivated. For this the human being had to have himself to thank, as much for the

cultivation of his talents as for the benevolence of his will. Endowed with
great capacities, but with the application of these capacities left to himself,
such a creature must certainly be of significance. One can expect much of
him; but on the other hand no less is to be feared. He can perhaps raise himself above a whole host of will-less angels, but he may also degrade himself so
that he sinks even below the irrational animals.[61]

Freedom thus allows human beings to achieve a transcendent good above
even that enjoyed by the "will-less angels": the virtuous conquest of instinct.
Kant here is clearly paraphrasing Rousseau's Vicar, who had likewise insisted
that, freed from the temptation to sin, man "would be happy, no doubt, but
his happiness would not attain to the highest point, the pride of virtue, and
the witness of a good conscience within him; he would be but as the angels
are, and no doubt the good man will be more than they."[62] Kant concludes
that it would accordingly "not occur to any human being who is aware of
the powers and impulses in himself toward activity to exchange his state for
this supposed happiness [of slothful ease], even if he had to struggle with all
sorts of discomforts."[63]

For the same reason, Kant observes strikingly, "a novelist always permits
his hero to withdraw from the stage once he has overcome his many difficulties and has finally achieved tranquility. For the novelist is quite conscious
of the fact that he cannot describe happiness as mere enjoyment. Rather it
is labor, difficulty, effort, the prospect of tranquility and the striving toward
the achievement of this idea which is happiness for us and a proof already of
God's benevolence."[64] This is the "strenuous liberty" of Milton's *Samson Agonistes*—a text near and dear to Kant's heart[65]—and it points us to the
pedigree of Kant's famous claim that "morality, and humanity insofar as it
is capable of morality, is that which alone has dignity [*Würde*]."[66] "Dignity"
is defined, for Kant, as that which is "raised above all price" and possesses
an "unconditional, incomparable value."[67] This set of things, it turns out,
has only one member: our capacity for morality, the transcendent value of
which outweighs everything that merely has a "price"—including the entire
spectrum of "human inclination and need."[68] Whatever we suffer is therefore
as nothing compared with our glorious autonomy. The discourse of dignity
is, first and foremost, a theodicy.

II

Two vitally important conclusions followed from this set of Pelagian arguments, one in the realm of religion itself and the other having to do with the political context in which religious life must unfold. Both became constitutive of liberalism in the nineteenth century and beyond. The first of these is rational religion, or what Kant called "religion within the boundaries of mere reason." Scholars have usually regarded this phenomenon as a symptom of secularization, provoked in large part by skepticism concerning the authenticity of scriptural revelation. But this view is, I think, mistaken. The turn to a pure religion of reason was instead a Pelagian response to the theodicy problem: the conviction that everything necessary for salvation must be accessible to human reason was yet another inference from God's justice. If the transcendent value of human life (outweighing all of the world's suffering) was to be found in the freely chosen right—and if God was justified in punishing the sins of human beings—then the metaphysical freedom of the human will was necessary, but not sufficient. Human beings must also have been given reasonable access to the content of the law that they were expected to follow. For just as it would be straightforwardly unjust for a human sovereign to punish a subject for violating a law of which he was blamelessly ignorant, so too would it be unjust for God to punish us for sinning if we could not know that we were doing so. Choice requires both a free will and relevant information—what Kant called "publicity." You can't compete for a prize unless you know the rules of the game.

Milton was, for this reason, eager to insist that God had placed within human beings after the Fall "My umpire conscience; whom if they will hear, / Light after light, well used, they shall attain, / And to the end, persisting, safe arrive."[69] But it was Locke who first offered a full exploration of this line of thought. In order to understand his argument, we first have to recognize that by "the reasonableness of Christianity" he emphatically did *not* mean that everything necessary for salvation is accessible to unaided human reason. On the contrary, he argued, *"Natural Religion* in its full extent was no-where, that I know, taken care of by the Force of Natural Reason. It should seem, by the little that has hitherto been done in it, That 'tis too hard a task for unassisted Reason to establish Morality in all its parts upon its true foundations; with a clear and convincing light."[70] Locke's claim is, rather, that everything contained in scriptural revelation can be seen to be consistent with reason *once we have received the former*—much as we can see why an impenetrable mathematical proof works once someone has given us the solution. Locke is extraordinarily eloquent on the subject of our epistemic limitations and the blameless moral ignorance from which human beings can suffer. Moral principles may exist objectively, but our access to them is imperfect. The human race has made progress in moral understanding throughout its history, but precisely for this reason it is unjust to blame past generations for failing to understand what we have come to understand, no matter how obvious a given moral requirement may now appear to us. Locke thus gives us the first extended treatment of a philosophical problem that contemporary theorists have rediscovered under the heading of "moral luck":[71]

> When Truths are once known to us, though by Tradition, we are apt to be favourable to our own Parts; And ascribe to our own Understandings the Discovery of what, in reality, we borrowed from others. Or, at least, finding we can prove what at first we learnt from others, we are forward to conclude it an obvious Truth, which, if we had sought, we could not have missed. Nothing seems hard to our Understandings, that is once known; And because what we see, we see with our own Eyes, we are apt to over-look or forget the help we had from others, who shewed it us, and first made us see it; as if we were not at all beholden to them for those truths, which they opened the way and led us into. . . . Thus the whole stock of Human Knowledge is claimed by every one, as his private Possession, as soon as he (profiting by others Discoveries) has got it into his own mind; And so it is; But not properly by his own single industry, nor of his own Acquisition. He studies, 'tis true, and takes pains to make a progress in what others have delivered; But their pains were of another sort, who first brought those Truths to light, which he afterwards derives from them. He that Travels the Roads now, applauds his own strength and legs, that have carried him so far in such a scantling of time; And ascribes all to his own Vigor, little considering how much he owes to their pains, who cleared the Woods, drained the Bogs, built the Bridges, and made the Ways passable; without which he might have toiled much with little progress. A great many things which we have been bred up in the belief of from our Cradles, (and are Notions grown Familiar, and as it were Natural to us, under the Gospel,) we take for unquestionable obvious Truths, and easily demonstrable; without considering how long we might have been in doubt or ignorance of them, had Revelation been silent.[72]

The Gospels, for Locke, first gave humanity an "unerring Rule" and a "sure Standard" of what God's law (the law of reason) requires:[73] "such a Body of *Ethicks,* proved to be the Law of Nature, from principles of Reason, and reaching all the Duties of Life; I think no body will say the World had before our Saviour's time."[74] Prior to this revelation, we could only access the natural law partially and inexactly by means of "the same spark of the Divine Nature and Knowledge in Man, which making him a Man, shewed him the Law he was under as a Man."[75] If God is just, on Locke's account, it follows that obedience to this more limited, naturally accessible moral law must be sufficient for salvation for all those who have not heard the Gospel—whether they lived before the time of Christ or in parts of the globe to which the good news had not come. If one asks "what shall become of all the rest of Mankind; who having never heard of the Promise or News of a Saviour, not a word of a *Messiah* to be sent, or that was come, have had no thought or belief concerning him?" the answer is straightforward: "God will require of every man, *According to what a man hath, and not according to what he hath not.* He will not expect the Improvement of Ten Talents, where he gave but One; nor require any one should believe a Promise, of which he has never heard. . . . He that made use of this Candle of the Lord, so far as to find what was his Duty, could not miss to find also the way to Reconciliation and Forgiveness, when he had failed of his Duty."[76] Thus we infer from God's justice that a purely rational religion suffices for salvation.

Rousseau, for his part, goes even further, arguing that the moral law *in its entirety*—and with it all that is necessary for salvation—must be accessible to unaided human reason. For only a "God of darkness" would have denied access to the truth about moral obligation to any human being:

Either all religions are good and pleasing to God, or if there is one which he prescribes for men, if they will be punished for despising it, he will have distinguished it by plain and certain signs by which it can be known as the only true religion; these signs are alike in every time and place, equally plain to all men, great or small, learned or unlearned, Europeans, Indians, Africans, savages. If there were but one religion upon earth, and if all beyond its pale were condemned to eternal punishment, and if there were in any corner of the world one single honest man who was not convinced by this evidence, the God of that religion would be the most unjust and cruel of tyrants.[77]

Thus Rousseau's Vicar declares that "in my exposition you find nothing but natural religion; strange that we should need more! How shall I become aware of this need? What guilt can be mine so long as I serve God according to the knowledge he has given to my mind, and the feelings he has put into my heart?"[78] "What purity of morals," he asks, "what dogma useful to man and worthy of its author, can I derive from a positive doctrine which cannot be derived without the aid of this doctrine by the right use of my faculties?"[79]

Kant rather cagily attempted to position himself between Locke and Rousseau on this question. He offers what appears to be a straightforward paraphrase of Locke's argument, but, on closer inspection, it contains a Rousseauian twist. A revealed religion, Kant writes in *Religion within the Boundaries,* can be considered appropriately "natural"

> if it is so constituted that men *could and ought to have* arrived at it [*auf sie . . . hätten kommen können und sollen*] on their own through the mere use of their reason, even though they would not have come to it so early or as extensively as is required [*ob sie zwar nicht so früh, oder in so weiter Ausbreitung, als verlangt wird*], hence a revelation of it at a given time and in a given place might be wise and very advantageous to the human race, for then, once the thereby introduced religion is at hand and has been made publicly known, everyone can henceforth convince himself of its truth by himself and his own reason. In this case the religion is *objectively* a natural religion, though subjectively a revealed one; hence it truly deserves also the former title. For that there once was such a supernatural revelation might subsequently be entirely forgotten without the religion in question losing the least thereby, either in comprehensibility or certainty, or in its power over minds.[80]

The Lockean notion of a "reasonable" religion is recognizably present, but Locke himself had emphatically denied that men who lived before the time of Christ "could and ought to have arrived at" the complete moral system of the Gospels through the use of their rational faculties. Kant plainly sides with Rousseau in this respect, a point that becomes clearer when he writes that the Gospels merely brought "into public currency a doctrine whose authenticity rests upon a record indelibly registered in every soul and which stands in need of no miracle."[81] Historical, revealed religions have a role to play, "but it is essential that, in the use of these historical accounts, we do not make it a tenet of religion that the knowing, believing, and professing of them are themselves means whereby we can render ourselves well-pleasing to God." Such a doctrine, Kant agreed, was inconsistent with God's justice. We must accept that the "moral predisposition in us" is the "foundation and at the same time the interpreter of all religion" (*die Grundlage und zugleich Auslegerin aller Religion*), and that "in the end religion will gradually be freed from all empirical determining grounds and from all statutes which rest on history . . . and thus at last the pure religion of reason will rule over all, 'so that God may be all in all.'"[82]

With this argument in place, we can turn at last to politics. It will come as news to no one that Milton, Locke, Leibniz, Rousseau, and Kant were all deeply committed to religious toleration; my suggestion is that this set of Pelagian views explains why. If we believe that only freely chosen religious observance has salvific value—if, in Milton's words, God has no use for "obedience paid, / When will and reason (reason also is choice) / Useless and vain, of freedom both despoiled / Made passive both, had served necessity, / Not me"[83]—and if it is universal rational religion, rather than a particular revealed faith that saves, we will find it very difficult indeed to justify religious coercion. In such a case, as Locke puts it, "there would be not so much as a pretence left for Compulsion."[84] But the implications of this neo-Pelagian view are in fact far more sweeping. Once the religious life is redefined in Pelagian terms as the cultivation of moral virtue throughout a complete life, then what needs protecting is not simply worship and preaching, but an entire sphere of private action. If what has transcendent value is the freely chosen right, then individuals must be allowed to make choices in every facet of their lives. They must be left alone to join the fray and try to win the garland, so long as their actions deprive no one else of the like opportunity.

Each of our authors had his own distinctive vocabulary for expressing this thought. For Milton, God commits the ordering of our moral lives "without particular law or prescription, wholly to the demeanour of every grown man . . . God uses not [man's actions] to captivate under a perpetual childhood of prescription, but trusts him with the gift of reason to be his own chooser."[85] For Locke, "the way to salvation not being any forced exterior performance, but the voluntary & secret choice of the minde . . . it cannot be supposed that god would make use of any means, which could not reach but would rather cross the attainment of the end."[86] "Even in things of this world over which the magistrate has an authority, he never does, & it would be unjustice if he should, any farther then it concerns the good of the

publique, injoyne men the care of their private civill concernments, or force
them to a prosecution of their owne private interests, but only protects them
from being invaded & injured in them by others, (which is a perfect toleration)."[87] Kant makes the same point by invoking his well-known distinction between the "ethical" and the "political" state:

> In an already existing political commonwealth the political citizens, as such,
> are in an ethical state of nature [*im ethischen Naturzustande*] and are entitled
> to remain therein; for it would be a contradiction *(in adjecto)* for the political
> commonwealth to compel its citizens to enter into an ethical commonwealth,
> since the very concept of the latter involves freedom from coercion. Every
> political commonwealth may indeed wish to be possessed of a sovereignty,
> according to laws of virtue, over the spirits [of its citizens]; for then, when its
> methods of compulsion do not avail (for the human judge cannot penetrate
> into the depths of other men) their dispositions to virtue would bring about
> what was required. But woe to the legislator who wishes to establish through
> force a polity directed to ethical ends! For in so doing he would not merely
> achieve the very opposite of an ethical polity but also undermine his po-
> litical state and make it insecure. The citizen of the political commonwealth
> remains therefore, so far as its legislative function is concerned, completely
> free to enter with his fellow-citizens into an ethical union in addition [to the
> political] or to remain in this kind of state of nature, as he may wish. Only
> so far as an ethical commonwealth must rest on public laws and possess a
> constitution based on these laws are those who freely pledge themselves to
> enter into this ethical state bound, [not indeed] to accept orders from the
> political power as to how they shall or shall not fashion this ethical constitu-
> tion internally, but to agree to limitations, namely, to the condition that this
> constitution shall contain nothing which contradicts the duty of its members
> as citizens of the state.[88]

And so theodicy leads us to build a protective perimeter around each questing
human being. This perimeter we call "rights."

III

The commitments that we now regard as distinctively liberal have been defended on a variety of different grounds in the intervening centuries. For
the line of English utilitarian philosophers that runs from Jeremy Bentham

to Henry Sidgwick, for example, civil liberties and religious toleration were to be endorsed because they promoted the greatest happiness of the greatest number. A later tradition would, rather ironically, justify these same liberal institutions instead on the explicitly Augustinian grounds that human beings are so degraded in their nature that they cannot be trusted to wield coercive power over their fellows without inflicting great suffering. This is what Judith Shklar called the "liberalism of fear."[89] But the Pelagian arguments I have sketched out remained basic to all subsequent attempts to ground liberal commitments in the distinctive value of human autonomy. Or rather, they did until 1971. In that year, John Rawls produced the twentieth century's most significant statement of liberal political philosophy. Yet, unlike all of his predecessors in what we might call the "dignitarian" liberal tradition, his orientation was stridently anti-Pelagian. The young Rawls, as we shall see, first developed the idea of what he called "moral arbitrariness" in order to justify his rejection of the claim that human beings can merit election and earn God's favor. Such a conceit, on his account, was merely the product of pride and "egotism," which denied the fundamental reality of human fallenness and original sin.[90]

Before turning to Rawls and his many followers, however, I need to say a bit more about the early-modern origins of liberal ideas. For the picture I have offered thus far is importantly incomplete. We have seen that broadly Pelagian theological commitments prompted an array of theorists in the seventeenth and eighteenth centuries to insist upon the metaphysical and political freedom of individuals as a necessary condition of their being held to account by a just and benevolent God. But liberal political philosophy, as it emerged in the modern period, involved more than a simple account of the transcendent value of human freedom. It also relied upon a particular theory of the state—one that promised to explain why the existence of coercive political institutions need not compromise our essential autonomy. The Pelagian theological tradition duly provided this further account as well, in the form of a distinctive argument about the character of political representation. It is to that second momentous intervention that we now turn.

CHAPTER TWO

Representation and the Fall

JOHN LOCKE OPENS HIS ESSAY on *The Reasonableness of Christianity* (1695) with a striking claim. Since it is "obvious," he writes, that the Christian "Doctrine of Redemption, and consequently of the Gospel, is founded upon the Supposition of *Adam's* Fall," it follows that, in order to understand "what we are restored to by Jesus Christ, we must first consider what the Scripture shows we lost by *Adam*."[1] The orthodox answer to this question had been supplied by Augustine's doctrine of original sin, according to which all of humanity fell with Adam; our will is in bondage to sin as a result, and it is only God's grace that spares the elect from their just and eternal punishment. But Locke makes clear that he cannot accept this Augustinian doctrine. It is, he insists, "little consistent with the Justice or Goodness of the Great and Infinite God" to suppose that "all *Adam's* Posterity" could have been "doomed to Eternal Infinite Punishment for the transgression of *Adam,* whom Millions had never heard of, and no one had authorized to transact for him, or be his Representative."[2]

Locke thus grounds his momentous rejection of the doctrine of original sin in a claim about the theory of representation. A representative, on this account, is one who is "authorized" by some group of people to "transact" in their name. To ask whether Adam legitimately represented the human race when he fell is therefore simply to ask whether humanity ever authorized Adam to act as their agent. And because the answer to this question is unambiguously negative, Locke concludes that Adam acted solely in his own right and, consequently, that his sin cannot have been attributed by a just God to anyone else—let alone to the entire human race. Locke's terminology in this passage clearly reflects an encounter with the well-known discussion of "Persons, Authors, and things Personated" in Thomas Hobbes's *Leviathan* (1651). A *"Representer,* or *Representative,"* Hobbes tells us, is a person whose "words or actions" are *"Owned* by those whom they represent."[3] In such a case, "the Person is the *Actor;* and he that owneth the words and actions, is the AUTHOR," as a result of which the representative may be said to act "by Authority."[4] If we take this theory seriously, we will conclude that, "when the Actor maketh a Covenant by Authority, he bindeth thereby the Author, no lesse than if he had made it himself; and no lesse subjecteth him to all the consequences of the same."[5] But the converse holds equally well: if the Actor has *not* been authorized to transact in the name of another person, he acts only for himself. "For no man is obliged by a Covenant, whereof he is not Author; nor consequently by a Covenant made against, or beside the Authority he gave."[6]

We have recently been reminded of the highly polemical character of Hobbes's intervention.[7] The political and military contest between King and Parliament in the 1640s had turned substantially on a debate about the proper understanding of representation. Parliamentarian writers argued that a legitimate representative must be a good representation, or image, of those represented. Representation, on this view, is a matter of degree: A is more representative of B the more he resembles, or constitutes a good image of B. Accordingly, this view insisted that an assembly reflecting the complex composition of the "body of the people" could be said to represent them better than could a single monarch—and that such an assembly might represent the entire body of the people even if many citizens did not elect members to it. The theory thus conveniently established two vital propositions: that the King could not compete with Parliament for the title of "representative of the people," and that the House of Commons could be the representative of the whole people, despite the fact that nine-tenths of the English population did not elect members to Parliament. But if the King was not the representative of the people, it followed that the existence and exercise of his various prerogative powers (particularly the "negative voice") would place Englishmen in a state of servile dependence upon an arbitrary and alien will—that is, in the condition of slavery.

Royalists countered this Parliamentarian onslaught by deploying a rival theory of representation, according to which it is authorization, not resemblance (or "representativeness"), that is both necessary and sufficient to establish the legitimacy of a representative. If any authorized agent can be said to speak or act in the name of the people just as well as any other, then plainly a king, no less than a popular assembly, is capable of "representing" his people—from which it follows that the people can be said to be "sovereign" under the rule of a monarch who wields prerogative powers. Representation, on this account, is not a comparative concept, or a matter of degree. It is either wholly present or wholly absent, depending solely on whether the one claiming to act for another has in fact been authorized by that person to do so. Hobbes's discussion of "personation" in chapter 16 of *Leviathan* plainly aimed to systematize and develop this Royalist line of argument.

I wish to suggest that this debate over political representation in the 1640s was deeply intertwined with a theological debate over the Fall. The "signification" or "resemblance" theory of representation adopted by Parliamentarians began life as Calvinist apologetics. It was first formulated to make the case that Adam could justly be regarded as the representative of humanity, despite the fact that humanity had never authorized him to act in their name. He had been appointed by God to act as trustee for the human race, and had then covenanted with God on humanity's behalf. God's appointment of Adam to this office was, in turn, just and equitable, because Adam and his descendants shared an image and nature. Adam was thus an adequate "representation" of his descendants, each of whom was "in" him "virtually" or "interpretively." He was the "sign" and humanity was the "signified." In virtue of their shared image, Adam and humanity likewise possessed shared interests, from which it followed that the former could be expected to act in accordance with the (eventual) will of the latter. The Royalist rejoinder began life instead as a Pelagian response to this Calvinist orthodoxy. Arminian and Laudian theologians developed the authorization theory to explain why Adam could not have represented his descendants, despite their shared image, and, accordingly, why a just God could not have held humanity at large responsible for Adam's sin. At stake in this confrontation were central articles of Christian faith—the Incarnation, the Atonement, and the doctrine of grace—along with the millennial hope of a theodicy.

Indeed, as we shall see, it is not merely that the theological debate over theodicy and original sin gave rise to a set of concepts and arguments that would later be deployed by other theorists in the political context. Rather, the theological and political debates about representation were, to a remarkable degree, two fronts in a single war. The Parliamentarian writers who formulated the "imaging" theory of representation were themselves Calvinists dedicated to the defense of Augustinian orthodoxy against Pelagianism and "Popery," whereas the Royalist polemicists who defended the "authorization" theory were overwhelmingly Laudian and Arminian opponents of Calvinism. When Locke insisted in 1695 that Adam could not have represented the human race, he was aligning himself self-consciously with a Pelagian / Royalist tradition of thought that placed consent and "authorization" at the center of both the civic and religious enterprises.

I

The earliest Christian accounts of the Fall make no use of the concept of representation, for the simple reason that they accept the organic, familial notion of personality that is found in the Hebrew Bible itself. Abraham, on this view, just *is* his family; they are essentially the same person, from which it follows that his descendants can be rewarded for his virtues and punished for his vices.[8] It is this collective concept of personality that underlies the famous claim in the Decalogue that God "visits the iniquities of the fathers upon the children to the third and fourth generations" (Ex. 20:5), and likewise explains why Adam's offspring might be said to have fallen with him. If we assume that Adam and his descendants are the same person, we need not grapple with the question of why the sins of one person (Adam) are visited upon a set of wholly distinct persons (his descendants) who never sinned. When the Epistles assure us that "all sinned" in Adam (Rom. 5:12), they are not speaking metaphorically. Adam, on this account, simply *was* humanity.

This familial, collective understanding of personality was already a subject of controversy in the later Biblical books. It is, for example, clearly the target of Ezekiel's celebrated insistence that each individual should only suffer for his own personal sins: "What do you people mean by quoting this proverb

about the land of Israel: 'The parents eat sour grapes, and the children's teeth
are set on edge'? As surely as I live, declares the Sovereign Lord, you will no
longer quote this proverb in Israel. . . . The one who sins is the one who will
die" (Ez. 18:1–4).[9] But the collective understanding remained powerfully
present among the church fathers. When Augustine turns to the subject of
the Fall in *The City of God,* his intellectual allegiances are straightforwardly
on display:

> For God, who is the author of nature, and certainly not of vices, created man
> righteous. Man, however, depraved by his own will, and justly condemned,
> produced depraved and condemned children. For we all were in that one
> man, since we all were that one man who fell into sin through the woman
> who was made from him before they sinned. The particular form in which
> we were to live as individuals had not yet been created and distributed to us;
> but the seminal nature from which we were to be propagated already existed.
> And, when this was vitiated by sin and bound by the chain of death, and
> justly condemned, man could not be born of man in any other condition.
> Thus, from the evil use of free will there arose the whole series of calamities,
> by which the human race is led by a succession of miseries from its depraved
> origin, as from a corrupt root [*radix corrupta*], even to the ruin of the second
> death, which has no end, and from which those who are redeemed by the
> grace of God are exempt.[10]

For Augustine, the Pauline claim that we all sinned in Adam must be understood to mean that "we all were that one man." Our subsequent
individuation—"the particular form in which we were to live as individuals"
that was eventually "created and distributed to us"—was an incidental development that did not vitiate our organic unity in Adam.

This collective understanding of human personality remained central to
orthodox accounts of the Fall until well into the sixteenth century. Indeed,
Calvin himself endorsed it unreservedly (although this is a subject on which
there has been a good deal of scholarly confusion).[11] "The whole human race,"
he writes in the *Institutes of the Christian Religion,* "was lost in the person of
Adam."[12] "We must, therefore, hold it for certain, that Adam was not merely
a progenitor of human nature, but, as it were, a root, and that, accordingly,
by his corruption, the whole human race was deservedly vitiated."[13] Here
again, Adam was our "root" *(radix)* and we were therefore "radically" present
in him when he fell. But for Calvin's disciples, both continental and English,

this collective understanding of personality began to seem untenable. Adam and humanity, they increasingly felt obliged to concede, were not the same person. Rather, what now had to be explained was why we could have fallen with Adam *despite* our undeniable separateness.[14] And it was the concept of representation that gave them their explanation. God, they claimed, had appointed Adam the representative of the human race and entered into a covenant *(foedus)* with him, according to which humanity would be rewarded with immortality if they remained obedient to his law and punished with death and damnation if they proved rebellious.[15]

As William Perkins canonically put the argument in the *Golden Chaine* (1600), "all his posteritie sinned" in Adam because "Adam was not then a priuate man, but represented all mankind."[16]

> Sinnes are either personall, or generall. Personall are such, as are peculiar to one or some fewe persons and make them alone guiltie. Generall, that is common to all men: and such is Adams fall. It is a sinne not onely of the person of one man, but of the whole nature of man. And Adam must be considered not as a priuate man, but as a roote or head bearing in it all mankind; or as a publike person representing all his posteritie, and therefore when he sinned, all his posteritie sinned with him; as in a Parliament whatsoeuer is done by the burgesse of the shiere, is done by euery person in the shiere. As Paul saith, *By one man sinne entred into the world, and so death went ouer all for as much as all haue sinned.* And here lies the difference betweene Adams fall and the sinnes of men, as Cains murder, which makes not the posteritie of Cain guiltie, because he was neuer appointed by God to be the roote of his posteritie, as Adam was: and therefore his sinne is personall, whereas Adams is not. Yet this which I say, must not be vnderstood of all the sinnes of Adam, but onely of the first.[17]

Perkins thus invoked the concept of representation to address what struck him as a dangerously powerful objection to the doctrine of original sin. If the familial, collective account of personality and responsibility is to be accepted, then surely we must be just as responsible for the sins of Cain, and all of our other ancestors, as we are for the sins of Adam. But that looks absurd—we don't ordinarily hold people accountable for the crimes of their grandfathers. Perkins's answer is straightforward: we are accountable for Adam's sin, and not Cain's, because only the former was a "public person" designated by God to represent us. Adam therefore spoke and acted for us in the same way that "in a Parliament whatsoeuer is done by the burgesse of the shiere, is done by euery person in the shiere."

Perkins's argument in this respect was immediately taken up by a range of Calvinist divines. "We must know," announced Thomas Tuke in 1609, "that *Adam* was no priuate person, but represented all mankinde. And therefore we stood and fell with him. For hee was the root and we are his branches: he was the spring, and we the streams: he was as the head, and wee are as the members. As the King, his Nobles, Knights and Burgesses doe represent the whole realme in the Parliament: euen so did *Adam* represent the person of his whole posteritie."[18] John Yates offered both the organic argument and the representation argument in *Gods Arraignement of Hypocrites* (1615). On the one hand, "he was our father, & we his heires; he was the root of all mankind, and we were in his loynes: the manner is by imputation of the transgression, and so consequently of blame, guilt, and punishment."[19] But, anxious to reassure those who might be skeptical of this claim about collective personality, he adds that Adam "couenanted with God for vs, as well as for himself."[20] Paul Baynes, Perkins's Puritan successor as minister in the Church of St. Andrew the Great in Cambridge, likewise insisted in 1618 that "a publique person standing for him and his, doth agree to *Adam,* as a thing appropriated to him."[21] In this regard, Adam was crucially a "Type of Christ," who was likewise a "public person" representing humanity on the cross: "as the Subiects of England, Scotland, Ireland, are in our King vnited, and all made one body politicke, so it is with the members of Christ in heauen and earth."[22]

Pierre du Moulin offered precisely the same argument from analogy in *The Anatomy of Arminianisme* (1620):

> The punishments which all men suffer in the name of *Adam,* doe argue that the sinne of *Adam* is imputed to vs: This the Apostle teacheth, *Rom.* 5.12. *Death passed on all men, by one man, in whom all men sinned, or because all men sinned in him:* For the sinne of *Adam* was not onely personall, neither did hee sinne as a singular person, but as carrying all mankinde in the stocke and originall; no otherwise then Christ satisfying for vs on the crosse, hath not suffred as a priuate person, but as sustaining and representing the whole Church in the head.[23]

And like Perkins before him, du Moulin makes use of the notion of representation to address the reductio that we are legally and morally accountable for the sins of all of our progenitors: "I say that that place in *Ezechiel* [18:1–4, where Ezekiel declares that "the one who sins is the one who will die"] makes nothing to the present matter: for hee speaketh of the sinnes of the fathers, whose sinnes are personall, and who in sinning doe not sustaine the persons of their children . . . the sinnes of my Grand-father and great-Grandfather were personall sinnes; neither did they in their sinning sustaine the persons of their posterity, which cannot be said of *Adam*."[24] "Surely," du Moulin continues, "I think that it cannot be said that *Ezechias* or *Iosias*, who were the posterity of *Dauid*, did in *Dauid* murther *Vrias*." Indeed, "*Adam* while hee liued committed many sinnes, yet I thinke that onely that first sinne of *Adam* was imputed to his posterity, because onely by this sinne he violated that couenant which was made with him, as with the author of mankind."[25]

As this tradition of thought gathered pace, its expositors grew increasingly eager to characterize the office of a representative more systematically and to distinguish it from other, apparently similar juridical roles. Thus Thomas Goodwin, writing in *Christ Set Forth* (1642), offers a meticulous, highly technical definition of a "common person":

> A *Common person* with, or for another hee goes for, is one who represents, personates, and acts the part of another, by the allowance and warrant of the Law: so as what he doth, (as such a common person, and in the name of the other) that other whom he personates, is by the Law reckoned to doe: and in like manner, what is done to him, (as being in the others stead and roome) is reckoned as done to the other. Thus by our Law, an Attorney appears for another, & money received by him, is reckoned as received by him whom it is due unto. Thus the giving possession of an estate, a re-entry made, and possession taken of land, &c. if done by, and to a man who is his lawfull Attorney, it stands as good in Law unto a man, as if in his owne person it had been done. So Embassadours for Princes represent their Masters: what is done to them, is reckoned as done to the Prince; and what they do according to their Commission, is all one as if the Prince, whose Person they represent, had done it himselfe.[26]

But Goodwin was equally keen to prevent a particular kind of misunderstanding. A "common person," or representative, is sharply to be distinguished from a mere "surety"—a point of some importance in this theological discourse, where Christ was routinely said to have acted as a surety for mankind.[27] "A Surety," Goodwin explains, "undertakes to pay a debt for another, or the like; but a Common person serves to perform any common act, which by the Law is reckoned, and virtually imputed to the other, and is to stand as the others act, & is as valid, as is he had done it: So as the good and benefit which is the consequent of such an act, shall accrew to him whom he personated, and for whom he stood as a Common person."[28] It is therefore crucial to understand that "*Adam* was not a *Surety* for all Mankind, he undertook not for them, in the sense fore-mentioned; but he was a *Common person* representing all Man-kind; So as what he should do, was to be accounted as if they had done it."[29] Adam was "herein a lively type of our Lord Christ," who was likewise a "common publique person," rather than a mere surety.[30] The Larger Catechism of the Westminster Assembly codified this set of assertions in 1648, declaring that "the covenant being made with Adam as a public person, not for himself only, but for his posterity, all mankind descending from him by ordinary generation, sinned in him, and fell with him in that first transgression."[31]

But Calvinist theorists confronted a challenge at this stage of the argument. God, they agreed, had appointed Adam as a representative of the human race and had then entered into a covenant with humanity through him. But why exactly was it just for God to do this? What was it about Adam that gave him a justifiable claim to represent his progeny in the sweeping fashion presupposed by the first covenant? A small number of divines were prepared simply to accept God's appointment of Adam as an arbitrary exercise of sovereign power. For Anthony Burgess, "*Adam's* will may be said to be our will two ways." First, "by way of delegation, as if we had chosen him to be our common parent, and had translated our wills over to him, as amongst men, it is usual in arbitrations, and then they are said to will, that which their Arbitrator hath done, though it may be they dislike it."[32] But, clearly, "in this sense, *Adam's* will is not our will, for we had no actual being or existence in him." Fortunately, however, there is another option: "*Adam's* will may be said to be ours interpretatively, God appointing him to be the universal principle of mankind; what he did is interpreted, as if we had done it, and the equity of making *Adam's* will ours, ariseth from the instituting will and Covenant of God, that would have it so."[33] Burgess adds later that "neither was it requisite that God should expect *Adam's* consent, or ours to this agreement, seeing God is the absolute Sovereign and Lord of all"[34]—or "supream Lord over all Mankind."[35] Thomas Brooks agreed, writing in *A*

Golden Key to Open Hidden Treasures (1675), "And so was *Adam* a common person, and that by an act of God's Sovereignty; appointing him, in making a covenant with him so to be, and he did represent all Man-kind."[36]

But most Calvinists were unwilling to leave matters here. They were not voluntarists, after all, and so did not believe that God's will was itself the measure of just and unjust.[37] Rather, they accepted that God, being perfect, would unerringly conform his conduct to an objectively valid natural law. His designation of Adam as representative of humanity therefore must have been just and legitimate. Some explained the justice of the divine appointment by stressing its "equity." God, on this account, would have credited the human race with Adam's obedience, had the latter resisted temptation, so it was only fair that He should have attributed Adam's Fall to his descendants as well. As in any partnership, partners should stand ready to bear the losses if they hope to share in the gains. As John Polhill put the case, "if one Man may put his Will into another Man's Will in a Comprimise, why may not God (who is more Lord of our Wills than our selves) put all our Wills into *Adam's* by a Covenant? and here God did it with abundant Equity, because our Wills were put into *Adam's* as well for the obteining blessedness upon his Obedience, as for the incurring punishment upon his Disobedience."[38] Burgess canvassed this view as well, explaining that "*God when he made* Adam *thus the common trustee for mankind, did herein consult our good;* It was for mans advantage that all this was done for him, he intended original righteousness, immortality and happinesse should descend from him to his posterity, upon his perseverance, so that no more evil is now inflicted upon *Adam's* off-spring then good was designed and provided for him, if he had continued in obedience."[39]

Fair enough, one might reply, but the mere fact that the terms of a partnership are equitable does not suffice to show that persons may be designated as partners without their consent. The question remains: why was God acting in accordance with the principles of justice when he designated Adam as our partner in this fashion? As a first step toward an answer, a number of theorists began to emphasize that Adam and humanity shared a set of interests. Adam could, for this reason, be supposed to act as his descendants would have chosen to act. Gabriel Towerson, for example, insisted that the law "must be supposed to have been given to *Adam,* as that too not only in his *private,* but *publick* capacity, and as he may be thought to have been the *representative* of all Mankind."[40] "By the *publick* capacity of *Adam,*" Towerson goes on to explain, "I mean such a one, whereby as he was design'd to be the Father of all Mankind, so God made him a kind of Trustee for it; In order thereunto both giving him what he did for their benefit, as well as his own, and obliging him for their sakes, as well as his own, to see to the preservation of it, and act agreeably to it. Which if he did, his Posterity as well as himself should have the benefit thereof, and God's favour together with it, but if not, forfeit together with him what God had so bestow'd upon him, and incurr the penalty of his displeasure."[41] Since it was in Adam's own interest to act as a good steward and "trustee" of humanity's patrimony, it was just and proper for God to assign him that office.

But here again, the argument seemed to need something more. The laws of trusteeship, after all, were well known, and they plainly did not allow the crimes of trustees to be attributed to beneficiaries.[42] Adam was not merely a trustee, but a representative whose actions were to count as the actions of his progeny. Why was it legitimate for him to have been assigned this office? To answer this further question, Calvinist divines turned to a discourse of representation that they had inherited chiefly from the Protestant theology of the sacraments and from Biblical typology. To "represent" something, in this discourse, was to make an image or "representation" of that thing. As George Lawson put the crucial point, "something in relation to another thing, whereof it is *an Image* or likenesse . . . is represented by it. For the form of an image, or likenesse as such is to represent some other thing."[43] The Eucharist, rightly understood, functions "by Representation, because it's a Sign and Figure of [Christ's] Body. . . . The reason of this expression, is the similitude and agreement between the sign and the thing signifyed."[44] Christ, he adds in an important turn of phrase, is therefore "here Virtually, and Really present" by representation.[45] Perkins had likewise written fifty years earlier that "figures" represent in just the same way that words "signifie," and he had offered precisely the same example: in "the Lords Supper, as in euery sacrament, there is a relation or analogie betweene the outward signes and the things signified. The action of the minister giuing the bread and wine to the hands of particular communicants, representeth Gods action in giuing Christ with his benefits to the same particular communicants."[46] Or as he put the same argument in the form of a catechism, "Q. What is a Sacrament? A. A *signe* to represent, a *seale* to confirme, an *instrument* to conuey Christ and all his benefits to them that doe beleeue in him. Q. Why must a Sacrament represent the mercies of

God before our eies? *A.* Because we are dull to conceiue and to remember them."[47]

Whatever is said about the representative character of the sacraments can, on this account, likewise be said about Biblical "types" more broadly—each of which "was a figure and a shadow in foreshewing some represenment of those things which should have a future existence under the new covenant."[48] Thus, Lancelot Andrewes (writing in his most Calvinist register) could insist that "King *David* . . . is in Scriptures, not *persona Regis* onely, the person of a *King;* but *persona Regum,* a person representing all *Kings* to come after him; such specially, as with *David, serve and worship* GOD *in truth.* We doe safely therefore, what is said to him, applie to them all, since he is the *type* of them all."[49] A type represents its antitype by virtue of resemblance or "signification." In precisely this sense, Edward Reynolds argued that "as Christ was the substantiall and universall Mediator betweene God and Man: So *Moses* was to that people a *representative, typicall, or national* Mediator."[50] Note that the word "representative" in this context appears as a synonym for "typicall." John Owen employed the term identically when he wrote that "Christ was *like to Moses,* as he was a Prophet, and like to *Aaron,* as he was a Priest, and like to *David,* as he was a *King.* That is, he was represented and *typified,* by all these, & had that likenesse to them, which the *Antitype* (as the thing typifyed is usually, but improperly called) hath to the *Type.*"[51]

But if representation is understood in this fashion, the notion of "authorization" simply drops out. If, in Perkins's words, "the name of the thing signified is giuen to the signe, as vpon a stage he is called a king that represents the king,"[52] then the question of whether Adam represented humanity cannot possibly turn on whether he was authorized by humanity to act in that role. After all, the actor upon the stage who "represents the king" has not been authorized *by the king* to speak and act in his name. He represents the king by "signification" and resemblance. To adjudicate the question of whether Adam represented humanity in this sense, we must therefore ask whether he adequately "signified" or resembled humanity—whether he and his descendants shared an image, such that he could "appear" in their stead and "act their part." Was Adam, in other words, an acceptable "representation" of his descendants?

Calvinists had no doubt that he was, and they could turn for support to the established Christian discourse of the Incarnation. Christ, in this tradition of thought, had taken on human form—the image of humanity—precisely so that he could "bear the person" of humanity as Adam had, thus undoing the consequences of the Fall for the elect. As Calvin himself had written, "our lord came forth a true man, adopted the person of Adam, and undertook in his stead to obey the Father."[53] Or as Patrick Gillespie put the claim, Christ "act[ed] our part, not in a scenick, but in a real manner; he came upon the stage to represent our person, and in our nature and Law-place he really acted our part."[54] He could only "act our part" because he was able to "represent" our person, precisely as Adam had. "In whatsoever state and condition Christ was," Gillespie explains, "in that state and condition he doth sustain our persons, and is surrogate in our place and condition . . . when he was in a state of *humiliation* here, upon the earth, in that low condition, he did sustain the persons, and bear and represent the state and condition of his poor broken people."[55] Likewise, after the crucifixion, "in his *exaltation,* Christ doth sustain the persons, and represent the condition of the Elect, unto the which they are advanced by the Covenant through him: and therefore the Scripture holds him forth in his resurrection and ascension, &c. as representing the state of the Elect: He is in heaven this day, saith the Scripture, *for us,* sustaining our state, and glorified condition, till we come there."[56] His passion was therefore an "instance and parallel of Adams sustaining the condition of all men, and therein being a type of Christ."[57]

Thomas Goodwin unpacked the comparison in even greater detail. "In their two severall conditions, qualifications, and states," both Adam and Christ "were *Common persons:* That is, look what state or condition the one or the other was made in, is by a just Law to be put upon those whom they represented. So the Apostle reasons from it, *ver.* 48. [*As*] *is the earthly man,* (namely, the first man, *Adam*) [*such*] *are the earthly:* namely, to be earthly men as well as he; because he who was a Common person representing them, was in his condition but an *earthly man:* And oppositely, by the same Law, it follows, [*As*] *is the heavenly man,* (namely, the second man, Christ) [*such*] *are and must be the heavenly,* who pertaine to him, because he also is a Common person, ordained to personate them: and *Adam,* who came after him, was therein but his Type."[58] Humanity was "virtually, and representatively" in both men, with the result that "as in *Adam* we were all virtually condemned, *(In Adam all dye)* . . . and yet we are not actually in our owne persons condemned, till we are borne of him; nor doe we personally dye, untill we lay downe our flesh: Even so is it in the matter of our Justification;

it was done virtually in Christ, and afterwards when we beleeve, is actually passed in and upon our selves."[59]

Calvinist divines were at great pains to insist that Christ could not have represented humanity had he not taken on their image, just as Adam could not have represented his descendants had he not shared theirs. As Lawson explained in his *Theo-Politica* (1659):

> If we enquire of the manner, how Righteousness and Life is derived from Christ being One, unto so many, we shall find that this cannot be, except Christ be a general Head of Mankind, and one person with them, as *Adam* was. And this He could not be, as He was the Word properly; but as the Word, made Flesh: for if He will sanctifie them, he must take Flesh and Bloud with the Sanctified, and so be Man. Yet He may be Man, and not a general Person, so as to be one with them: and we do not read of any, but onely two, who were general Heads, and, in some respect, virtually all Mankind, *the first and second Adam.* Such Christ, was not but by the Will of God, and His own voluntary Consent. The Will of God appoints Him to be the Head of Mankind, and their Surety and Hostage, and so accounted Him; and He did willingly submit, and took upon Him the Person of others. And the principal cause of this Representation, whereby He is one Person with us, is the Will of God, who, as Lord, made Him such; and, as Lawgiver, and Judge, did so account Him.[60]

Sharing the image of man was therefore a necessary condition of Christ's acting as a representative, "general Person." It was not, of course, a sufficient condition: not everyone who shares A's image is A's representative. Only those "image-sharers" who are duly appointed or designated to speak and act in A's name, and who voluntarily accept the office, may be said to bear his "Person" (note, however, that A's consent is not necessary for this arrangement). But one cannot be a "representation" of A if one doesn't share his image.

Indeed, some Calvinists went so far as to argue that Adam and Christ were "representations" of humanity in an extraordinary sense. John Owen, for example, emphasized in his *Vindiciae Evangelicae* that the manner in which both Adam and Christ possessed "a likenesse of *nature* to *all* men" is to be understood in relation to the Biblical claim that "*Adam begat a Sonne in his own likenesse,* Gen. 5. 1."[61] Glossing this verse, Owen writes that "an *Image* is either an *Essentiall* Image, or Accidentall. A Representation of *a* thing in the *same substance* with it, as a Sonne is the Image of his Father, or a Representation in some *resemblance* like that of a Picture."[62] A picture merely "resembles" its subject—that which it represents—while a son is the "representation" of his father "in the same substance." The two share an "essential" image, rather than merely "accidental" features. Adam and Christ, on Owen's account, were able to represent humanity in this deepest of senses; they were "representations in the same substance."

This, then, was the Calvinist explanation of the Fall. Humanity fell with Adam because the latter was a "public" or "common" person who represented them; and Adam represented them because he was an adequate "representation" or "signification" of his descendants. He and they shared an "essential" image, as a result of which posterity was "virtually" or "interpretively" present in Adam. These polemicists deployed precisely the same language and arguments to explain their support for the Parliamentarian cause in the 1640s and 1650s. Henry Parker, a committed Calvinist who insisted that man was "depraved by the Fall of Adam"[63] and straightforwardly endorsed the "similitude" account of representation in his 1641 attack on the Catholic veneration of relics and icons,[64] declared in his political pamphlets that "the Parliament is indeed nothing else, but the very people it self artificially congregated, or reduced by an orderly election, and representation, into such a Senate, or proportionable body."[65] "Tis true, in my understanding," he grants, "the Parliament differs many wayes from the rude bulk of the universality," but the former is "so equally, and geometrically proportionable, and all the States doe so orderly contribute their due parts therein" that "in power, in honour, in majestie, in commission, it ought not at all to be divided, or accounted different as to any legal purpose."[66] Parliament, on this view, is "vertually the whole kingdome it selfe."[67] Indeed, the similitude between people and Parliament is not merely accidental, but "essential": "in the truth," Parker observes, "the vvhole Kingdome is not so properly the Author as the essence it selfe of Parliaments."[68] "For the Parliament being the representative of the people becomes thereby their living soul, including the will and desires of all the people, as comprehending them all."[69]

It is important to recognize that Parker and his allies did not claim that a single person could *never* "represent" or "signify" a multitude. Such a conclusion would obviously have had the effect of undermining the entire Calvinist project, since it entails that only an assembly, and not Adam alone, could have represented humanity in falling. Parker argues instead that a "proportionable" assembly will always be a *better* representation of the people than a single man—so good, in fact, that it will infallibly act as the natural body of the people would have acted—and that, given a choice between the two, one should therefore always choose the former.[70] When no such choice is available, a single person can indeed adequately represent the people. In the early ages of the earth, Parker explains, "till some way was invented to regulate the motions of the peoples moliminous body, I think arbitrary rule was most safe for the world. But now since most Countries have found out an Art and peaceable Order for Publique Assemblies, whereby the people may assume its owne power to do itselfe right without disturbance to it selfe, or injury to Princes, he is very unjust that will oppose this Art and order."[71] That is, "we cannot imagine that publique consent should be any where more vigorous or more orderly than it is in Parliament," but when no orderly, "proportionable" assembly is on offer, a single person will do.

Parker can thus hold that "the King does not represent the people, but onely in such and such cases: *viz.* in pleas of a common nature betwixt Subject and Subject. Wherein he can have no particular ends; and at such or such times, *viz.* when there is not a more full and neer representation by the Parliament."[72] The King, in other words, *can* count as a "representation" of the people when "a more full or neer" one is unavailable. By the same reasoning, since there was clearly "not a more full and neer representation" of humanity available in the first days of creation, a just God could have appointed Adam, who "signified" us, to bear our person. Once designated in this manner, Adam (like the House of Commons) became our representative, despite the fact that we ourselves never chose him for the role—for, as the parliamentarian John Herle helpfully explained, "designation to a trust in anothers stead," just as much as "the deputation of a man by way of election," makes "him to represent that other."[73]

II

Royalists of the 1640s answered this parliamentarian challenge by rejecting the "virtual," signification theory of representation in favor of a pure authorization account. Anyone authorized by the people to speak and act in their name must count as their representative, whatever the authorized party may look like—and no amount of "similitude" or resemblance in any way enhances the claim of an agent to represent a given author. Thus the fact (if it

is one) that the House of Commons constitutes a better image of the people
than the King becomes completely irrelevant. Both King and Commons
were authorized by the people, and both therefore count as representatives.
The popular authorization in question could not have come in either case
by way of election, since, as Royalists delighted in pointing out, nine tenths
of the Englishmen "represented" in Parliament did not possess the franchise.
And, of course, no one ever voted for the King. Rather, the people gave their
tacit consent to the overall institutional scheme of which both King and Parliament were a part.

Thus, when Sir John Spelman sought to refute Parker's claim that Parliament alone was "virtually" the whole kingdom in 1643, he offered as evidence the language of a statute of Henry VIII: "the truth is, the King, Lords
and Commons in conjunction are *vertually the whole Kingdome,* for that all
the people did at first submit themselves to their determination. 25 *H. 8.
21. your royall Majestie and your Lords and Commons representing the whole
Realme, in this your most high Court of Parliament, have power, &c.* So that
in the King principally, but yet in conjunction with the Lords and Commons, is the vertue and power of the whole Kingdome contained."[74] For
Spelman, the King as well as the Lords and Commons represented the people
for the simple reason that "all the people did at first submit themselves to
their determination."[75] Henry Ferne likewise mocked Parker's insistence
"that *the two Houses upon the absence and refusall of the other part, are virtually the whole*": "This tearm *virtually* doth often stand him instead, for under
that he can enlarge the power of the Houses to the extent of his fancie."[76] In
fact, Ferne agrees with Spelman, the King is every bit as much the representative of the people, since "we are sure it is declared 25 *H. 8.21. Your Royall
Majesty, and Your Lords and Commons represent the whole Realm.*"[77] Dudley
Digges was, if anything, even more emphatic on this point. The Commons
claim the "virtue of Representation," but "is not this cleerly the Kings case,
who is entrusted certainly as highly as they?"[78] To be sure, the Commons
"represent the people to some purposes," but so too does the King.[79] Both
have been "entrusted" in precisely the same sense.

At the very same moment, Royalist divines were also applying this set of
arguments to the case of church councils. A representative, Henry Hammond
announced, "hath its authority" from the agent it represents.[80] That is all
there is to it. Yet "low church" councils dared to claim "infallibility" on the
grounds that they constituted a perfect image of the church universal. They

fancied themselves "the *Compendium* and quintessence of the Church, and
the body representative thereof," as Parliament was of the "whole Kingdome," and therefore claimed "that the *Councell is the Church in substance.*"[81]
In truth, Hammond explains, the council is a "*representation* onely" and
"nothing is the Church in substance, but the Church in its full extent, of
which . . . the Church is onely the *quintessence,* which sure is not the same
in *substance* with that whose *quintessence* it is, but onely the *representation of
it.*"[82] Laud himself had made an identical case as early as 1639:

> *Every Body Collective that represents, receives power, & priviledges from the
> Body which is represented,* els a *Representation* might have force without the
> thing it *represents;* which cannot be. So there is no *Power* in the *Councell,* no
> *Assistance* to it, but what is in, and to the *Church.* But yet then it may be
> Questioned, whether the *Representing Body* hath all the *Power, Strength,*
> and *Priviledge,* which the *Represented* hath? And suppose it hath all the *Le-
> gall* Power, yet it hath not all the *Naturall,* either of strength, or wisdome,
> that the whole hath. Now because the *Representative* hath power from the
> *Whole,* and the *Maine Body,* can meet no other way; therefore the *Acts,
> Lawes,* and *Decrees* of the *Representative,* be it *Ecclesiasticall,* or *Civill,* are
> *Binding* in *their Strength.* But they are not so *certaine,* and free from *Errour,*
> as is that *Wisdome* which resides in the *Whole.* For in *Assemblies* meerely
> *Civill,* or *Ecclesiasticall,* all the able and sufficient men cannot be in the *Body*
> that *Represents,* And it is as possible, so many able, and sufficient men (for
> some particular businesse) may be left out, as that they which are in, may
> misse, or mis apply that *Reason,* and *Ground,* upon which the *Determination*
> is principally to rest. Here, for want of a cleare view of this ground, the *Rep-
> resentative Body* erres; whereas the *Represented,* by vertue of those *Members*
> which saw and knew the ground, may hold the *Principle* inviolated.[83]

If, as Laud argues, representation is simply a mechanism whereby some agent
authorizes some other agent (individual or collective) to act in his name, then
all of the complex metaphysics of image-sharing and consubstantiality must
be rejected out of hand. A representative body is no more the "virtual whole"
than a single, authorized magistrate is.

It is, I want to suggest, no accident that the Royalist writers and divines
who deployed these arguments were all Arminian anti-Calvinists who rejected the Augustinian doctrine of original sin.[84] Beginning in the early seventeenth century, continental opponents of Calvinism had developed the

authorization argument in order to deny that Adam could have represented the human race when he fell. Thus, the Remonstrant Simon Episcopius reasoned in his *Institutiones Theologicae* (left unfinished at his death in 1643) that "it is impossible that the actual and personal sin of Adam could have been originally ours," on the grounds that another's sin cannot be attributed to an agent "unless he contributes authority [*imperium*], or counsel, or consent, either tacit or express, or at the very least . . . knowledge of the crime or sin. And none of these could have any place in that sin."[85] As Josué de la Place (Placeus) likewise insisted in his well-known *De imputatione primi peccati Adami*, it cannot be said that Adam represented his posterity "by a legal pact" *(foedus legalis)*.[86] "Did he sin in our place? . . . Did we ever accept this by any act of our mind and will?"[87] Turning to the English context, Samuel Hoard reached the same conclusion in *Gods love to Mankind, Manifested, by Disproving his Absolute Decree* (1633): our guilt for Adam's sin must be rejected out of hand on the grounds that *"Adams sinne is the sinne of mans nature onely and no mans personall transgression, but Adams:* it was neyther committed nor consented to, by any of his posterity in their own persons."[88] Such an "absolute decree is repugnant to Gods *Iustice."*[89]

This argument became hegemonic in Arminian circles in the 1640s and 1650s. "Why," Henry Hammond asked in 1645, "should God inflict that punishment upon all mankinde, for (or upon occasion of) the sinne of that one man? though he used his talent so very ill, others of his posterity might have used it better, and why should they all be so prejudged, upon one mans miscarriage?"[90] Such a decree could not have been an expression of "distributive justice," because humanity never authorized Adam to act in their name. Jeremy Taylor likewise reasoned in 1656 that "condemnation cannot pass upon a man for any sin but his own: therefore it did not pass upon man for *Adam's* sin; because *Adam's* sin, was *Adam's*, not our own."[91] Calvinists may ground their doctrine of original sin in a *"Covenant made between Almighty God and* Adam, *as relating to his posterity,"* but Taylor finds "in Scripture no mention made of any such Covenant as is dreamt of about the matter of original sin: only the Covenant of works God did make with all men till Christ came; but he did never exact it after *Adam;* but for a Covenant that God should make with *Adam,* that if he stood, all his posterity should be I know not what; and if he fell, they should be in a damnable condition, of this (I say) there is *nec vola nec vestigium* in holy Scripture, that ever I could meet with."[92] He then makes the crucial claim:

If there had been any such covenant, it had been but equity that to all the persons interested it should have been communicated, and caution given to all who were to suffer, and abilities given to them to prevent the evil: for else it is not a Covenant with them, but a decree concerning them; and it is impossible that there should be a covenant made between two, when one of the parties knowes nothing of it.[93]

In other words, only "he that is *author* or the *perswader,* the *minister* or the *helper,* the *approver* or the *follower,* may derive the sins of others to himself, but then it is not their sins only, but our own too."[94] Humanity was not the "author" of Adam's sin, because Adam had never been authorized by humanity to covenant on its behalf.

What, then, of the Calvinist claim that our wills were in Adam "by interpretation" because he shared our image? On this point, Taylor is scathing:

Now if so, I ask, Whether before that sin of *Adam* were our wills free, or not free? For if we had any will at all, it must be free, or not free. If we had none at all, how could it be involv'd in his? Now if our wills were free, why are they without our act, and whether we will or no, involv'd in the will of another? If they were not free, how could we be guilty? If they were free, then they could also dissent. If they were not free, then they could not consent; and so either they never had, or else before *Adams* fall they lost their liberty. But if it be inquired seriously, I cannot imagine what can be answered. Could we prevent the sin of *Adam?* could we hinder it? were we ever ask'd? Could we, if we had been ask'd after we were born a moneth, have given our negative? Or could we do more before we were born then after? were we, or could we be tied to prevent that sin? Did not God know that we could not in that case dissent?[95]

"Why then," Taylor wonders in conclusion, "shall our consent be taken in by interpretation, when our dissent could not be really acted; But if at that time we could not dissent really, could we have dissented from *Adams* sin by interpretation? If not, then we could dissent no way, and then it was inevitably decreed that we should be ruin'd: for neither really, nor by interpretation could we have dissented. But if we could by interpretation have dissented, it were certainly more agreeable to Gods goodnesse, to have interpreted for us in the better sense, rather then in the worse."[96]

This theological debate provided a crucial context for Hobbes's celebrated intervention in *Leviathan.*[97] Hobbes was closely associated with the circle of

Arminian Oxford divines who met regularly to discuss theology in Viscount Falkland's house at Great Tew in the 1630s, among them William Chillingworth, George Morely, Gilbert Sheldon, and Hammond himself.[98] He was also quite familiar with the writings of Perkins, Tuke, du Moulin, and other federal theologians.[99] It is therefore difficult to believe that, when he asserts in chapter 16 that a representative is merely an "actor" who has been authorized by another agent to "bear his person," Hobbes is unaware that he is endorsing and systematically developing a position that is not only Royalist, but also deeply Arminian / Pelagian. And, indeed, important passages in this much-studied chapter take on a new resonance once they are seen as volleys in the battle over representation and the Fall. Thus, Hobbes's claim that "no man is obliged by a Covenant, whereof he is not Author; nor consequently by a Covenant made against, or beside the Authority he gave" amounts to a straightforward rejection of the central claim of Calvinist covenant theology—namely, that Adam could have entered into a covenant with God on humanity's behalf.[100] Hobbes likewise had an unambiguous answer for those who argued that Adam might have represented us as a "trustee" in virtue of sharing our image. It is true, he grants, that those who are not capable of acting in their own right may be "represented by Fiction," and "Likewise Children, Fooles, and Mad-men that have no use of Reason, may be Personated by Guardians, or Curators."[101] But such non-agents "can be no Authors (during that time) of any action done by them, longer then (when they shall recover the use of Reason) they shall judge the same reasonable."[102] Even if Adam had been our trustee before we existed, we would not have counted as "authors" of his actions unless and until we endorsed them *after* we had developed our own agential powers. And, in any event, Hobbes tells us that non-agents of this kind "cannot be Personated, before there be some state of Civill Government"—that is, until "the Actors may have Authority to procure their maintenance, given them by those that are Owners, or Governours of those things."[103] And Hobbes is clear that no such state existed when Adam fell.

In consequence, Hobbes nowhere refers to Adam as a representative of the human race, and, given his numerous and extensive discussions of the Fall, the silence would have been deafening to his contemporaries (he likewise systematically avoided using the language of representation in his lengthy discussions of the sacraments).[104] In chapter 35, for example, Hobbes writes that God "*reigned* over Adam, and gave him commandment to abstaine from the tree of cognizance of Good and Evill; which when he obeyed not, but tasting thereof, took upon him to be as God, judging between Good and Evill, not by his Creator's commandment, but by his own sense, his punishment was a privation of the estate of Eternall life, wherein God had at first created him: And afterwards God punished his posterity, for their vices."[105] Adam is punished personally for his transgression, and his posterity are punished for their own "vices"—not for their ancestor's.

Likewise, we read in chapter 38 that "it seemeth to me, (with submission neverthelesse both in this, and in all questions, whereof the determination dependeth on the Scriptures, to the interpretation of the Bible authorized by the Common-wealth, whose Subject I am), that Adam, if he had not sinned, had had an Eternall life on Earth: and that Mortality entred upon himself, and his posterity, by his first Sin."[106] Two points are worth stressing about this comment. First, Hobbes makes clear that he understands the depths of the controversy into which he is wading; hence his insistence that, his own view notwithstanding, he is prepared to accept the interpretation of his sovereign. Second, his argument here is radically Arminian, indeed almost Socinian. Adam, on this account, would have lived forever in Eden, had he not sinned, "for there was the *Tree of life;* whereof he was so long allowed to eat."[107] Once denied access to the tree, his existing mortal nature entailed that he would die, as would his posterity. Humanity was not depraved in spirit as a punishment for the sin of Adam.[108] Indeed, the Fall wrought no change in human nature at all.

Hobbes was equally emphatic that Christ himself could not, properly speaking, be regarded as a representative of mankind at the time of the crucifixion. To be sure, "Jesus Christ hath satisfied for the sins of all that beleeve in him; and therefore recovered to all beleevers, that ETERNALL LIFE, which was lost by the sin of Adam,"[109] but, as Hobbes took pains to establish in chapter 16 (quoting Thomas Goodwin almost verbatim), there is a central difference between an "Author" who is represented by an "actor" and one "that owneth an Action, or Covenant of another conditionally; that is to say, he undertaketh to do it, if the other doth it not, at, or before a certain time."[110] "These Authors conditionall," Hobbes explains, "are generally called SURETYES, in Latine *Fidejussores,* and *Sponsores;* and particularly for Debt, *Prædes;* and for Appearance before a Judge, or Magistrate, *Vades.*"[111] A "surety" who appears before a judge to settle a "debt" on another's behalf is not a "representative"—and, as we have seen, Christ was understood to be the archetypal surety. Indeed, the Latin term *sponsor* was invariably used to translate the crucial passage in the Septuagint in which Christ is described as "the surety (ἔγγυος) of a better covenant" (Heb. 7:22), and Reformed theologians of the seventeenth century added, more specifically, that Christ had entered into a *fideiussio* on behalf of humanity—that is, a conditional suretyship, in which the debtor remains liable for his debt until the designated *sponsor* pays the creditor.[112] Hobbes's use of this vocabulary is quite deliberate.

Thus, while Jesus was a surety, he was not the "public person" of Calvinist theology, any more than Adam had been. "The King of any Countrey," Hobbes clarifies, "is the *Publique* Person, or Representative of all his own Subjects," and in the ancient "Kingdom of God" by covenant, this public person was "God the King of Israel," not his son.[113] "It is manifest," for Hobbes, "that our Saviour (as man) was not King of those that he Redeemed, before hee suffered death; that is, during that time hee conversed bodily on the Earth."[114] The incarnate Christ was never authorized by covenant to represent the faithful, from which it follows that he was not their representative at the time he mounted the cross. "The Kingdome of Christ is not to begin till the generall Resurrection," at which point he will become sovereign representative "peculiarly of his own Elect, by vertue of the pact they make with him in their Baptisme."[115] During his ministry, Christ was only the representative of "God the Father," who had authorized him to bear his person "during his abode on earth," in precisely the same sense that "Moses, and the High Priests, were Gods Representative in the Old Testament" and "the Holy Ghost, that is to say, the Apostles, and their successors . . . have Represented him ever since."[116] In this sense—and *only* in this sense, as Hobbes notoriously argued—"God, who has been Represented (that is, Personated) thrice, may properly enough be said to be three Persons; though neither the word *Person,* nor *Trinity* be ascribed to him in the Bible."[117]

Hobbes thus offered the most sophisticated and influential defense of the Arminian / anti-Calvinist theory of representation to appear in the seventeenth century, but he plainly did *not* do so because he wished to vindicate a set of Pelagian views about theodicy and the undiminished metaphysical freedom of human beings. On the contrary, he famously advocated a wholly deterministic picture of human agency that appalled his more Pelagian interlocutors. The solution to this apparent riddle is to point out that Hobbes, unlike virtually any of his interlocutors, was a voluntarist. The Calvinists and anti-Calvinists we have been discussing all agreed that God's actions must be judged with reference to a transcendent, objective principle of justice. If he is to punish us, it must be that we have sinned, because it is contrary to justice to punish someone who is not guilty of a transgression. The problem with the doctrine of original sin, from this point of view, is that it holds that God punished us for the sins of another person—and that as a consequence of this first sin, we are now unable to avoid committing sins of our own (for which we will then be punished). The Calvinist solution was to insist that Adam was our representative, and that our depravity was thus itself a just punishment for our own sin; the anti-Calvinist rejoinder was to assert that Adam was not our representative, and therefore that God, being just, could never have depraved our spirit as punishment for the Fall.

Hobbes, in contrast, holds that God's will is itself the only measure of just and unjust, and that, accordingly, "though it be said, *That death entred into the world by sinne,* (by which is meant, that if *Adam* had never sinned, he had never dyed, that is, never suffered any separation of his soule from his body,) it follows not thence, that God could not justly have Afflicted him, though he had not sinned, as well as he afflicteth other living creatures, that cannot sinne."[118] If God is perfectly within his rights to afflict us at will, even when no sin has been committed, there is simply no theological reason to insist that Adam was our representative (God could, without injustice, have decided to afflict us even if he had not been). As Hobbes puts the point in his response to Bishop Bramhall, "the power of God alone is sufficient Justification of any act he does. . . . That which he does is made just by his doing it."[119] Hobbes could therefore safely embrace the Arminian / Pelagian theory of representation for political purposes without fearing that any of his religious views would come undone as a result.

It is for this reason wholly unsurprising to find vocabulary that looks quite Hobbesian in a great many Arminian and Socinian texts of the late seventeenth century.[120] Thomas Pierce, writing in *Divine Purity Defended* (1659), demanded of the Calvinist / Augustinian "party": "Is it not at least as *just* a thing, to decree the *misery* of the farr *greatest part* of *mankinde* for those personal *Impieties* which they do *wilfully commit,* as for the *meer sin* of *Adam,* which was committed by *Adam* before his *posterity* had a *Being,* much less a *Will,* and a *Personality?*"[121] Those who are not "persons" cannot have their person "born" or "sustained" by another, and so cannot be represented. Locke's friend Philipp van Limborch used similar language when he sought to answer the Calvinist claim that "Adam was the Representative of all Mankind [*repraesentavit totum genus humanum*], which was then in his Loins." "No man," for Limborch, "can by any Action represent the Person of another, unless impower'd by him so to do: For in this case only whatsoever Offence the one commits, may be imputed to the other: but Adam was not impower'd with any such Authority by his Posterity."[122]

Stephen Nye likewise may have been alluding to Hobbes in his *A brief history of the Unitarians, called also Socinians* (1687) when he insisted that Christ had been God's representative, not man's: "Christ may well be named *Immanuel,* taking it for *God with us;* as God was most plentifully with his People, by sending the Lord Christ to be his Ambassador and Representative, and our Redeemer. Several of the most learned *Trinitarians* acknowledg, that no more than this was intended by this Name."[123] Gilbert Burnet, writing in 1700, presented himself as an unapologetic opponent of Hobbesian voluntarism: "in Moral Matters, in God's foederal dealings with us, it seems unreasonable and contrary to the Nature of God, to believe that there may be a Mystery contrary to the clearest Notions of Justice and Goodness; such as the condemning Mankind for the Sin of one Man, in which the rest had no share; and as contrary to our Ideas of God . . . Justice and Goodness being as inseparable from his Nature, as Truth and Fidelity can be supposed to be."[124] But in rejecting "the supposed Covenant with *Adam* as the Representative Head of Mankind," Burnet was nonetheless endorsing an account of representation identical to Hobbes's own.[125]

III

Let us end as we began, with Locke's claim at the outset of *The Reasonableness of Christianity* that, if we believe in a just God, we cannot suppose that "all *Adam*'s Posterity" could have been "doomed to Eternal Infinite Punishment for the transgression of *Adam,* whom Millions had never heard of, and no one had authorized to transact for him, or be his Representative."[126] I hope it is now clear that, in making this argument, Locke was associating himself with a long-standing Royalist and Arminian / Pelagian tradition of thought, according to which a representative is simply one who has been authorized by an actor to "bear his person"—not a "similitude" or image of the represented party. But Locke, whose *Two Treatises of Government* appeared barely four years earlier, was also a committed defender of the Whig,

Parliamentarian cause, which remained ideologically invested in the discourse of "virtual representation" throughout the long eighteenth century.[127] His challenge, therefore, was to marry two positions that had grown up in comprehensive opposition to each other: (1) the notion that an assembly chosen by a small number of voters represents the people to a far greater degree than a single monarch ever could, and (2) the claim that Adam could not have represented the human race by virtue of sharing their image. The more Locke spoke the Pelagian language of representation, the more he threatened to undermine his own defense of parliaments; and the more he invested in the ideological defense of parliaments, the less stable his anti-Calvinism became.

This fact may well explain the notoriously muddled set of arguments about representation that we find in the *Second Treatise*. On the one hand, Locke straightforwardly agreed with his parliamentarian predecessors that "there can be but *one Supream Power*, which is *the Legislative*, to which all the rest are and must be subordinate," and he further affirmed their view that this power ought to be placed "in collective Bodies of Men, call them Senate, Parliament, or what you please"—and that only under such circumstances could "every single person" regard himself as "subject, equally with other the meanest Men, to those Laws, which he himself, as part of the Legislative had established."[128] Locke thus made it clear that subjects must be governed by laws promulgated by an assembly in order to count as self-governing, and he likewise tended to reserve the term "representative" for the members of such an assembly.[129]

But at the same time, Locke states emphatically in chapter 10 that the people may "put the power of making Laws into the hands of a few select men . . . or else into the hands of one Man, and then it is a *Monarchy*" if they choose, and, a fortiori, "the Community may make compounded and mixed forms of Government, as they think good."[130] These "mixed" forms may, in turn, legitimately assign the monarch a negative voice, along with the other sweeping prerogatives outlined in chapter 14 ("Of Prerogative"). Whatever the description of the instituted legislative power, the subject "authorizes the Society, or which is all one, the Legislative thereof to make laws for him as the publick good of the Society shall require."[131] Or again: "the *Constitution of the Legislative* is the first and fundamental Act of Society, whereby provision is made for the *Continuation of their Union*, under the Direction of Persons, and Bonds of Laws, made by persons authorized thereunto, by the Consent and Appointment of the People, without which no one Man, or number of Men, amongst them, can have Authority of making Laws, that shall be binding to the rest."[132] Here we recognizably find ourselves back in the conceptual world of the Royalist / Pelagian tradition, where authorization is a necessary and sufficient condition of representation. In such a world, "one man" or a "number of Men" can represent the people equally well.

The scholarly temptation has always been to try to find some way of reconciling these apparently contradictory claims, but that exercise has, I think, prevented us from appreciating the significance of the muddle itself. Locke, who had already in the *First Treatise* expressed his contempt for the view that Adam was the "Representative" of "all mankind" when he fell,[133] could not wholeheartedly embrace the Parliamentarian language of resemblance and "signification" without imperiling his assault on the doctrine of original sin. He was driven, instead, to engage with a Royalist discourse that placed the concept of authorization at the very center of the human experience, in both politics and theology. What mattered, in this discourse, was not what people *would have* agreed to—or what others just like them may have agreed to—but, fundamentally and exclusively, what people themselves had *in fact* agreed to. We call the resulting tradition of thought "liberalism."

CHAPTER THREE

"The Bargain Basis"

Rawls, Anti-Pelagianism, and Moral Arbitrariness

IF THE LIBERAL POLITICAL tradition initially derived its character from Pelagian commitments to the metaphysical freedom of human beings and the authorization account of political representation, it becomes clear that contemporary liberal political philosophy has strayed quite far from its ideological origins. The distance in question is best exemplified by what has arguably become the central normative premise of recent Anglophone political theory: John Rawls's idea of "moral arbitrariness." Rawls and his many disciples regard society as a cooperative scheme among free and equal individuals, none of whom has any freestanding entitlement to a larger share of the social product than any other. These theorists concede that some citizens are more productive than others, but they deny that unusually productive members of society have a claim to the greater value that they produce. The fact that some citizens are more productive than others is dismissed as "arbitrary from a moral point of view," on the grounds that we cannot be said to deserve, or be responsible for, the features of our person that cause us to be better or worse at producing value. These features include not only our degree of intelligence and our talents, but also (for some) our level of industriousness and commitment. All of these facts about us are regarded as "given" from outside, the products of some combination of heredity and environment. Egalitarianism has thus come to depend, for many of its proponents, upon the conviction that our actions and decisions in the realm of production cannot be attributed to us in the morally relevant sense; we cannot claim to have earned or merited the fruits of our labor, from which it is taken to follow that these fruits should be distributed by the "basic structure" of society in an egalitarian fashion.

To be clear, I intend the foregoing account of the relationship between egalitarian political philosophy and the doctrine of moral arbitrariness to be neutral with respect to two competing understandings of the latter's role in Rawls's theory. On one view (shared by many "luck egalitarians"), "justice as fairness" is best understood as an attempt to mitigate, or correct for, the morally arbitrary distribution of talents and endowments among citizens. That is, the doctrine of moral arbitrariness is taken to motivate, or even ground Rawls's theory of justice. On the rival conception, Rawls merely introduces the notion of moral arbitrariness in order to rebut a potential objection to justice as fairness—namely, that it pays insufficient respect to free-standing claims of desert. Rawls's theory, on this second account, is grounded instead in a substantive commitment to equality among citizens.[1] My own view is that Rawls is inconsistent on this point; different passages in *A Theory of Justice* may plausibly be adduced to defend both positions. But the reliance of egalitarianism on the doctrine of moral arbitrariness is clear in any case: either it affirmatively grounds egalitarian commitments, or it is invoked to rebut what would otherwise be a serious objection to the moral plausibility of those commitments.

As several theorists have observed, it is rather odd that this approach to moral agency should have found its way to the center of contemporary liberal political philosophy. There is, at the very least, a prima facie tension between liberalism's commitment to the fundamental dignity of human beings as choosers and the conviction that vast numbers of choices cannot be attributed to human agents in the morally relevant sense. I take no position here on whether this tension rises to the level of an incoherence (although I suspect that it does); rather, I hope that the fact of this tension will suffice to make us curious about how the alliance between liberalism and moral arbitrariness should have come about. Up until quite recently, it would have been prohibitively difficult to answer this question, but the publication of

John Rawls's undergraduate senior thesis, *A Brief Inquiry into the Meaning of Sin and Faith,* has given us an invaluable new perspective on his intellectual formation. The young Rawls, who planned to become an Episcopal priest, spent his Princeton years immersed in neo-Orthodox Christian theology and dedicated his thesis to an exploration of its themes. It was in this essay that Rawls first developed his idea of "moral arbitrariness," and it is significant that he did so in the context of a fierce attack on the Pelagian heresy.

The theological issues involved in this dispute go back, as we have seen, to the very beginnings of the Christian church. Early Christians confronted a question of theodicy: how can we vindicate the justice of an omnipotent God, given the terrible suffering we see all around us—and given His apparent intention to punish many of us with eternal damnation? A natural way of answering this challenge would be to insist upon the radical freedom of human beings. God, being good, has created us to be capable of morality, but we cannot be capable of morality without being free to choose to do evil. Human suffering (or a great deal of it, at any rate) is the result of the free choice of free men, and, precisely because it is always in our power to merit God's favor by doing right, we cannot deny that God justly punishes us when we sin.

This general approach to the question of election we have called Pelagianism. While it seemed to offer a promising way out of the theodicy tangle, critics immediately recognized that it also posed a grave threat to orthodox Christian doctrine. The problem, put simply, was as follows: if human beings are free to sin or not sin, and thereby to merit God's favor or punishment on their own, what was the purpose of the Atonement? Why did Jesus have to come to earth to be crucified to redeem us from sin, if we were always perfectly capable of redeeming ourselves? Pelagianism was thus associated from the very beginning with anti-trinitarianism and other heresies denying the divinity of Jesus. For precisely the same reasons, Pelagianism was always regarded as a "Judaizing" or "Hebraizing" doctrine. Its enemies saw in it the sin of "pride"—the prideful insistence of the "chosen people" that one can follow God's law and earn election without Christological intercession. Augustine responded to this Judaizing Pelagian challenge by formulating the doctrine of original sin: human beings, on his account, are deformed in their nature and incapable of avoiding sin and achieving election without the intercession of grace. Calvinists would later develop a yet more stringent version of the doctrine, according to which it is grace *alone* that saves us, and God "predestines" which of us will be recipients of this unmerited and irresistible favor (Augustine himself endorsed something like this position in his late works).[2]

The Augustinian and Calvinist approaches promised to rescue the Atonement, but only at the cost of exacerbating the initial theodicy problem. For how can a just God punish us for sinning if we cannot *help* but sin, if doing right is simply *beyond our power?* The tendency of predestinarian theories to turn God into a tyrant explains the persistence of Pelagianism in the Christian world, in the form of radical Arminianism, Socinianism, and, later, Unitarianism.[3] It is, indeed, no coincidence that all of the early-modern theorists who laid the philosophical foundations for what we have come to call "liberalism"—from Milton and Locke to Kant—were committed Pelagians. Their shared conviction that human beings are radically free and responsible for their choices before God and man undergirds both their contractarian politics and their commitment to religious toleration. For these theorists, it is only the human capacity for morality that could ever "justify the ways of God to men," and human suffering is the fair price we pay for it.

The striking fact about Rawls, in contrast, is that, although he would go on to produce the twentieth century's most significant statement of liberal political philosophy, his orientation was stridently anti-Pelagian. Distraught that "Pelagius rendered the Cross of Christ to no effect,"[4] the young Rawls wished to reject the idea that human beings can "merit" election and "earn" God's favor. Such a conceit, on his account, is merely the product of pride and "egotism," which denies the fundamental reality of human fallenness and original sin. Rawls, quite conventionally, associated this Pelagian pridefulness above all with Judaism. Picking up Marx's terminology from *On the Jewish Question*—but developing the argument of his source in a highly original direction—he denounced the "bargain basis" which "manifests itself in the barrier of legalism in religion [i.e., Judaism] and in contract theories in politics."[5] It was the apostle Paul, Rawls explained, who first recognized "how easily legal righteousness comes to be infected by pride. He knew that the best efforts in Judaism were so corrupted—not the worst, but the best."[6] A central project of Rawls's thesis was, in short, to rescue orthodox Christian doctrine from a Judaizing Pelagianism (one that "construct[s] the Cross as a new law and as a new rule to be obeyed and rewarded")[7] by denying the possibility of human merit. The mature Rawls of *A Theory of Justice* (1971) was no longer a Christian and certainly had no interest in vindicating the doctrine of original sin. But his essential anti-Pelagianism remained intact as a habit of mind. When outlining his principle of moral arbitrariness, he straightforwardly returned to the very same language and arguments he had first employed at Princeton thirty years earlier. This fact, I shall argue, explains a notoriously puzzling feature of Rawls's theory of agency, and should also prompt us to reassess the attractiveness of that theory as a whole.

I

Rawls submitted the *Brief Inquiry* to the Princeton philosophy department almost exactly one year after the bombing of Pearl Harbor. It was discovered by Eric Gregory shortly after Rawls's death and then published in 2009, along with a lucid introduction by Joshua Cohen and Thomas Nagel.[8] Also included in the edition was an important essay by Robert Adams that identified Rawls's intellectual debts to a set of neo-Orthodox Christian theologians, chiefly Reinhold Niebuhr and Philip Leon. Rawls does indeed make extensive use of these twentieth-century writers, but his own emphasis is actually quite different from theirs, and his crucial engagement is with a much earlier text.

The case of Leon is particularly instructive in this respect. The second half of Rawls's thesis, which addresses the questions of "sin" and "faith" in turn, is organized around a distinction between "egoism" and "egotism" that is drawn straightforwardly from Leon's *The Ethics of Power* (1935). Roughly speaking, Leon's egoist seeks to satisfy his appetites without regard to the interests and well-being of others, while the egotist seeks *superiority* over his fellows (Leon is clearly indebted here to Rousseau's distinction between *amour de soi* and *amour propre*). Rawls agrees with Leon that the egotist is the "sinner par excellence," whose vainglorious pride accounts for "all the great sins."[9] In order to resist the pathology of egotism, on Leon's account, we must first be brought to recognize that it draws nourishment from a false picture of morality. Contrary to the teachings of virtually all philosophers in the Western tradition, "blaming and condemning and remorse and approving and honouring and self-respect and the glow of the satisfied conscience and merit and worthiness have nothing to do with morality or the good life but rather belong to its opposite."[10] As Leon puts it elsewhere, "a thoroughgoing criticism of egotism does not merely bring down the high, noble, glorious, etc., but asks for the scrapping of the very notions of these."[11] A true morality is one "without any idea of merit or greatness (without egotism)."[12]

Much of this language, as we shall see, reappears with great precision in Rawls's thesis. But it is important to observe that Leon's focus is not on denying the *truth* or *possibility* of claims to merit or desert. He aims, rather, to demonstrate that an obsessive focus on relative standing and moral heroics disfigures our relationships with other people, and with God, in distinctive and dangerous ways. We become, in essence, our own idols, allowing our inner conviction of superiority to estrange us from our fellows, thus undermining community. (Rawls too is deeply worried about the effects of egotism on community, but he is worried about other things as well.) Like Rawls, Leon treats the pre-Damascene Paul as "an egotist," but, for Leon, Paul's egotism consisted in his prideful embrace of "his People, the Chosen People, and its code of Law. It was in defence of his people's absoluteness, with which his own was identified, in defence of its threatened soleness and exclusiveness, that he persecuted, as may be judged from the fact that he afterwards made it his special mission to do away with that soleness and exclusiveness."[13]

Here, the Jewish pride that Paul eventually rejects is the pride of "chosenness," which is taken to be a communal / national manifestation of the individual's sense of superiority over his fellows. Just as an individual's self-idolatry estranges him from other people, the self-idolatry of the nation estranges it from humanity at large. What is *not* at issue here is the "Jewish pride" of anti-Pelagian polemic: the prideful assertion that we can earn God's favor without the intercession of grace, simply by following His law. Indeed, the absence of this anti-Pelagian anxiety from Leon's account may well explain his strikingly favorable treatment of Judaism as a religious system. Leon writes that the cure for egotism is to be found in "the Judaeo-Christian tradition with its realization of God who is personality and Love or Goodness."[14] Rawls's account of Judaism is very different indeed, and reflects his distinctive encounter with a rather surprising source: Marx's essay *On the Jewish Question* (1844).

II

Marx's famous reply to Bruno Bauer memorably turned the familiar question of Jewish emancipation on its head. Whereas most interventions in the debate about the *Judenfrage* had posited an incompatibility between Judaism and liberalism (on the familiar grounds that Judaism amounted to a chauvinistic rejection of Enlightened universalism), Marx argued instead that Judaism and liberalism were in fact a perfect match. Liberalism, on his account, is simply an expression of Judaism. Man in liberal civil society is "active as a *private individual,* treats other men as a means, reduces himself to a means, and becomes the plaything of alien powers."[15] Religion in civil society is therefore "the sphere of egoism, of the *bellum omnium contra omnes.* It is no longer the essence of *community,* but the essence of *division.* It has become the expression of man's *separation* from his *community,* from himself and from other men."[16] The notion of "the rights of man," as understood within the liberal order, presupposes a picture of man as "an isolated monad, withdrawn into himself," into "his private interest and private choice, and separated from the community."[17] The pathological focus of liberal citizens on their private, isolated needs estranges them from their fellows, whom they encounter as mere "means" to the advancement of their own interests. The result is the distinctive commodification of human life that Marx associates with the bourgeois, liberal order.

But this fact about the liberal state, for Marx, is to be explained as a manifestation of its essential "Jewishness." The "secular basis of Judaism," Marx argues, is *"practical need,* self-interest. What is the worldly cult of the Jew? Bargaining. What is his worldly god? Money."[18] The degeneration of "civil society" into a "sphere of egoism" is to be explained as a "Judaizing" of society, from which it follows that "emancipation from *bargaining* and *money,* consequently from practical, real Judaism, would be the self-emancipation of our era," or, as he also puts it, "the emancipation of mankind from Judaism."[19] The key term in this argument is "bargaining" [*Der Schacher*]—the German term has the sense of "hucksterism" or "street barter."[20] Judaism, on this account, takes the "bargain" as its paradigmatic form of encounter between agents, both divine and human. The Jew approaches God as an "egoist" aiming to satisfy "practical needs"; he promises obedience to "an unfounded, superficial law" in return for the satisfaction of those needs, and tries to get the best deal possible from the party opposite—often using the "cunning" of "Jewish Jesuitism" to find loopholes in the law he purports to honor.[21] "The bill of exchange," as Marx puts it, "is the real god of the Jew. His god is only an illusory bill of exchange." The liberal contractarian tradition is, in turn, merely the application of this Jewish "bargain" mentality to the relationship between citizens; each approaches the other as an "egoist" trying to extract the best possible terms from his fellows. Marx's conclusion is that "an organization of society which would abolish the preconditions for bargaining, and therefore the possibility of bargaining, would make the Jew impossible."[22]

When Marx associates the "bargain" mentality with Judaism, he thus primarily has in mind an egoistic fetishism of needs that reduces both the self and other people to "means," rather than ends. Jews particularly adore money, on this account, because it is the efficient medium through which human beings (particularly their labor) can be commodified and exchanged.[23] The purported fact that the Jew conceives of God as just another party with whom to bargain is introduced as evidence of a more general pathology. But, despite Marx's own silence on the subject, the attack on Jewish "bargaining" harmonizes very nicely with the anti-Pelagian critique of Judaism. What, after all, is the Jew bargaining *for,* if not election, or divine favor? And how can he imagine himself to have anything *with which* to bargain if he does not regard his meritorious actions as truly his own? This (allegedly) Jewish understanding of the divine-human encounter presupposes that human beings can come to have *claims* on God's favor; we can fulfill our side of the bargain and thereby merit our reward. The sin of "pride" might therefore seem to underlie the "bargain" mentality, in both its religious and political manifestations. It is perhaps not coincidental that, thirty years after composing *On the Jewish Question,* it was Marx himself who first applied something resembling the doctrine of moral arbitrariness to the realm of distributive justice. In his *Critique of the Gotha Program* (1875), Marx argued that, even if the problem of exploitation could be overcome—that is, even if every worker could reliably receive back the full value of his labor from the productive process—the result would still be subject to a "bourgeois limitation":

> The right of the producers is *proportional* to the labor they supply; the equality consists in the fact that measurement is made with an *equal standard,* labor. But one man is superior to another physically, or mentally, and supplies more labor in the same time, or can labor for a longer time; and labor, to serve as a measure, must be defined by its duration or intensity, otherwise it ceases to be a standard of measurement. This *equal* right is an unequal right for unequal labor. It recognizes no class differences, because everyone is only a worker like everyone else; but it tacitly recognizes unequal individual endowment, and thus productive capacity, as a

natural privilege. *It is, therefore, a right of inequality, in its content, like every right.*[24]

"In a higher phase of communist society," Marx famously concluded, the conceit of desert would at last be transcended: "only then can the narrow horizon of bourgeois right be crossed in its entirety and society inscribe on its banners: From each according to his ability, to each according to his needs!"[25] When the young Rawls read Marx, it was this anti-Pelagian undercurrent that most interested him.

III

There can be little doubt that Rawls's attack on Pelagianism in the *Brief Inquiry* reflects an encounter with Marx's essay.[26] The primary target here is once again "the barrier of the bargain basis," or "the bargain scheme of redemption," a term that does not appear in any of the neo-Orthodox or Lutheran sources with which the thesis engages. Rawls likewise follows Marx in insisting that this mentality "manifests itself in the barrier of legalism in religion [i.e., Judaism] and in contract theories in politics."[27] He agrees that these two phenomena are connected insofar as they both reflect a tendency to regard the "other," whether divine or human, as a mere "means" to selfish ends. Both therefore destroy "the foundation-ground of community" and "throw one into the abyss of isolation and separation in which man ceases to be man."[28] Or, as Rawls puts it elsewhere, the "scheme of the bargain" shuts "the individual person within himself, which isolates him from his fellows and which leaves him deserted amid the frenzied wreck of community."[29] But Rawls leaves Marx behind when he adds (deploying Leon's distinction) that "egoism, which seeks to use people, is justified in the mind of the sinner by a previous self-worship, a self-worship which seeks to abuse people. Egoism merely uses the other, the 'thou'; egotism abuses the 'thou.' Egotism seeks to set the 'thou' below itself, to turn the 'thou' into an admirer or an object of admiration. Once the other has been abused, the other can be used."[30] The tendency to reduce others to mere "means" reflects a more fundamental sin of pride, or "egotism," that is itself rooted in false ideas about the possibility of merit.

It is striking that Rawls's example in this context is the "capitalist" (indeed, he feels it necessary to reassure his reader at this point that he is not "spreading Marxist propaganda").[31] To be sure, Rawls agrees with Marx, "the capitalist seems merely to use his employees. He treats them as so many cogs in the machine which piles up wealth for him. Hence, he seems merely to be an egoist; he seems to want nothing more than concrete wealth, bodily comfort, to which end those he hires are means." That is, in Marx's terms, he is motivated by "practical need" and "self-interest." But Marx had failed to note a deeper fact:

> All the time this use of persons is justified by a tacit abuse of them. In the mind of the capitalist those persons are inferior, while he is superior. Further, the employees are not being used as means to concrete egoism, that is, to help amass large properties and estates; no, the end is not purely appetitional, but is spiritual. The capitalist takes great pride in his wealth; he loves to show it off. He likes to walk about his estate praising himself on his success. . . . Underlying all this sinful striving is the egotist lie, namely that he is a person distinct and superior.[32]

The hegemony of "self-interest," which Marx had taken to be foundational in the liberal state, appears here as a symptom of a more basic moral / theological mistake: the belief in the possibility, and moral relevance, of merit—what Rawls calls "the real core of Pelagian falsity."[33]

Rawls offers two distinct critiques of the language of "merit." The first is quite reminiscent of Leon's: the emphasis on merit and desert, on this view, is both a cause and a symptom of human isolation. The "scheme of the bargain" is always based on fear, rather than love. To assert a claim against either man or God presupposes a "lack of trust and faith" in the other; the goal is always "to bind the 'other' and to protect his own self. Bargaining springs from fear, and fear is the most self-centering of all the emotions. Thus, to use the method of legalism [i.e., Pelagianism in religion and contractarianism in politics] is to thrust us further into aloneness and separation."[34] We might refer to this as the "communitarian" critique of the language of claims, merit, and desert.[35] If we think in these terms, Rawls agrees with Leon, our relationships with both God and our fellow citizens will be disfigured.

But, unlike Leon, Rawls has a second critique to offer as well. He wishes to establish the falsehood, or impossibility, of human claims to merit and desert. The fundamental error, Rawls insists, is to suppose that we can have legitimate claims against God or against our fellows: "the errors which infect traditional doctrines of election arise by attacking the problem from the standpoint of individualism. Misunderstandings of election proceed therefore from the barriers constructed by sin."[36] "Lying beneath all these barriers," Rawls explains, "there remains the sin of egotism." This "infection" is most powerfully on display in "the pride of those who think they have been successful at the bargain scheme of redemption." Here, like Leon before him, Rawls turns to the case of Paul. But the lesson he draws from the Pauline conversion is very different indeed:

> In the Epistle to the Romans, Paul speaks severely of those who pride themselves on being upholders of the law. He attacks those who pride themselves on their good works, and he criticizes the Jews as strongly as the Gentiles. The Jew finds compensation in bearing the name of Jew; he relies upon the law, considers himself a "guide to the blind" and "a light to darkened souls" [Rom. 2:19]. Paul himself had experienced the pride of the Jew in his pre-Christian days. He tells us how he strived to be "immaculate by the standard of legal righteousness" [Philipp. 3:6]. Paul after his conversion came to realize that the ideal of his religious endeavors had been at bottom the sinful attitude of boastful self-confidence. The Apostle knew how easily legal righteousness comes to be infected by pride. He knew that the best efforts in Judaism were so corrupted—not the worst, but the best.[37]

For Rawls, the "Jewish pride" that Paul rejected was in fact Pelagianism. The "boastful self-confidence" of the Jew arises from his conviction that he can fulfill the law and be "immaculate by the standard of legal righteousness." Rawls's crucial claim is that "the best efforts in Judaism were so corrupted—not the worst, but the best"—that is, even when Judaism avoids the snare of national chauvinism that preoccupied Leon, it cannot free itself from the delusion of merit and desert. The conclusion is straightforward: "Man cannot allow any merit for himself. If Pelagianism is marked by a lack of faith, it is also condemned by its pride."[38]

The Pelagian doctrine of merit must be false, on Rawls's account, because it would "render the Cross of Christ to no effect."[39] If human beings could merit election through their freely chosen acts, the Atonement would be an absurdity. "As a result we conclude that man alone cannot save himself. . . . The sinner himself is helpless, as we have tried to show. Therefore, salvation depends on God. If He holds back His word, then man must continue in his blindness and in his aloneness. Man lies at the mercy of God, although in his egotistical closedness he does not know that he lies at His mercy. His pride tells him that he possesses power on his own part."[40] As Rawls puts it more succinctly elsewhere, God "comes to us not on account of merit on our own part. We have no claim upon Him."[41] Rawls's account of why man lacks the ability to earn election is straightforward and traditional: he agrees with Augustine that man is fallen. We are by nature sinners, and so, left to our own devices, we would do nothing but sin. "Such, then, is our bondage."[42] Moreover, we are responsible for our sins—that is, we own them in a way that we do not own our good or virtuous acts—because they are not caused from outside.

> We have to admit that the spirit simply corrupts itself. Personality depraves itself for no reason that can be found external to it. There is nothing in the natural cosmos, nothing in man's nature as such to explain egotism, envy, vanity, pride, and so forth. We must say, no matter how mysterious it may seem, that the spirit depraved itself by itself; that it turned in upon itself to love itself from no external suggestion. The apparent inevitable tendency to do this we may term, if we care to, Original Sin. The beginning of sin must be conceived as taking place in this unfathomable "causeless" way.[43]

Here we reach the asymmetry that lies at the heart of the anti-Pelagian account of human agency. Our sins should of course be attributed to us in the morally relevant sense, because we are sinners—our nature is to sin. What needs to be explained "from outside" is why sinners such as ourselves would ever fail to sin. Our good, virtuous, and productive actions cannot be thought to emerge from us; they must be attributed instead to the intercession of grace. Indeed, on Rawls's account, the experience of conversion is simply the recognition of this fact:

> The human person, once perceiving that the Revelation of the Word is a condemnation of the self, casts away all thoughts of his own merit. He sees that the givenness of God is everywhere prevenient, and that he possesses nothing that he has not been given. He knows that what he has received has been given by some "other," and that ultimately all good things are gifts of God. Therefore in the face of this givenness of God, in the face of His perfect and righteous mercy, he knows that he has no merit. Never again can he hope to boast of his good deeds, of his skill, of his prowess, for he knows that they are gifts. The more he examines his life, the more he looks into himself with

complete honesty, the more clearly he perceives that what he has is a gift. Suppose he was an upright man in the eyes of society, then he will now say to himself: "So you were an educated man, yes, but who paid for your education; so you were good and upright, yes, but who taught you your good manners and so provided you with good fortune that you did not need to steal; so you were a man of a loving disposition and not like the hard-hearted, yes, but who raised you in a good family, who showed you care and affection when you were young so that you would grow up to appreciate kindness— must you not admit that what you have, you have received? Then be thankful and cease your boasting.[44]

The facts about us that cause us to do good are attributable only to God's grace, working (importantly) through the medium of those around us. They are "received" from outside; if they were not, we would be able to make claims against God on the basis of our actions, thereby undermining the Christian salvific scheme. "No man can claim good deeds as his own, since the very possibility of his goodness presupposes someone's giving to him. . . . Even when we have desert it is because [God] first gives it to us."[45] Animating Rawls's discussion here is a verse from the Epistles that the late Augustine had likewise emphasized in this context: "Who makes you to differ from another? And what do you have, that you did not receive? Now, if you received it, why do you glory as if you had not received it?"[46] "Merit," Rawls concludes, is therefore "a concept rooted in sin, and well disposed of." "To hold on to the concept of merit is to turn Christianity upside down."

It is easy to lose sight of the force of this polemical argument in the *Brief Inquiry*, because the young Rawls also apparently embraces a doctrine of universal election. Ultimately, on Rawls's account, God has ordained a "community joining all together under God," from which none will be excluded.[47] The notion that some are predestined for salvation while others are damned is just as unacceptable to Rawls as Pelagianism—and like the latter "renders the cross of Christ to no effect" (in that the Atonement, on such a view, makes no difference to the fate of the damned).[48] This defense of a universal salvation might seem to place Rawls on the "liberal," rather than orthodox side of the theological divide.[49] But that appearance is misleading. Universalism about election is perfectly compatible with the most strident insistence on the general depravity of man. The claim is that God freely chooses to redeem all of fallen humanity, rather than a small community of saints. The grace in question is no less irresistible (at least in the long run), and no less necessary, than Calvin's. It is simply bestowed on all by God as a sovereign "act of mercy," as Rawls explains.[50] A universalist of this kind must therefore still hold that God could (if he chose) justly punish all of humanity for sinning, despite the fact that human beings cannot help but sin. To be sure, a belief in God's generalized grace makes Rawls's eschatology more benign than Calvin's, but it leaves no more room than its predecessor for human merit or freedom.

IV

Readers of Rawls will recognize the extraordinary degree to which this account is reproduced in *A Theory of Justice*. Immediately after having unveiled the difference principle—that is, the principle that departures from equality in the division of resources will only be justified if they improve the position of the least well-off social group—Rawls writes as follows:

> Perhaps some will think that the person with greater natural endowments deserves those assets and the superior character that made their development possible. Because he is more worthy in this sense, he deserves the greater advantages that he could achieve with them. This view, however, is surely incorrect. It seems to be one of the fixed points of our considered judgments that no one deserves his place in the distribution of native endowments, any more than one deserves one's initial starting place in society. The assertion that a man deserves the superior character that enables him to make the effort to cultivate his abilities is equally problematic; for his character depends in large part upon fortunate family and social circumstances for which he can claim no credit. The notion of desert seems not to apply to these cases. Thus the more advantaged representative man cannot say that he deserves and therefore has a right to a scheme of cooperation in which he is permitted to acquire benefits in ways that do not contribute to the welfare of others. There is no basis for his making this claim.[51]

This passage is notoriously complex, not least because Rawls problematically elides the notion of "desert," in the sense of coming to have claims, with "Desert" in the sense of possessing "virtue" and what he calls "moral worth." Not all productive actions are virtuous, and not all virtuous actions are productive (although the same facts about us that make us responsible, or not, for the former must also surely make us responsible, or not, for the latter).

But Rawls's mature view essentially replicates his position from the *Brief Inquiry*. Not only are our raw natural abilities undeserved, but we have no "claim" to the productivity made possible by our "superior character," because the latter is to be regarded as given from outside. It is something for which we can "claim no credit."[52] As the young Rawls had put it, "no man can claim good deeds as his own, since the very possibility of his goodness presupposes someone's giving to him. . . . Even when we have desert it is because [God] first gives it to us."[53] In the later Rawls, grace has simply become chance.

One objection to this reading would focus on Rawls's assertion that our "superior character" depends "in large part" on external factors. That is, Rawls appears to concede that *some* proportion of our character is *not* dependent on such factors and is, therefore, truly of our own making. Is this not to deny the basic anti-Pelagian conviction and leave room for preinstitutional desert claims, however modest? The answer is "no," but, in order to see why, we need to return for a moment to the details of the theological debate.

The anti-Pelagianism of the young Rawls, we should recall, was not Calvinist in character.[54] His central claim was that "man alone cannot save himself," not that man has *nothing* to do with his own salvation.[55] He was, in short, attracted to the somewhat softer, but still robustly anti-Pelagian argument that election is a matter of grace, but that human beings are nonetheless free to accept or reject it (although this commitment is in obvious tension with his doctrine of universal election: surely, if all human beings are predestined for salvation, then no human being will be capable of resisting or rejecting grace forever).[56] We hear the call, and then we answer. Or, as the young Rawls put it, "because [God] acted first, we can act."[57] But our reciprocal acts are so profoundly indebted to the intercession of grace that they cannot ground claims to desert or merit. Our contribution is simply too small. The proper analogy, on this account, is to a man who is offered $10 by a stranger on the street; he must agree to accept the money in order to acquire it, but there is no sense in which he has earned it. The doctrine is designed to explain why the impossibility of human desert is compatible with some account of human freedom, and thereby to resist what Rawls called "harsh predestinarian conclusions" (i.e., Calvinism).[58] The coherence of this view is, of course, open to serious question, but it is perfectly continuous with the mature Rawls's position as stated in this passage. In order to establish that "the notion of desert" does not apply in the realm of distributive justice, and that claims based on preinstitutional desert have "no basis," it is sufficient to demonstrate that our own contribution to the development of our "superior character" is exiguous (rather than nonexistent). We are free to some extent, on Rawls's account, but not free enough to be deserving.

Rawls does, however, appear to offer an importantly different argument about this set of issues in a second well-known passage from *A Theory of Justice:*

> None of the precepts of justice aims at rewarding virtue. . . . The distributive shares that result do not correlate with moral worth, since the initial endowment of natural assets and the contingencies of their growth and nurture in early life are arbitrary from a moral point of view. The precept which seems intuitively to come closest to rewarding moral desert is that of a distribution according to effort, or perhaps better, conscientious effort. Once again, however, it seems clear that the effort a person is willing to make is influenced by his natural abilities and skills and the alternatives open to him. The better endowed are more likely, other things equal, to strive conscientiously, and there seems to be no way to discount for their greater good fortune. The idea of rewarding virtue is impracticable.[59]

Once again, this passage is far from ideally clear, but, in this iteration, Rawls's objection to distributive claims based on merit or desert appears to be epistemic in character. In principle, Rawls seems to concede, each person *might* have a desert-based claim to the value produced by whatever share of his "conscientious effort" is not attributable to "his natural abilities and skills and the alternatives open to him" (and, since Rawls here treats effort as "influenced" by these external factors, rather than determined by them, this share is presumably not nil).[60] But, as a practical matter, we cannot appropriately "discount" for the "greater good fortune" of the "better endowed"—from which Rawls seems to think it follows that, by default, no preinstitutional claims based on desert ought to be acknowledged.

It is difficult to know what to make of this argument, not least because Rawls never returns to it. But it is strikingly similar to a passage from Kant's late essay "The End of All Things" (1794).[61] Having invoked a distinction between soteriological "unitists"—who believe that all men will be saved—and "dualists," who believe that some will and some will not, Kant argues that practical reason disposes us to the latter position. "For as far as [man] is acquainted with himself, reason leaves him no other prospect for eternity than that which his conscience opens up for him at the end of this life on the basis of the course of his life as he has led it up to then."[62] That is, the moral law gives rise in us to a conviction that a "supremely good original being" will elect us if our conduct in life has merited election. But we ourselves can never know, as a matter of "objective," theoretical reason, whether we are indeed meritorious, let alone whether anyone else is—which is to say, we can't *know* (although we should suppose) that some human beings will be elected and others damned:

> For what human being knows himself or others through and through? Who knows enough to decide whether if we subtract from the causes of a presumably well-led course of life everything which is called the merit of fortune [*Verdienst des Glücks*]—such as an innately kind temperament, the naturally greater strength of his higher powers (of the understanding and reason, to tame his drives), besides that also his opportunity, the times when contingency fortunately saved him from many temptations which struck another—who knows if he separates all these from his actual character (from which he must necessarily subtract them [*nothwendig abrechnen muß*] if he is to evaluate it properly, since as gifts of fortune he cannot ascribe them to his own merit)—who will then decide, I say, whether before the all-seeing eye of a world-judge one human being has any superiority over another regarding his inner moral worth?[63]

This looks quite a lot like Rawls's worry that we cannot adequately "discount" for the "good fortune" enjoyed by those blessed with "natural abilities and skills" and favorable "circumstances." And Rawls's claim that "the idea of rewarding virtue is impractical" echoes Kant's conclusion that the determination of who merits election cannot be a matter of reason's "practical use."[64]

But Kant's argument is very different from Rawls's in two important respects. First, Kant does believe, as a matter of practical reason, that there is indeed an all-seeing "world-judge" who *can* do the discounting in question—and who, indeed, will do. But, more importantly for our purposes, Kant also declines to draw anything like Rawls's distributive conclusion, perhaps because it simply does not follow. Consider by way of analogy a standard case of "unjust enrichment." Suppose we know that, as a result of a banking error, some amount of money to which Fred is not entitled has mistakenly found its way into his account, but we do not know how much. It would seem quite strange to conclude that, given our uncertainty about the proportions of tainted and untainted funds in the account, all of Fred's money should be confiscated. Indeed, wouldn't broadly liberal views about the requirements of permissible coercion point us in precisely the opposite direction? Liberals tend to suppose that we need better reasons to coerce than to refrain from coercion; this is the grounding supposition behind our insistence that the burden of proof ought always to be on the state or plaintiff in judicial proceedings, whether civil or criminal. If even the "preponderance of the evidence" cannot establish the proportion of tainted funds in Fred's account, surely we would be inclined to resolve the case by declining to confiscate any of his money (this would seem to be true a fortiori of a case in which *no one else* has an identifiable claim to the tainted funds). Why, then, would it not be at least as plausible to conclude that, in light of our uncertainty as to what share of an individual's effort and achievement are attributable to underserved external factors, we ought to leave him in possession of the full value of his productive labor (particularly since, on Rawls's account, no one else has an identifiable claim to that value)?

I take it, however, that this epistemic argument is something of a red herring in Rawls's account. Indeed, Rawls suggests in the very next paragraph that he has offered it merely arguendo: that is, he means to establish that, even if we were to concede (wrongly) the existence of preinstitutional desert claims, it would not follow that the basic structure should set itself the task of vindicating such claims in the realm of distribution. His more basic argument—and certainly his more philosophically interesting one—is not that we should ignore claims of desert because we are, in practice, incapable of disaggregating "external" and "internal" causes of human action, but rather that, because the internal contribution to human action is so vanishingly small, it cannot in principle ground *any* claims to merit or desert.[65] It was this argument that began life as an attack on the Pelagian heresy in Rawls's senior thesis.

The question arises: what does this matter? Perhaps the origin of Rawls's pattern of thought in Christian apologetics is historically interesting, but it may be that this pedigree presents no real problem for the contemporary idea of moral arbitrariness. Perhaps anti-Pelagianism is the sort of doctrine that can be secularized without any philosophical trouble. This is certainly the view defended by Cohen and Nagel in their fine introduction to Rawls's thesis. They briefly note "a particularly striking continuity between the thesis and Rawls's later views: the rejection of merit," and they further observe that this continuity is most apparent in "Rawls's opposition to Pelagian and semi-Pelagian doctrines."[66] But they conclude that the young Rawls's arguments, "though linked here to revelation, can be given a purely secular significance" without any difficulty. After all, as they point out, the thesis asks the "upright man" to notice that his meritorious actions have been made possible by *other people:* "So you were an educated man, yes, but who paid for your education; so you were good and upright, yes, but who taught you your good manners and so provided you with good fortune that you did not need to steal . . . ?" It seems facially plausible that this sort of view could safely be extracted from its theological context and put to work in a secular theory.

The thought is indeed plausible, but, in my judgment, it is nonetheless mistaken. Rawls in fact offers us a paradigmatic case of the perils of secularization: when religious arguments are secularized, they tend to leave behind the set of premises that initially made sense of them. Rawls's doctrine of moral arbitrariness suffered precisely this fate. It is perfectly true that, in Rawls's thesis, the uprightness of the upright man is said to be the consequence of the actions of others—but these others are merely conduits of God's grace. It is God acting through others who makes us act in ways that seem "deserving." This fact is far from trivial, and it explains a famous incoherence in the account of agency that Rawls defends in *A Theory of Justice.*

Having vindicated the difference principle by rejecting the notion of "merit" or "desert" in the realm of distributive justice, Rawls offers a strikingly asymmetrical defense of blame in the realm of retributive justice. Indeed, he foregrounds and explicitly defends the asymmetry in question. We make a mistake, Rawls argues, in "thinking of distributive justice as somehow the opposite of retributive justice":

> It is true that in a reasonably well-ordered society those who are punished for violating just laws have normally done something wrong. This is because the purpose of the criminal law is to uphold basic natural duties, those which forbid us to injure other persons in their life and limb, or to deprive them of their liberty and property, and punishments are to serve this end. They are not simply taxes and burdens designed to put a price on certain forms of conduct and in this way to guide men's conduct for mutual advantage. It would be far better if the acts proscribed by penal statutes were never done.

Thus a propensity to commit such acts is a mark of bad character, and in a just society legal punishment will only fall upon those who display these faults. . . . To think of distributive and retributive justice as converses of one another is completely misleading and suggests a moral basis of distributive shares where none exists.[67]

This passage is, again, quite difficult, but, as several commentators have observed, it must be seen to introduce an incoherence into Rawls's account of agency. Rules governing punishment in "justice as fairness" are evidently meant to track a preinstitutional sort of blameworthiness; the criminal violates "basic natural duties" as a result of a "bad character" for which just institutions should punish him. Yet, as Michael Sandel put the objection long ago, "do not the same arguments from arbitrariness exclude desert as a basis for punishment as for distributive shares? Is the propensity to commit crimes, any less than the propensity to do good, the result of factors arbitrary from a moral point of view? And, if not, why would the parties in the original position not agree to share one another's fate for purposes of criminal liability as well as distributive arrangements?"[68] Samuel Scheffler, a more sympathetic reader of Rawls, likewise remarks that "Rawls appears to suggest that reliance on a preinstitutional conception of desert is appropriate in the case of retributive justice, despite the fact that it is inappropriate in the case of distributive justice."[69] Scheffler regretfully concedes that "it is very difficult to see what basis Rawls has for making this distinction."[70] The move is simply "curious," a "small and insufficiently motivated departure" from his doctrine of moral arbitrariness.

I agree with Scheffler that Rawls's departure is insufficiently motivated, but I do not regard it as "small." Rather, I would suggest that this seemingly minor incoherence exposes the central fault line that runs through Rawls's mature theory—a fissure that results from what we might call the "incomplete secularization" of his early theological views. For the asymmetry in the account of agency that Rawls incorporated into "justice as fairness" is, as we have seen, fully present in the *Brief Inquiry*. But in that context it is not insufficiently motivated. It is, quite simply, the doctrine of original sin. Our bad acts, on this view, should of course be attributed to us, because we are sinners; our sins simply reflect our deformed nature (our "bad character") and are not caused from outside—as Rawls puts it, the "spirit corrupts itself for no reason that can be found external to it. There is nothing in the natural cosmos, nothing in man's nature as such to explain egotism, envy, vanity, pride, and so forth. We must say, no matter how mysterious it may seem, that the spirit depraved itself by itself; that it turned in upon itself to love itself from no external suggestion."[71] But for precisely the same reason, our *good* acts must be accounted for in some other manner, as the fruits of grace (why would a sinful nature not sin?).[72] All merit is "given": "No man can claim good deeds as his own, since the very possibility of his goodness presupposes someone's giving to him. . . . Even when we have desert it is because [God] first gives it to us."[73] The point is not that the mature Rawls continued to accept the doctrine of original sin, but rather that he continued to write and think *as if he did.* And to the extent that his many disciples have tended to regard human responsibility as quite robust in the retributive realm and highly attenuated in the distributive realm, they are likewise operating under the shadow of a theological claim.

V

I close by returning once more to Scheffler's essay on notions of responsibility in liberal political philosophy. He notes that "the main lines of contemporary philosophical liberalism agree in avoiding any appeal to a preinstitutional conception of desert—any appeal, that is, to an independent standard of desert by reference to which the justice of institutional arrangements is to be measured."[74] How is this fact to be explained? Scheffler offers a fascinating suggestion: lying beneath this consensus, he argues, is "the influence of naturalism."

> The widespread reluctance among political philosophers to defend a robust notion of preinstitutional desert is due in part to the power in contemporary philosophy of the idea that human thought and action may be wholly subsumable within a broadly naturalistic view of the world. The reticence of these philosophers—their disinclination to draw on any preinstitutional notion of desert in their theorizing about justice—testifies in part to the prevalence of the often unstated conviction that a thoroughgoing naturalism leaves no room for a conception of individual agency substantial enough to sustain such a notion. . . . Desert and responsibility are the moral notions that are most conspicuously threatened by a thoroughgoing naturalism.

Scheffler is careful to stress that, on his view, naturalism is only "in part" responsible for the phenomenon in question, and I have no doubt that it is. But it will be clear by now that my own primary explanation is quite different, indeed almost the reverse. The attack on preinstitutional desert in contemporary liberal political philosophy is fundamentally a legacy, not of naturalism, but of Christian apologetics. It is the product of the young Rawls's desire to neutralize the perceived threat to Christian doctrine posed by a Judaizing Pelagian heresy. The Cross could only be rescued by an insistence on the radical fallenness of human beings and a corresponding denial of the possibility of human merit and desert. The Rawls of *A Theory of Justice* had left Christianity behind, but he had retained, for good or ill, the anti-Pelagian account of human agency.

The question remains whether there is such a thing as a coherent anti-Pelagian liberalism. In a sense, the answer is clearly "yes." As I mentioned in Chapter 1, we are familiar with any number of theorists who have reasoned from a heavily Augustinian conception of human nature to a defense of liberal political institutions. Such theorists favor a regime of civil rights, religious toleration, and limited government precisely *because* they regard human beings as fallen, degraded creatures who cannot be trusted to wield coercive power over their fellows without inflicting great suffering.[75] But I take it that this is not the sort of liberalism in which we are interested here. We have in mind, rather, the sort of liberal political philosophy that takes as its basic commitment the fundamental dignity of persons as autonomous choosers and therefore assigns paramount importance to the value of freedom. Can one be a "dignitarian" liberal and an anti-Pelagian at the same time?

This vitally important question must remain open for the time being, but it is surely suggestive that all of the great progenitors of dignitarian liberalism were committed Pelagians, just as it is revealing that the young Rawls reserved some of his harshest criticism for precisely these figures, from the Renaissance humanists to Kant (whose "world full of noumenal selves" he dismissed as "a theology which intellectually attempts to justify man's cardinal sin [i.e., pride]").[76] Indeed, for the mature Rawls, the only "usable" Kant was a "constructivist" Kant—which is to say, a Kant purged of the Pelagian insistence upon a noumenal realm.[77] In this sense, perhaps Robert Nozick was on to something when he observed of Rawls's defense of moral arbitrariness that "one doubts that the unexalted picture of human beings Rawls's theory presupposes and rests upon can be made to fit together with the view of human dignity it is designed to lead to and embody."[78]

To put the same point a bit differently, there is something deeply inegalitarian about Rawlsian egalitarianism. In place of the Pelagian insistence on the equal moral power of all human beings to shape their lives in accordance with virtue, Rawls gives us an essentially hierarchical account of human nature in which the "better endowed" take the place of the Augustinian elect. And he himself was quite aware of the fact. In 1973, two years after the publication of *A Theory of Justice,* he extensively annotated a copy of Kant's *Religion within the Limits of Reason Alone,* prefaced by an essay of John R. Silber's. At one point, Silber offers a summary of Kant's essential claim about theodicy: "*The moral quality of the will is completely self-acquired.* No matter how bountifully or stepmotherly a human being is treated by nature, he is fundamentally the equal of, and his opportunities are basically the same as those of all other men in the development and expression of his moral personality."[79] Below this heavily underlined passage, which he likewise marked with a question mark and three bars for emphasis, Rawls writes, "It is hard to see how this <u>can</u> be true." And in the margin next to the passage from Kant's own text to which Silber was referring, he simply writes: "Pelagian-ism."[80]

The final irony is that, if Rawls's own account is to be believed, he was driven to reject Christianity in 1945 because he found himself unable to make moral sense of the anti-Pelagian God.[81] In old age, he described this moment of rupture in an unpublished essay entitled "On My Religion":

> I came to think many [of "the main doctrines of Christianity"] morally wrong, in some cases even repugnant. Among these were the doctrines of original sin, of heaven and hell, of salvation by true belief and based on accepting priestly authority. Unless one made an exception of oneself and assumed one would be saved, I came to feel the doctrine of predestination as terrifying once one thought it through and realized what it meant. Double predestination as expressed in its rigorous way by St. Augustine and Calvin seemed especially terrifying, though I had to admit it was present in St. Thomas and Luther also, and actually only a consequence of predestination itself. These doctrines all became impossible for me to take seriously, not in the sense that the evidence for them was weak or doubtful. Rather, they depict God as a monster moved solely by God's own power and glory. As if such miserable and distorted puppets as humans were described could glorify anything![82]

The post-1945 Rawls, in other words, reasoned that: (1) Christianity requires anti-Pelagianism, (2) anti-Pelagianism turns God into a tyrant, (3) tyranny is incompatible with any plausible idea of the divinity, therefore (4) Christianity is false. Hannah Arendt famously quipped that, while she was not a practicing Jew, Orthodox Judaism was the Judaism she didn't practice. Likewise, we might say of the mature Rawls that, while he was not a believing Christian, anti-Pelagian Christianity was the Christianity he didn't believe in. He could never quite bring himself to take seriously the possibility of a Pelagian deity, who creates men free to sin or not as they choose, and who will judge them according to their deeds. It is bittersweet to imagine what might have become of liberal political philosophy if Rawls had come to disbelieve in a different sort of God.

CHAPTER FOUR

Egalitarianism and Theodicy

> It is evident that the hatred of God accrues even to Atheists. For
> whatever they think and say, given only that the nature and state
> of things is displeasing to them, by that very fact they hate God,
> even if they do not call what they hate God.
>
> —Leibniz, *Confessio philosophi*[1]

THE HUMAN WORLD IS AN uneven place. Some people live longer than others; some are smarter, healthier, and more easily pleased; others more beautiful and talented. For these reasons and many besides, some people are also richer than others. Over the last thirty years, a substantial number of political philosophers have defended the view that this set of facts about the world amounts to injustice. Any distribution of well-being or advantage that leaves some worse off than others for reasons beyond their control is taken to be unjust. Since the existing distribution of natural assets appears to do precisely this, the theorists in question conclude that we all lie under an obligation of justice to reshuffle the "cards" we are dealt and, to the greatest practicable extent, deal them out again in such a way as to secure an equal division (or, to be more precise, a division that exhibits no inequalities derived from anything other than choice).[2] This philosophical position, now widely known as "luck egalitarianism," has had its committed critics. Some object that the view is overly permissive of inequalities that are *not* beyond the control of agents. If someone gambles his fortune on a losing bet, these critics ask, does the principle of justice really absolve us of any responsibility to alleviate his resulting poverty? Others complain that any attempt to implement the principle would require "humiliating disclosures" by the worse-off. In order to qualify for redistributive assistance, an individual would have to establish that he has been unfortunate for reasons beyond his control—say, because he is less intelligent or talented than others. But being forced to admit as much publicly would involve a degree of humiliation that is thought to be incompatible with the norms of liberal citizenship. Egalitarian justice, in other words, runs up against the requirement that we treat each other with equal respect.[3]

But by far the most common objection to luck egalitarianism points instead to the epistemic difficulties involved in identifying and rectifying an unequal distribution. How, it is asked, can we reliably know which of two people has in fact been more naturally "favored" on balance? What is the capacity for a happy family life worth as against a higher IQ, or good health as against the ability to throw a football or play the violin? There does not seem to be a common currency into which we can readily convert all of the facts about our lives, so that we can then make plausible comparative judgments and determine who should be compensating whom. Moreover, how can we judge in practice which proportion of a given result (say, a financial gain) is the result of natural endowment as opposed to conscientious effort or skill (or socioeconomic circumstance, which is yet another matter)?[4] Some luck egalitarians, to be sure, are open to the possibility that all aspects of human life (effort as well as native endowment) should be regarded as outside of our control: that is, they accept the normative principle that only "true" choice would be capable of justifying inequalities, but then endorse the descriptive claim that human beings, as a matter of fact, never truly choose anything. Permissible inequality thereby becomes a null set.[5] But for those who wish to hang on to a robust account of human freedom, the problem of disaggregation becomes daunting indeed. Where do "I" end and where does "my talent" begin?

Another common way of putting this final objection is to say that luck egalitarians are guilty of "playing God." They reason about justice as if they had access to the viewpoint of an omniscient and omnipotent Distributor, who searches the heart and knows exactly what has been given to each. Egalitarians of this stripe "long for a theodicy," as one critic has put it,[6] aiming to replace what chance has produced with what a just God would have ordained, had he existed. Yes, these skeptics concede, life is unfair. But it is not in the power of finite human beings to right this wrong. Luck egalitarianism stands accused of confusing what John Rawls called an "ethics of creation" with a theory of justice for human beings.[7] It is true that the existing distribution of endowments and advantage among human beings cannot be justified; what luck egalitarians fail to see is that it needn't be.

I agree that luck egalitarianism confronts daunting epistemic challenges of this kind, but I have come to believe that, in an important sense, this criticism misses the point. The objection that luck egalitarians are "playing God," like virtually all of the other objections that have been offered against their view, leaves intact the fundamental, apparently commonsensical intuition that gives the approach its continuing allure: the thought that, to the extent that the existing distribution of native endowments or advantage is unequal, it is unjust. When the critic complains that the injustice of this distribution is beyond our power to rectify (or that any attempt to rectify it will run up against prohibitions imposed by other values), he concedes what should be in dispute. It is in fact far from obvious that the existing distribution of native endowments and advantage is incompatible with justice (as egalitarians understand that principle), even if it is unequal. I shall argue that luck egalitarians have failed to notice this problem, not because they have indulged in too much theology, but because they have engaged in too little. On closer inspection, luck egalitarianism turns out to incorporate a silent and controversial theological premise: namely, that no theodicy is possible.

This claim will strike many readers as strange, or even perverse. For all of their critics' talk about "playing God," luck egalitarians plainly suppose that moral and political philosophy ought to proceed on the assumption that no cosmic Distributor exists. It is "luck," not God, that generates the putative injustices to which these egalitarians address themselves. But the theodicy debate can be had whether or not one supposes that God exists—and, in this case, it *must* be had. For to say that the existing distribution of well-being and natural advantage among human beings is unjust or unfair is to say that, had the distribution been intentionally brought about by an agent, that agent would be guilty of injustice or unfairness. It is to say, in other words, that the distribution is inconsistent with the existence of a just and omnipotent God.[8] But this claim has been the subject of fierce dispute for two millennia, and it implicates a range of epistemic and metaphysical puzzles of which egalitarians appear to be unaware. My argument will not be that the existing distribution of natural assets is in fact just, but rather that we cannot know that it is unjust (even on the debatable assumption that we *can* know that it is unequal). We cannot reason from the character of the existing distribution to the nonexistence of a just and omnipotent Distributor. And if this is the case, it ceases to be clear that there is any injustice for luck egalitarians to rectify. Moreover, I will suggest that, even if the injustice of the distribution were (wrongly) to be granted, it would not follow that human beings are under an obligation of justice to engage in rectification. In short, this form of egalitarianism is not merely inoperable; it is ineligible.

The argument that follows is therefore an attempt to relate an important strand of contemporary egalitarian thought to what was identified in Chapter 1 as the second branch of the theodicy problem: that having to do with God's distributive justice. It is vital to understand, as early-modern theorists did, that this issue is orthogonal to the question of God's *punitive* justice. The latter asks whether we are responsible for our actions and their consequences, such that a just God could hold us accountable for them. The former asks, in contrast, whether the distribution of goods and evils in the world is fair or optimal, such that a just God could have elected it.

The temptation to run these two distinct questions together has been pervasive in recent political theory. Rawls, for example, argues that "the distributive shares that result" from the process of production "do not correlate with moral worth, since the initial endowment of natural assets and the contingencies of their growth and nurture in early life are arbitrary from a moral point of view."[9] The word "since" in this passage is unfortunate. The character of the distribution of natural assets (i.e., whether it is fair or arbitrary) does not speak to the question of whether, or to what degree, our productive efforts reflect our "moral worth" or give rise to claims of desert. Suppose that the distribution of natural assets and favorable social circumstances were perfectly fair: it would not follow in such a case that the "distributive shares" that resulted from production would "correlate with moral worth." If we believe (with the Augustinians) that our actions are simply the product of these natural assets and circumstances—that everything we do is determined by the cards we are dealt—then plainly our productive actions cannot reflect our moral worth or give rise to claims of desert, no matter how fair or equal the distribution of natural endowments and opportunities may be. Conversely, if we believe (with the Pelagians) that our respective allotments of natural assets and social circumstances do not determine our actions, then the fact that the distribution of these assets is "arbitrary from a moral point of view" would not prevent us from making coherent claims about desert and responsibility. Here again political philosophy has something to learn from theology.

I

Since my aim in this chapter is to provide an internal critique of luck egalitarianism—that is, to explain why the principle of justice, as understood by luck egalitarians, does not necessarily impeach the existing distribution of natural endowments and advantage, as they suppose—the most direct route for my argument would be to deny that luck egalitarians ought to regard the distribution of natural assets as a matter of justice in the first place. There are several possible versions of this argument, but I believe that all of them fail. Luck egalitarians are right, given what they think about justice, to think that the natural distribution is a matter of justice. More precisely, they are right to conclude that it is capable of being unjust.

The first and most prominent defense of the view that the natural distribution cannot be unjust comes from Rawls himself. In *A Theory of Justice*, he argues in a well-known passage that "the natural distribution is neither just nor unjust; nor is it unjust that men are born into society at some particular position. These are simply natural facts. What is just and unjust is the way that institutions deal with these facts."[10] This argument can be construed in two importantly different ways. On one reading, the natural distribution is not a matter of justice, because justice is only a matter for institutions. This reading privileges the "political" conception of justice delineated by Rawls and championed by several of his disciples. It insists that only citizens of the same state can be said to stand in relations of justice with each other, and that it is only their shared rules of social organization that can be just or unjust. If one accepts this view, it obviously follows that there is no principle of justice governing the distribution of native endowments and advantage among human beings in general—and, accordingly, that the distribution of these assets cannot be unjust.

But luck egalitarians clearly deny the political conception of justice, and so must reject this tidy solution to the problem.[11] They accept, as I do, that the principle of justice governs (or ought to govern) the conduct of all rational agents toward one another—including God, if one exists. These theorists therefore work within the parameters of what Leibniz called a "universal jurisprudence."[12] The "institutional" rejoinder cannot form part of an internal critique of their position.

Rawls's remarks can, however, be taken in a second sense, and this alternative construction introduces a different argument for why luck egalitarians might be wrong to suppose that the natural distribution can be unjust. When Rawls states that the "natural distribution is neither just nor unjust," he might be taken to mean, not that justice applies only to institutions (i.e., only those who partake of shared institutions stand in relations of justice to one another), but rather that judgments of justice or fairness apply only to states of affairs brought about by agents. Supposing there is no God, the existing distribution of endowments and advantage ought to be understood as a matter of contingent nature, and therefore as an inappropriate object of moral evaluation. When a tree branch falls on my head, we don't raise the question of whether anything "unjust" or "unfair" has occurred, unless we have in mind an agent (God) who either causes or permits the branch to fall. As Jan Narveson has put the point, "No one is responsible for [the natural distribution of endowments]: we are who we are, we could not conceivably have had any choice in the matter, and *therefore*, considerations of fairness *simply do not apply*."[13]

This argument thus asserts that, contrary to what I have suggested, the theodicy debate and the secular debate about egalitarian justice must come radically apart. If there is a God, then the "natural" distribution is (at least potentially) a matter of justice; if not, then not. And since luck egalitarians assume that there is no God, they should concede that the natural distribution—being merely natural—is not a matter of justice or fairness and, a fortiori, gives rise to no valid claims for rectification.

Here, however, it seems to me that the luck egalitarian has a convincing response to offer. To be sure, if there is no God, the distribution of natural endowments is not in itself an injustice (indeed, it isn't even a "distribution," properly speaking), but the point is trivial. The moment that human beings have to decide what to do with, or in light of, a distribution produced by chance or nature, it becomes a human distribution and therefore a matter for moral evaluation (this, on the second reading, is what Rawls means when he goes on to say that "what is just and unjust is the way that institutions deal with" the natural distribution). The agents in question must consider whether there are good reasons to let the division stand, or whether it ought to be adjusted in some way. They ask themselves, in effect, whether the distribution is such that it could have been produced by a just and fair distributor.[14] Indeed, from the point of view of these agents, it matters not at all whether the distribution was *in fact* brought about by an agent or by chance.

Consider the following two cases: (1) During a given growing season, the farmers on the right bank of a river enjoy superb weather conditions and therefore produce abundant crops, while those on the left bank suffer through lousy weather and, consequently, a poor harvest. (2) Precisely the same thing happens to the two sets of farmers, but in this case the divergent weather patterns were produced by a malevolent rogue scientist. It is true that the left-bank farmers in the second case might be said to be victims of injustice, whereas those in the first are not—and therefore we might want to say that the mere fact of the distribution in case 2 represents or embodies an injustice, whereas the mere fact of the distribution in case 1 does not. But when the two sets of farmers deliberate about how to deal with the identical distributions in the two cases, the issue becomes a red herring.[15] Any consideration that is relevant to the adjudication of the first case is relevant to the second, and vice versa (assuming that reparations cannot be sought from the rogue scientist in scenario 2). The farmers may or may not decide that it is unjust or unfair to allow the resulting distribution to stand. Perhaps the previous harvest treated the left-bankers far better than the right-bankers, in which case they might conclude that all's well that ends well; or perhaps they reach the same conclusion because they subscribe to a parsimonious theory of justice, according to which individuals are only obliged to engage in rectification when they themselves have been the cause of harm. What these rival principles of adjudication share with each other, and with all plausible alternative principles, is an indifference to the question of whether the relative fortunes of the two sets of farmers in this case had a natural cause or a (third-party) agential cause. The answer to this question adds nothing of moral interest to the case.

There is, however, one additional argument that might be offered in support of the view that the distribution of natural endowments and advantage cannot be unjust: namely, that no human being has any claim to a given share of these goods in the first place, and therefore that the principle of justice is silent with respect to their distribution among people. To get this argument more clearly into view, consider the famous opening scene of *King Lear*. Lear initially means to divide his kingdom equally among his three daughters, Regan, Goneril, and Cordelia. But when Cordelia refuses to flatter him as the others do, he resolves instead to divide the entire kingdom between Regan and Goneril, leaving Cordelia with nothing. There is no question in this case that Lear has behaved capriciously and unfairly, but is he guilty of injustice? The argument we are now considering would answer "no," on the grounds that the kingdom (by hypothesis) belongs to Lear, and he is therefore free to assign it to whomever he wishes. None of his daughters has a justice-based claim to any portion of his realm. Some possible divisions of Lear's estate would clearly be unfair, inequitable, and ungenerous, but none can be unjust. To the extent that the principle of justice is involved in this case at all, it simply instructs everybody else to respect whichever division Lear selects—and, in in so doing, to vindicate his property rights in his kingdom.

By analogy, one could argue that the distribution of natural endowments and advantage does not, properly speaking, implicate the question of theodicy, even counterfactually. If there is a God, he owns all natural assets (because he created them), and therefore any distribution that he produces will be consistent with the principle of justice. Like Lear's daughters, we human beings have no justice-based claim to any share of these advantages. To be sure, if the distribution that God selects is seen to be unfair or arbitrary, this will pose a theological problem. But the problem would arise because such a distribution is inconsistent with God's *goodness,* not with his justice. (The distribution of natural assets would only become a matter of God's justice, on this view, if it were shown to undermine our responsibility for our actions, thereby calling into question God's *punitive* justice in punishing us when we sin.)

Whatever its merits, however, I take it that, once again, this position is not available to luck egalitarians. To argue that God (if one exists) is free to dispose of his creation as he sees fit, and that no other agents can be said to have justice-based claims to any part of it, is to embrace a kind of "cosmic libertarianism" (or entitlement theory) that is plainly incompatible with the way in which these egalitarians understand justice. (Indeed, a luck egalitarian would presumably argue that it is "arbitrary from a moral point of view" that God, and no other creature, happened to be able to create a world.) But even if this problem of intellectual coherence could be set aside, the objection in question would remain unavailable to luck egalitarians, insofar as it only goes through if God *actually* exists. Here we reach a point at which the secular debate about distribution of natural assets and the theodicy debate do indeed come apart. The cosmic libertarianism that promises to explain why the existing distribution of natural endowments cannot be unjust requires the premise that there is in fact a cosmic proprietor whose rights we vindicate by respecting whichever distribution he chooses to make. Absent this premise, the case of the natural distribution of advantage simply becomes a variant of the case of the farmers that we have already considered: one in which we are required to determine the proper allocation of resources dispersed unevenly by chance, to which *no one* has an antecedent claim. And we have already established that, for luck egalitarians, such allocations can in principle be unjust. The following dilemma therefore presents itself: either the distribution of natural endowments and advantage can be unjust, or there is a God. I take it that this dilemma holds no terror for luck egalitarians.

II

Luck egalitarians are therefore rightly (by their lights) committed to the view that a distribution of natural advantage can in principle be unjust. But their case against the existing distribution rests on two further assertions: (1) that a distribution of natural advantages is unjust if it is unequal (in other words, that inequality is a sufficient condition of injustice); and (2) that the existing distribution is in fact unequal. Any attempt to establish the second of these claims will raise formidable epistemic challenges, but, since I am more interested in exploring the first, I will concede for the sake of argument that the current distribution is in fact unequal. Our question therefore is: given the way in which luck egalitarians understand the principle of justice, are they right to suppose that an unequal distribution of natural endowments is necessarily unjust?

Let us begin with a simple two-person case. Suppose for the sake of argument that Bob and James have exactly equivalent shares of natural assets,[16] but for the fact that Bob is more intelligent than James. On the luck egalitarian account, this distribution is unjust to the degree that it is unequal, and, by implication, an agent responsible for bringing about this distribution would be guilty of injustice. It is simply unfair (and therefore unjust), on their view, for one agent to be rendered better off than another for reasons beyond his/her control—and to be more intelligent than someone else is (let us further suppose) to be better off than that person. Any such distribution fails to express the equal concern owed to all human beings. As a result, luck egalitarians conclude that Bob lies under a duty of justice to compensate James for the latter's inferior intelligence.

To begin with, it is worth pointing out that the previous sentence contains a non sequitur. It does not follow from the fact that assets are unjustly distributed that those who hold larger shares under that distribution must lie under an obligation of justice to "make whole" those with smaller shares. It is more plausible to suppose that such a duty arises in some cases, but not in others. Return for a moment to our *King Lear* example. Suppose we grant that Lear is guilty of injustice (and not merely unfairness or some other, lesser moral transgression) in assigning Cordelia's share of his kingdom to Regan and Goneril. Do Regan and Goneril therefore lie under an obligation of justice to give a third of their resulting shares to Cordelia? I myself doubt that the answer to this question is straightforward, but to the extent that we are tempted to answer "yes," it is clearly because Regan and Goneril's shares and Cordelia's stand in a particular kind of relation to each other. It is not merely that Regan and Goneril have been made better off than Cordelia, but rather that they have been made better off *at Cordelia's expense.* They have been given the very resources that, under a putatively just distribution, would have gone to Cordelia. They got her share. Or, to put it another way, their having gotten more is the flip side of her having gotten less. The game is zero sum.

Now suppose instead that Lear's kingdom is infinite. He can give as much to each daughter as he chooses; what he gives to one imposes no sort of constraint on what the others can receive. In such a case, if Lear were capriciously to give substantial assets to Regan and Goneril, but not to Cordelia, a luck egalitarian would still rightly charge Lear with injustice—from which it seems to follow that the resulting distribution would itself be classified as unjust. But in this kind of case it is far less clear that Regan and Goneril would lie under an obligation of justice to transfer a third of their assets to Cordelia. Here, Regan and Goneril's having more is not the result of Cordelia's having less. Indeed, in a world in which Goneril and Regan did not exist, Cordelia would presumably have received exactly the same bequest from Lear (namely, nothing). There is no sense in which Regan and Goneril have wrongly been given *her* share; to the contrary, their having gotten exactly what they got is fully co-possible with Cordelia's having gotten an equal or greater share. Under this scenario, it would no doubt be praiseworthy of

Regan and Goneril to share their holdings with their wronged sister; they might even be said to lie under a moral obligation of some kind to do so. But it seems quite forced to suppose that they must relinquish a third of their assets to Cordelia, on pain of being guilty of *injustice.*

It should be clear that the case of Bob and James resembles this altered Lear case far more than it does the original. Absent further information, a luck egalitarian would be right to regard the distribution of intelligence between Bob and James as unjust (because unequal), and to conclude that an agent responsible for producing such a distribution would be guilty of injustice. But it does not seem plausible to suppose that, simply for this reason, Bob is under an obligation of justice to compensate James. What exactly would he be compensating James *for?* There is no sense in which Bob got James's intelligence. Bob's having less intelligence would not mean James's having more. Moreover, for all we know, Bob and James might live in different countries; they might never meet or hear of each other, let alone compete for scarce positions. In such a case, Bob's intelligence cannot even be a cause of envy or diminished self-esteem for James. The latter's life would be precisely the same—no better and no worse—if Bob did not exist at all.[17] If Bob is under any sort of duty to James, it must surely be far less strong than the one he would be under if James's level of intelligence were somehow a *function* of his.

Indeed, we should go further. On closer inspection, the issue is not merely that James is not entitled to compensation from Bob; it is, rather, that he lacks standing to demand compensation per se, even from a counterfactual unjust Distributor. A valid claim to compensation for injustice requires a demonstration that an agent has been harmed (i.e., made worse-off) by the injustice in question, or, at least, deprived of something to which he is entitled.[18] If you owe me ten dollars but only pay me five, you have harmed me to the tune of five dollars, and corrective justice requires you to make me whole. But the alleged injustice of an unequal distribution of natural assets cannot be said to harm James in this sense: for, if the distribution had been just, James would not have existed at all. This is an instance of the so-called nonidentity problem.[19] Our natural assets and endowments are not things (like five-dollar bills) that we can replace or lose without ceasing to be who we are. James with a very different set of talents and aptitudes is not James, but someone else.[20] It follows that, even if the distribution is unjust—and even if its injustice consists in the fact that the natural advantages enjoyed by James are more meager than they should have been—James has not been harmed by this injustice: he has not been made worse off than he otherwise would have been (unless we suppose that it is worse for him to exist than not to have existed).[21] Why is James, as opposed to anyone else, entitled to compensation for the putative fact that a wholly different human being should have been created instead of him?[22]

But let us set these reservations to the side for a moment and return to the claim that, *absent further information,* a luck egalitarian would be right to regard the distribution of intelligence between Bob and James as unjust (because unequal). To say that further information might render this judgment incorrect is, of course, to challenge the luck-egalitarian claim that an unequal distribution of natural assets is necessarily unjust.[23] What sort of information could vindicate the justice of an unequal distribution of natural endowments, if we take as given the luck-egalitarian account of justice? To see the beginnings of an answer, let us adjust the case of Bob and James. In the initial version of the case, Bob is more intelligent than James, but this fact has no implications for the latter, whether positive or negative. James's life is the same as it would have been had Bob not existed. But suppose instead that Bob uses his superior intelligence to invent a drug that extends James's life, as well as his own, by twenty years. Is the distribution of advantage between them still unjust because unequal?[24] Or, to put it differently, is it still the case that, had this distribution been produced by an agent, that agent would have committed an injustice by assigning Bob more than exactly James's level of intelligence?

At issue here is the familiar intuition behind the Pareto Principle. It would seem odd to suppose that justice requires an equal distribution of some good among individuals, if such a division would leave all of them worse off than they would have been under some available unequal distribution. Egalitarian justice, in other words, should not require the comparative immiseration of the very people whose interests it is designed to advance; it ought to oppose, not unchosen inequality per se, but unchosen *disadvantaging* inequality. A world in which everyone has a larger slice of an unequally divided pie is, from the vantage point of justice, better than one in which everyone has a smaller slice of an equally divided pie. Put just this way, however, the principle is radically indeterminate: any number of possible distributions might make everyone better off than they would be under a regime of strict equality, and some of these distributions will strike us as unfair (if Distribution A delivers massive gains to a small group while delivering only one penny more to everybody else, it satisfies Pareto, but it might well seem unfair to prefer it to Distribution B, which distributes the gains more equitably). Several further specifications of the basic Paretian insight have accordingly been proposed. Rawls famously endorses his Difference Principle, with its maximin requirement: justice, on this account, instructs us to select whichever distribution of goods would make the least well-off as well-off as possible. This view is, however, open to the criticism that it allows perverse results of its own: should we really prefer Distribution P, in which the least well-off receive two pennies more while everyone else receives nothing, to Distribution Q, in which the least well-off receive only one penny more and everyone else enjoys massive gains? Anxieties of this kind have driven some theorists to explore weaker versions of "prioritarianism," in which the interests of the least well-off are given extra weight, but everyone else's interests count for something as well. What unites these diverse principles is the conviction that, under some circumstances, deviations from equality are not only permitted, but required by the principle of justice.

What should luck egalitarians think about the relationship between justice and "Paretianism," broadly understood? The answer to this question has proven surprisingly elusive. Consider the case of perhaps the most influential advocate of the luck egalitarian position, G. A. Cohen. Cohen criticized the Difference Principle, as deployed by Rawls, throughout his career, but the nature of his critique changed significantly over time. He initially objected only to the way in which Rawls and his disciples used the Difference Principle to justify the payment of unequalizing incentives to the talented. The Rawlsian argument in question goes roughly like this: (1) justice requires that we select whichever distribution of the social product will make the least well-off social group as well-off as possible, (2) the position of the least well-off will be maximized only if the talented mobilize their full productive capacities to increase the social product, (3) the talented will only agree to do this if they are paid more than others, therefore (4) justice permits (indeed, requires) that the talented be paid more than others. The early Cohen, along with other egalitarians, objected to the role played by the third premise in this argument. The problem, he argued, is that the talented themselves make it the case that unequalizing incentives need to be paid to them; they *demand* these incentives. But their demand, as Cohen puts the objection, "runs counter to the spirit of the difference principle" and is therefore itself unjust—from which it is taken to follow that any distribution that includes such payments under these circumstances is, to that degree, unjust.[25]

I take no position in this context on the merits of Cohen's objection to Rawls's argument for unequalizing incentives. The important point, for our purposes, is that the objection is not directed against the Difference Principle per se. Indeed, in this initial statement of his position, Cohen states forthrightly that he accepts the principle in what he calls "its generous interpretation."[26] He concedes that, in cases where it is *impossible* to maximize the well-being of the least well-off without distributing the social product unequally, justice permits (and requires?) an unequal distribution. He simply denies that the standard incentives case fits this description: the fact that the talented refuse to produce at the requisite level absent unequalizing incentives does not mean that they are *unable* to produce at that level without the incentives (rather, it implies the opposite). If, by contrast, maximal contribution by the talented depended on their being paid more, not because they held out for such payments, but, say, because "without enough money to buy superior relaxation some high-talent performances would be impossible"—then Cohen agrees that it would be consistent with justice to assign larger shares to the talented.[27] Justice, on this initial account, requires equality only when equality does not *necessitate* the comparative immiseration of the least well-off.

Yet Cohen ultimately came to regret this concession. In his later work, he argues in contrast that, while the Difference Principle (or some other Paretian alternative[28]) can indeed justify departures from equality, such departures are not themselves just. "Inequality," as he now puts it, "is always unfair and to that degree unjust" (more precisely, inequality of unchosen levels of advantage is always unjust).[29] The Pareto Principle often gives us moral reason to act in various ways, but it is not a principle of justice. It can, however, "trump justice"—by which Cohen means that, although Distribution A might be more just than Distribution B (because more equal), it might still be the case that our "all things considered" moral judgment (weighing such non-justice concerns as Pareto) should be that B is preferable to A.[30] Here we confront Cohen's strong pluralism about value: he supposes that justice is merely one of many independent values that must be balanced against one another in moral deliberation. On this later understanding, departures from equality may be morally permissible (and even required), but they will always amount to injustice (although Cohen adds, surprisingly, that one who introduces permissible inequalities, and therefore injustice, does not necessarily act "unjustly"[31]).

Quite a lot could be said (and has been said) about the merits of this position. It holds (1) that a world in which everyone is extremely and equally wretched for unchosen reasons is, in at least one respect, morally better than a world in which (again for unchosen reasons) everyone is deliriously, but not exactly equally happy[32]; (2) that the wretched world is morally better than the happy world (to the extent that it is) because it is fairer; and (3) that the wretched world is more just than the happy world because it is fairer, such that moving from 1 to 2 amounts to a (permissible) injustice. Most luck egalitarians would, I think, reject 3 at the very least, and I believe they would be right to do so.[33] Even if one grants that there is some element of unfairness in the happy world (because some people are better off in it than others for unchosen reasons), it does not follow that the wretched world is fairer overall, let alone more just.

Consider an example: we would all grant on reflection that there is an element of unfairness involved when we send a murderer to prison, since we know that some people who commit murders aren't sent to prison (because we don't catch them, or because they're acquitted for lack of evidence[34]). The murderer who is unlucky enough to be caught and convicted is made worse-off than the murderer who is lucky enough to get away, even though the two are equally culpable—and this looks less than perfectly fair. But it does not follow that it is fairer not to imprison the convicted murderer. There is unfairness involved in *declining* to imprison the murderer as well (unfairness to his victim, as well as to his potential future victims), and, in this case, we would not hesitate to say that it would be less fair overall not to imprison the murderer than to imprison him. Likewise, even if we were to grant that the slight unfairness involved in imprisoning the murderer amounts to an injustice (and I suspect most of us would not), it would not follow that putting him in jail would be less just overall than not doing so.

Luck egalitarians should, for analogous reasons, resist the later Cohen's argument. If the happy world is indeed in some respect less fair than the wretched world, the former must still be regarded, from their point of view, as fairer overall. The unfairness involved in preserving the wretched world is perfectly familiar: if I deny you something that is of no use to me and massively useful to you (and which it costs me nothing to give you)—if, as Locke put it, I allow my goods "to spoil or destroy" rather than to benefit another[35]—I act unfairly. This is the unfairness of a child who won't let her sister play with a toy of hers that she isn't using (and doesn't even like), "just because."[36]

But the unfairness of the wretched world is even more stark than this: for in the case of the two children, while it costs the first sister nothing to allow the second to play with her unused toy, the former presumably does not benefit thereby. This is therefore a "weak" Pareto improvement. But if denizens of the wretched world would allow others to make use of assets that are, by hypothesis, doing them no good—thereby (let us suppose) disrupting the equal distribution of advantage—the result would be delirious happiness, not just for the beneficiaries, but also for those who surrendered some of their (useless) goods. A refusal to make this bargain—that is, choosing not to eliminate extreme amounts of suffering while making oneself better off at the same time—must count as the very height of unfairness. It amounts to a denial that the lives and interests of others are entitled to equal concern; indeed, it seems to presuppose that one should go out of one's way to ensure that these lives go as badly as possible. To put the point another way, it is difficult to see how a distribution about which *no one* can reasonably complain can be fairer than one about which *everyone* can reasonably complain. The luck egalitarian is right, therefore, to insist that the happy world is better than the wretched world from the point of view of fairness (and justice) itself. A vindication of the former need involve no surreptitious dilution of justice with other values.

But even if one mistakenly accepts Cohen's later view, the consequence for our purposes is exceedingly modest. For, as Cohen frankly concedes, if there is *any* pro tanto reason of justice to prefer the wretched world to the happy world, it must be so very weak as to be incapable of outweighing our competing *moral* reasons for favoring the happy world—and chief among these "non-justice" moral considerations is the Paretian insight (broadly understood). A deviation from strict equality that is necessary to make everyone better off will therefore frequently count, by any plausible luck egalitarian standard, as "legitimate" and, indeed, morally required "all things considered"—even if it is not taken to be required by the principle of justice per se, as the late Cohen understands that principle.[37]

Returning, then, to the case of Bob and James, it follows that luck egalitarians should concede that an unequal distribution of intelligence between the two is not necessarily unjust (or, in the late Cohen's terms, "illegitimate"—

moving forward, I will drop this qualification for the sake of convenience, but the reader should have it in mind throughout). Justice requires *either* equality *or* (if there is one) a distribution that would make the least well-off better off than they would be under the best possible equal distribution. Indeed, justice would only permit an equal distribution of intelligence in this case if such a division could be shown to make James better off than any possible unequal distribution. We are dealing, in other words, with the application of a "Cosmic Pareto Principle" governing the distribution of natural endowments and advantages among human beings—one that does not run afoul of the early Cohen's critique, because there is clearly no sense in which recipients of greater natural advantages themselves *make it the case* that they must be given these in order to benefit the least well-off.

It is this fact that leads us squarely into the theodicy debate. For what we are really asking is whether a world characterized by the existing distribution of natural endowments among human beings is, from the point of view of justice, the best of all possible worlds. To be sure, if we assume that there is no God, it would seem monumentally improbable that the contingent world in which we live should just happen to feature precisely the distribution of natural assets that a perfectly just Distributor would have chosen. But this fact does not allow us to avoid the tangles into which the theodicy debate inevitably leads. We cannot say that the current (putatively) contingent distribution is unjust unless we establish that a counterfactual, perfectly just Distributor could not have chosen it. That is, the conclusion that the current distribution is unjust *simply is* the conclusion that no theodicy is possible. But we cannot establish this conclusion unless we can demonstrate that there is some possible world ("possible" in the sense that its description does not involve a contradiction) in which the possessor of the least valuable "bundle" of natural assets is better off than the possessor of the least valuable bundle in this world is—or, at least, no worse off, while others are better off. Otherwise, what would it *mean* to say that the current distribution is unjust?

But the point is deeper than this. It is not simply that we cannot determine whether the current distribution is unjust until we establish that there is a possible world in which the least advantaged person is better off. Even if we were to become convinced that such a counterfactual world was possible, we would still need to know quite a lot about the character of the distribution of natural endowments within it before we could determine *how far* our current distribution is from the one that justice demands. To say that the current distribution is unjust (supposing for a moment that it is) is not to say, *pace* luck egalitarians, that it is unjust because it is unequal. It could be that the Cosmic Pareto Principle favors a distribution that is unequal, but different from our own—in which case our disadvantaged would be owed (if anything) not equality, but rather the difference between the value of their current endowments and the value of the endowments they (or the people who would have existed instead of them) would have received under the just, but unequal distribution. The problem here, as in the theodicy debate, is establishing the baseline.

We can make this point more vivid by returning once again to Bob and James. We imagined that Bob is more intelligent than James, but that James benefits significantly from Bob's superior intelligence (i.e., because the drug invented by Bob extends James's life by twenty years—and Bob could not have invented this drug without his superior intelligence). The principle of justice would therefore clearly instruct us to elect this unequal distribution over one in which Bob has exactly James's level of intelligence. But the fact that James benefits substantially from Bob's intelligence does not suffice to show that the Cosmic Pareto Principle is satisfied. In order to vindicate the latter claim, we would need to demonstrate that James is benefited to the precise *degree* required by whichever specification of the Paretian insight we choose to adopt.

To make matters simple, I will suppose for the remainder of this discussion that the Difference Principle is the specification we want—not because I regard it as the most plausible version of Paretianism, but because I take it to pose the most difficult challenge to theodicy. It ought to be much easier to show that the current distribution of natural advantage might make the least well-off *somewhat* better off than they would be under an equal distribution, than it is to show that the least well-off are *maximally* benefited (i.e., one could not improve their position, even a bit, by adopting any alternative distribution). Indeed, if we can demonstrate that, for all we know, the current distribution might satisfy the Difference Principle, it follows a fortiori that it might satisfy any other candidate Paretian principle. So we should ask, in relation to the case of Bob and James, not whether the latter is merely better off than he would have been under an equal distribution of intelligence, but whether he has been maximally benefited by the unequal distribution. If he has not been maximally benefited, we will concede for these purposes that the distribution is unjust; and if the distribution is unjust, we might entertain the thought that James is owed the difference between the value of his current bundle of endowments and advantage (plus the benefit he receives from Bob's drug) and the bundle he would have received under the just distribution.

But how can we know whether he has been maximally benefited? The challenge posed by this question is very different indeed from the one posed by the application of the conventional Difference Principle to economic distributions. In market economies, the social product is not a fixed sum, but it is nonetheless finite. As a result, while it is always possible to achieve equality by "leveling down" (i.e., taking resources away from those who have more, thereby bringing them down to the level of those who have less), it is not usually possible to "level up" (raising the worst-off to exactly the level of the best-off, without taking resources away from the latter). This fact dramatically limits the set of possible distributions that we need to consider in order to apply the Difference Principle. If A has 5 and B has 10, we would compare this distribution to the following sorts of alternatives: (1) an equal distribution in which A has 7.5 and B has 7.5; (2) an unequal distribution in which market incentives are used to "grow the pie," such that B ends up with 20 while A ends up with 18; or (3) another possible unequal distribution, also market-driven, in which B ends up with 100 while A ends up with 8, and so on. But since there is an upper limit to the wealth that society can create—and because the creation of that wealth is apparently subject to various economic laws—most other options are excluded. A distribution in which the pie is maximally grown but shares remain completely equal is not possible, and therefore needn't be considered.

But in the case of the "Cosmic Difference Principle," this sort of option must be on the table—and this is what gives the theodicy debate its peculiar difficulty. When it comes to Bob and James, it is not the case that our only options are (1) Bob and James have the same level of intelligence, namely Bob's; and (2) James has greater intelligence than Bob, but Bob benefits thereby (relative to how his life would have gone under option 1). There must also be option 3: Bob and James have the same level of intelligence, namely the higher level that James alone enjoys under option 2. Indeed, there are potentially infinite further options: Bob and James could, in principle, both be made as intelligent as we please.[38] Here, then, would be the luck egalitarian rejoinder to the claim that an unequal distribution of natural endowments and advantage need not be unjust: since leveling up is possible with natural endowments (the supply of them is in principle infinite), it will simply never be the case that the least well-off are maximally benefited under an unequal distribution. We could always just give them more without thereby causing the "pie" to shrink.

But what exactly do we mean in this context by "the pie"? When Rawlsians apply the standard Difference Principle to the basic structure of society, the answer to this question is controversial, but clear. The "pie" refers to the total supply of "income and wealth." An unequal distribution of these goods is justified if it turns out that allowing some to have larger shares of them causes the total supply to increase—with the result that the representative least well-off person has more wealth than he would have had under an equal distribution. This person is then said to be made "better off." But this final claim depends for its force on two simplifying assumptions that Rawls makes. The first is that both intrapersonal and interpersonal comparisons can only be made (for purposes of the theory of justice) on the basis of what he calls "primary goods": goods that "every rational man is presumed to want," among them, "income and wealth."[39] The second is that everyone prefers "more rather than less" of these, no matter what amount of them he happens to possess.[40]

The first of these assumptions has been the subject of extensive criticism (is it really true, for example, that it is rational to desire wealth, no matter what one's conception of the good happens to be? What if one is a monk?). But the second is the crucial one for our purposes. It surely does not follow from the fact that one regards X as a good that one must always prefer more of it rather than less. The notion is implausible enough when applied to social goods such as wealth,[41] but, in the case of natural goods, it seems obviously wrong. White blood cells are good and, up to a point, having more of them is better than having fewer—but there is a threshold, past which having more becomes a disadvantage rather than an advantage. Indeed, a great many natural assets would appear to fall into this category: height, a rapid metabolism, a refined sense of pitch, a high tolerance for pain, and so on. But if this is true, then we cannot simply equate being "better off" with having more of some natural asset (or set of them), rather than less. Depending on the nature of the good, a distribution in which A has less rather than more of X, might be a Pareto improvement. This might be because having more than some amount of X would itself make A's life worse (as in the white cell example), or it could be because a world composed of people who all had more than some amount of X (or the same amount of X) would be a less advantageous world for A to live in.

Returning, then, to our example: the question is not whether an unequal distribution of intelligence might be necessary in order to maximize the *intelligence* of the least intelligent person. If this were the question, then the rejoinder of my imagined interlocutor would be persuasive (*viz.* that, in fact, one could always in principle give more intelligence to the least well-off without making it the case that there is less intelligence to go around). The question, rather, is whether an unequal distribution of intelligence might be necessary in order to maximize the level of *well-being* or *advantage* of the least well-off person; the total supply of the latter across persons is the "pie." To answer this question, we need to interrogate the relationship between intelligence (and other similar natural assets) and advantage. Is intelligence a "threshold" good, such that having more of it is only advantageous up until some point, or is it a good that it is always rational to want more of, rather than less? And would James in fact be better off if he lived in a world in which both he and Bob (and everyone else) were maximally intelligent?[42]

Put this way, the question might appear abstruse, but it is in fact a very familiar question in disguise. In the context of bioethics, philosophers have long debated whether we are permitted, or even required by justice, to engineer maximally intelligent, talented, or beautiful children. This debate and the theodicy question are mutually implicating in obvious ways. To the extent that we can offer ourselves reasons of justice for not engineering maximally intelligent children (supposing we had the technological capacity to do so), we thereby sketch the outlines of a possible theodicy. That is, we offer an explanation of why a just God might *not* have elected to "level up" when it comes to intelligence and other natural endowments—or, in other words, why a possible world in which people are all maximally intelligent is not more just than one characterized by some inequality in the distribution of intelligence.

Another way of putting the same point is that luck egalitarians are, by implication, committed to a very strong position in the bioethics debate: namely, that justice requires us to use available technologies to equalize human endowments, presumably by leveling up.[43] To say that it is unjust that A is more intelligent than B is necessarily to say that we should, as a matter of justice, equalize their levels of intelligence to the extent that we can. It is no good to respond: "I don't believe that justice requires that all people have the same genetic endowments; I simply believe that those who have inferior endowments should be compensated by those who have superior ones." A duty of compensation arises only if the distribution itself is unjust; if one concedes that it is not unjust, it follows that no compensation is owed. Moreover, it is important to remember that financial compensation must feature in luck egalitarian arguments as a "second best" option, to which we have recourse only because it is (putatively) impossible to "redistribute" natural endowments themselves among people. (In some cases, of course, the redistribution of such endowments is in fact possible: one could transplant an eye or kidney from A, who has two, to B, who has none. Egalitarians prefer financial compensation in such cases because the redistribution of organs involves the infliction of pain and a trespass against bodily integrity—i.e., because here justice runs up against other values.) But, to the extent that the actual augmentation of the capacities themselves is possible, a luck egalitarian must surely prefer that form of redress to mere financial compensation, for the same reason that the replacement of a leg mangled in a car accident would be superior, from the point of view of justice, to financial compensation for the loss of a leg.

But very few bioethicists have been attracted to the view that justice requires, or even permits, the engineering of maximally and equally gifted children.[44] Indeed, the thought strikes most of them (and, I imagine, us) as positively dystopian. What gives the human world its distinctive richness is the sheer range of possible experiences within it, as well as the very limitations under which we operate. A world in which we were all equally intelligent, and / or one in which the upper limit of our intelligence was far above what it currently is, would not, in any recognizable sense, be a human world. And very few of us would find this hypothetical world of supermen choiceworthy.[45] I would much rather be less smart than Einstein in a world in which there is only one Einstein, than as smart as Einstein in a world populated entirely by Einsteins. Still less would I want to be far smarter than Einstein in a world in which everyone was exactly equally smart. To be sure, I might prefer being the one and only Einstein in *this* world to being less smart than Einstein—but this is not to challenge the justice of the distribution of intelligence, but rather to desire a different place within that distribution. It is, in other words, to engage in special pleading: I want there to be *someone* in my position, just not me.[46] This is the line of argument mooted by those profound philosophers, Gilbert and Sullivan:

> If I were Fortune which I'm not
> B should enjoy A's happy lot,
> And A should die in miserie
> That is, assuming I am B.

If the less intelligent are better off in this world of unequal intelligence than they would be in a world inhabited only by equally and maximally intelligent people, then the mere fact that they would prefer to be smarter does not impeach the justice of the distribution of intelligence.

It is worth pausing to distinguish the argument I have just been sketching from a more familiar one that might look superficially similar. In the context of the theodicy debate, it has been common for theologians to argue that a just God would allow physical evil (pain / deprivation) into the world, if the resulting world would be better overall than one without such evil. For example, Milton might well have suffered terribly as a result of his blindness, but, had he not been blind, we would not have had his blindness sonnets or *Paradise Lost*—and the resulting world would have been worse overall. More broadly, one might argue in the same vein that, if there were no suffering in the world, we would not be able to cultivate the virtues of compassion, charity, and solidarity, with the result that our emotional lives would be badly impoverished. The problem with this argument is that it amounts to a kind of cosmic utilitarianism, in which the unfortunate suffer so that the rest of us can lead richer lives. It is as if, in Leibniz's formulation, God were "like a great architect whose aim in view is the satisfaction or the glory of having built a beautiful palace, and who considers all that is to enter into this construction."[47] While "the felicity of all rational creatures is one of the aims he has in view," it often happens that "the unhappiness of some creatures may come about . . . as a result of other greater goods.[48]

A Leibnizian theodicy thus allows the ill-fortune of some to be justified by the overall goodness of the resulting whole. But that is precisely not the logic of the Cosmic Difference Principle that I have been exploring, which fully respects what Rawls called the "distinction between persons." We do not say that the existence of less intelligent people is justified because, while they might have gotten a bad deal, the well-being or advantage enjoyed by everyone else is thereby increased—that is, because it is good for *us* to live in a world that includes less intelligent people (them). Rather, we say that the existence of less intelligent people is justified if, and only if, it makes those very people better off than they would have been in an alternate world in which everyone was equally, and maximally, intelligent. No one, in Alexander Herzen's powerful phrase, is to be condemned "to the sad role of caryatids supporting a floor for others . . . to dance on."[49] The theodicy we have in mind treats individuals as ends, rather than means. The claim is that the position of the less intelligent in our world may well, for all we know, be better than the position they (or the individuals who would exist instead of them) would occupy in a world of equally and maximally intelligent human beings.

At this point in the argument, a luck egalitarian might respond as follows: "I agree that a world in which everyone had precisely the same natural endowments and advantages would be dystopian, and, therefore, that such a distribution is not required by the principle of justice. But that is not the sort of world I have in mind. Rather, I envision a world in which everyone has an equal overall level of natural advantages and endowments. The precise endowments enjoyed by each would perforce be various, thus preserving the diversity and distinctive richness of human life. Some would be good chess players, others shrewd entrepreneurs, some more beautiful, others more athletic, and so on. But, when all endowments were added together, everyone would turn out to be exactly equally advantaged. To the extent that the distribution of natural assets in our world does not map onto this hypothetical one, it is unjust—and we should act to correct it where possible, either through genetic manipulation or (if that is not practicable) financial compensation."

It is tempting to suppose that the primary obstacle to the realization of such a scheme is epistemic in character. That is, we might imagine that, in principle, there is such a thing as "an overall equal level of advantage" that could obtain between different human beings, each of whom enjoys a unique and very different bundle of natural endowments and attributes. The difficulty, on this view, is simply that we human beings could never have the requisite level of information about the character of these bundles to allow us to do the sums (although an omniscient God presumably could). But it is in fact far from clear that this is the right diagnosis of the problem. In order to get a clearer view of the issue, we first have to clarify the sense in which the bundles in question are said to be equal or unequal. Is the claim that they are (or ought to be) *objectively* equal in value?—that each item in the bundle has some value in and of itself, and that the total value (thus understood) of each person's bundle should be equal to the total value of each other person's. Or is the claim that the subjective value attached by each person to his bundle should be equal to the subjective value attached to their respective bundles by all other people?

If we take ourselves to be discussing the objective value of natural endowments, the challenge here is not primarily epistemic, but metaphysical. It seems on its face implausible to suppose that there is such a thing as an equal division of heterogeneous natural endowments among individuals, if what we mean is that these different bundles can have identical objective value. Let us suppose (controversially) that we find the following things, among others, objectively valuable for human beings: (1) beauty, (2) longevity, (3) good physical and mental health, (4) capacity for intimacy, (5) intelligence, (6) athleticism, and (7) the ability to have children. Is there a common currency into which all of these assets can be converted, such that we can say in principle that the lives of two individuals possessing different "bundles" of these might feature identical overall levels of value? Is there some fact of the matter (however inaccessible to us) about what fraction of fertility a good jump shot is worth? Or how beautiful you would have to make a person in order to compensate for a lifespan that is (by genetic predisposition) five years shorter? The problem here is not that we can't identify the exchange rate, but rather that there isn't one. These are incommensurable goods; one cannot be cashed out in the currency of another.[50]

It does not, of course, follow from this that we cannot say that a person who is fated to die of a genetic disease at age four has an objectively worse "bundle" than a beautiful, brilliant, healthy, athletic mother of three, who is actuarially likely to live until eighty-five (although the claim is not without its difficulties). There are many cases in which we feel comfortable making ordinal, but not cardinal judgments—and in these cases we do not suppose that the cardinal values in question are "out there" somewhere, just inaccessible to us. I may have no anxiety about asserting that a Lucian Freud portrait is more beautiful than a Jeff Koons sculpture, without supposing that there is anything *exactly* as beautiful as a Lucian Freud portrait. And if I can't say that any two things are exactly as beautiful as one another—that is, if I think that looking for an exact measurement of beauty involves a category mistake—how much more implausible is it to suppose that some level of beauty might be exactly as valuable as some level of mental health? To the extent that natural endowments have objective value, the notion of equally valuable, but heterogeneous "bundles" of these endowments is a chimera.

But what if we consider instead the claim that the subjective value attached by each person to his bundle should be equal to the subjective value attached to their respective bundles by all other people? Here too we might understand the proposal in two different ways. The value of a particular bundle of natural assets for a given individual might be taken to refer to the *enjoyment* that the person derives from the bundle, in which case we would be talking about the individual's mental states (pleasure, primarily); or it might be taken to refer, more broadly, to the degree to which the person finds his natural assets to be valuable, in the sense of being choiceworthy (which would presumably involve some reflection on the mental states produced by the assets in question, but need not be reducible to a judgment about the value of those states). We might ask about each of these proposals in turn: (1) Is it coherent to talk about a distribution of natural assets being equal in the relevant sense? (or, to put it differently, would the primary obstacle to a scheme designed to equalize the subjective value of bundles of natural assets thus understood be epistemic in character?); and (2) If so, do we find it plausible that the principle of justice either demands, or is satisfied by, such a distribution (such that a possible world in which this distribution obtained would be more just than ours)?

If we take the "mental states" route, the program is at least possibly coherent, but also unattractive. It is possibly coherent because, in principle, there ought to be an answer to the question "how much pleasure does fluteplaying give the flautist?" if what we mean is simply the duration and intensity of a particular, neuroscientfically describable mental state called "pleasure" (for instance). To be sure, there are epistemic reasons why we could never find the answer to this question: since we don't spend our lives in MRI machines, our mental lives are not subject to this kind of analysis. And even if they were, we would still need to be able to disaggregate the pleasure caused by the mere possession of musical talent from the pleasure derived from, say, the decision to cultivate it (or from the social approval elicited by musical virtuosity of this kind in particular communities). But it does not seem obviously wrong to suppose that an omniscient God could distribute natural assets in such a manner that each bundle would produce (in itself) an equal amount of pleasure / enjoyment in each person. Perhaps one could.

The problem, as many philosophers have observed, is that justice cannot plausibly be a matter of the distribution of mental states. If someone is constituted by nature (or socially conditioned) so that his mental state while experiencing objectively appalling deprivation is as "pleasurable" as the one that most people require substantial resources to achieve, we don't suppose that a distribution that leaves him with next to nothing and everyone else with substantial resources is therefore just. In the context of the theodicy debate, if God blessed A with every natural advantage and B with none, save for an extraordinary ability to generate pleasurable mental states—such that A and B experienced identical amounts of "pleasure"—this fact on its own could hardly acquit God of the charge of injustice. An equally familiar objection is that pleasurable mental states can be generated by false beliefs: if I maintain a happy mental state in the midst of great suffering because I incorrectly believe that I am a great composer whose works will be played for centuries after my death, it would seem absurd to say that things have gone equally well for me as for someone who experienced equally pleasurable mental states as a result of holding true beliefs (i.e., John really is a great composer whose works will be played for centuries).[51] The point is that we care about more than mental states; we care about how our lives are actually going as well, and we don't all assign the same weight to pleasure as against other sorts of goods. Some of us care more about mental states than others do. Many would choose to undergo great suffering in order to be a great artist, while others would never make such a bargain.[52] So an equal distribution of enjoyment cannot be what justice requires.

We are left, then, with the rival claim that what should be equalized (by "leveling up") is not enjoyment, but rather the value that each person attaches to his bundle of natural endowments. On this view, justice demands that all people should regard their respective bundles as equally choiceworthy. For some, the mental states produced by the bundle will determine the degree to which it is choiceworthy, while for others (who attach great value to things that are not mental states) the character and duration of such states will be far less dispositive. But each person should be equally satisfied with what he's got. Now, this position initially looks more promising: it might be impossible to equalize the objective value of incommensurable goods possessed by different people, but it is surely a familiar thought that we can, in principle, equalize preference satisfaction. This is what markets do every day (at least in theory) through a system of prices. Indeed, the view we are currently considering is best described as an endorsement, at the cosmic level, of something like the hypothetical auction of natural resources proposed by Ronald Dworkin.

Dworkin famously sets himself the task of explaining how a society that wishes to equalize resources could go about doing so. His answer is that, ideally, each member of that society should be assigned an equal sum of an agreed-upon currency (clam shells, in his example) and each available natural resource should be auctioned off in such a manner that each lot clears (i.e., there is only one purchaser at any price, and every resource is sold). If the hypothetical auction is run correctly, each person will end up with an equal share of society's resources, as measured by the cost imposed on others by the satisfaction of that person's preferences.[53] Indeed, the result of the procedure is not only an equal distribution, but also one that passes what Dworkin calls the "envy test": no one prefers anyone else's bundle to his own. (One could of course imagine an equal distribution that fails the envy test: each person could end up with what he regards as the second-best bundle. The bundles would then be equally valuable to each person, but each person would prefer the bundle of exactly one other person.)

Why should we not argue by analogy that an equal division of natural assets and endowments among human beings can be identified in principle as the result of a hypothetical auction in which individuals, given equal amounts of an imaginary currency, are allowed to bid on talents and attributes until each lot clears? Each would then end up with an equal bundle that also passes the envy test. Here too, however, the problems turn out to be considerable.[54] The first and most obvious of these is metaphysical. Since our natural endowments and attributes are substantially constitutive of who we are, it is incoherent to suppose that there can be an "I," separate and apart from my attributes, who is capable of forming preferences concerning natural endowments and assets, and then bidding (even hypothetically) according to such preferences.

But there is in fact a far more basic reason why this argument cannot help the luck egalitarian in this context: Dworkin's claim, on closer inspection, is not about what constitutes an equal division of resources per se, but rather about what it would mean to assign people equal *shares* of finite resources. As he understands perfectly well, a system of prices (such as the one revealed by his hypothetical auction) presupposes scarcity. It measures the costs imposed on others by the satisfaction of one's preferences. If there are no such costs—if no one's share of a given good is a function of anyone else's (i.e., more of X for you does not in any way mean less of X for me)—there are no prices, and hence no conceivable auction of such goods. So we need to ask whether natural assets, such as intelligence and athletic ability, are to be understood as scarce goods in this sense. This question, as we shall see, poses a particularly acute dilemma for luck egalitarians.

In order to see why, let us recall precisely where we are in this rather intricate dialectic. I began by arguing that luck egalitarians are wrong, given what they think about justice, to claim that an unequal distribution of natural assets and endowments is necessarily unjust (when not a result of the choices of the individuals among whom the goods are distributed). The reason, I suggested, is that the logic of the Cosmic Pareto Principle (which I then specified, for the sake of argument, as the Difference Principle) must lead us to acknowledge that an unequal distribution of natural assets will be not only permitted, but indeed required by justice (as luck egalitarians understand the concept) if it maximizes the well-being of the least well-off. The challenge confronting luck egalitarians, I went on to suggest, is that we cannot say that the current distribution is unjust unless we can identify a possible world, featuring a different distribution, in which the least well-off is better off—and even if we could, it might turn out that the possible world in which the least well-off is made maximally well-off, features a different, but still unequal distribution, rather than an equal one.

But I then imagined a rejoinder from the luck egalitarian: the logic of the Difference Principle, I had him counter, will never be relevant to the question of the distribution of natural assets and endowments, because these (unlike economic goods) do not have a finite supply. One can always "level up" by making the worse-off better-off, without any adverse effects for anyone else. It will therefore simply never be the case, according to this argument, that an unequal distribution of these goods is required in order to maximally benefit the least well-off. I then responded to this objection by suggesting that a "leveled up" world in which all people were maximally and equally endowed would not be choiceworthy, even for those who are less well-off in this world (someone less smart than Einstein would, on reflection, probably not prefer to be smarter than Einstein in a world in which people were all equally smart). My imagined luck egalitarian interlocutor then countered that there is surely a way of making people maximally and equally well-off, without giving them identical natural endowments. We then moved on to consider various accounts of what this might mean—including, lastly, the claim that what should be equalized is the value that each person attaches to his bundle of natural endowments.

At this point, we should be able to get the dilemma confronting luck egalitarians clearly into view. If natural assets and endowments are regarded as "scarce goods" in the relevant sense (i.e., there is a finite supply of them, not just in the sense that, for any human being, there is a maximum level of, say, intelligence, but (more bizarrely) in the sense that the level of intelligence I can enjoy is somehow a function of the broader distribution[55]), then we could in principle use a Dworkin-style hypothetical auction to say what an equal distribution of these assets would look like.[56] But the cost of classifying these as scarce goods is that the luck egalitarian can no longer argue that "leveling up" will be possible for natural assets: if there is a finite supply, then equality cannot be achieved by assigning everyone maximal and identical levels of these goods (or maximally and equally valuable bundles of them). In other words, the luck egalitarian would need to surrender his objection to the claim that the Cosmic Difference Principle is capable of justifying inequalities in natural endowments—because, in a world where "leveling up" is not possible, it becomes far more plausible to suppose that the well-being of the least well-off could be maximized under an unequal distribution of natural assets.

So that is the first horn of the dilemma. But the second is equally unattractive for luck egalitarians. For now suppose that we regard natural assets and endowments (more plausibly) as goods that are not "scarce" in the relevant sense; we assume, to the contrary, that an omnipotent God (or philanthropic genetic engineer) could give any individual any amount of each he chooses, and no one's allotment is a function of anyone else's. If so, then we necessarily lack a system of prices (even in principle) for natural assets and endowments, and therefore cannot avail ourselves of a Dworkin-style hypothetical auction in order to vindicate the claim that there is such a thing as an "equal distribution of heterogeneous natural assets." And, as we have seen, none of the other possible glosses on the concept offers a better way out of the impasse. It would seem to follow that one can only equalize natural endowments among individuals by giving them precisely the same endowments. And since a world in which people all had the same endowments would not obviously be a better world (from the point of view of justice) than this one, we are left with the conclusion that the current world, characterized as it is (let us continue to suppose) by an unequal distribution of natural advantage, is not necessarily unjust.

But we can say a bit more than this. Even if one mistakenly rejected this argument and continued to insist that the distribution of natural advantage among human beings is unjust (that is, if one denied that a just Distributor could have chosen it), one would still be unable to show that redistribution or compensation is required, even in principle, if one accepts that natural assets and endowments are not "scarce" in the sense we have been exploring. For, as we learned from the *King Lear* example earlier, it is implausible to hold that those who have been assigned larger allotments under an unjust distribution are bound as a matter of justice to "compensate" those who have been assigned smaller allotments, unless the shares of the latter are somehow a function of the shares of the former (i.e., those with more have benefited *at the expense of* those with less). Luck egalitarians should concede, in short, that the current distribution of natural advantage is not, for all we know, unjust—or, as our forebears would have put it, that theodicy is possible—and that, even if it *were* unjust, no compensation from the better-off to the less well-off would be required by the principle of justice.[57] The problem with luck egalitarianism, it emerges, is not that we are unable to correct the injustice it identifies; it is that we cannot know whether there is an injustice to correct.

III

We should in closing entertain one final objection to the claim that theodicy is possible, and, therefore, that luck egalitarians cannot demonstrate that the current distribution of natural assets among human beings is unjust. A critic might reply that my argument becomes less plausible as the imagined condition of the least well-off becomes worse. In the example of Bob and James with which we began, it might after all be the case that, whereas Bob is smarter than James, James is still quite intelligent. If so, the notion that this unequal distribution makes James better-off than he would have been under an equal distribution of intelligence (or even maximally well-off) has a certain plausibility. But what if James is instead at the far left edge of the bell curve that maps the actual distribution of human intelligence? What if he has what we would describe as a cognitive disability? Is it really plausible to suppose that there is *no* possible distribution of intelligence that would leave the worst-off person better off than the *least* intelligent person under the current distribution? A reasonably intelligent person might not, for example, prefer to be smarter than Einstein in a world in which all people were equally smart, but can we say the same of a person with an IQ of 40?

Two points of clarification are in order before we turn to the merits of this objection. The first is that, here again, we need to distinguish the position in question from one that can appear superficially similar. My imagined interlocutor in this case is *not* defending a cosmic version of what has come to be called "sufficientarianism." That is, he is not arguing that, while justice does not require an equal distribution of natural assets and endowments among human beings, it does require that all individuals have "enough" of these assets—where "enough" is meant to mark out a threshold level of advantage, beneath which people ought not to be allowed to sink.[58] This view can look similar to the position with which I am now concerned, because both deny that a distribution in which the worst-off are as badly off as they are in our world can be consistent with justice. But they are nonetheless quite different. The sufficientarian objection (which has its own difficulties) is inadmissible in this context, because it necessarily involves a rejection of luck egalitarianism—and therefore cannot form part of an internal critique of that position. The sufficientarian argues that inequalities, even when unchosen, do not impeach the justice of a distribution of resources, unless the inequalities in question have the effect of leaving certain individuals without "sufficient" resources. The objection that we are now considering, in contrast, accepts that justice requires equality, unless an unequal distribution would make the least well-off as well off as possible (that is, it accepts the logic of the Cosmic Difference Principle). It simply holds that a distribution that includes the least valuable bundle of natural advantages actually possessed by a human being on this planet cannot plausibly be thought to maximize the well-being of the least-advantaged.

The second, equally important point of clarification has to do with what this objection concedes. Because my imaginary interlocutor accepts the Cosmic Difference Principle (denying only that the current distribution in fact satisfies it), he necessarily acknowledges that justice might require a different *unequal* distribution of natural assets, rather than an equal one. In other words, he concedes that, if the current distribution is indeed unjust, it does not follow that it is unjust because unequal. It is entirely possible, on his account, that the well-being of the worst-off could be maximized under an unequal distribution of natural endowments—it's just that our current distribution, he thinks, cannot be the one in question. This concession is quite important, insofar as it establishes that, to the degree that compensation is owed to the least well-off under our current, putatively unjust distribution, they are entitled, not to a "bundle" of natural assets equal in value to the most valuable extant bundle, but rather to the difference between the value of their present bundles (understood broadly, so as to include also the benefits that accrue to them as a result of the natural endowments of others) and those they would have possessed under the just, but still unequal distribution. In order to establish what they might be owed, we would need to know a good deal about the character of this counterfactual distribution—and, as we have seen, the metaphysical and epistemic difficulties involved here are prohibitive. Moreover, we have also demonstrated that the injustice of the current distribution (supposing it were granted) would not, in fact, give rise to obligations of justice to compensate the least well-off, if we assume that natural assets are not "scarce goods" in the relevant sense— or if we accept, on grounds of the nonidentity problem, that it is incoherent to claim that the least well-off can have been "harmed" by the putatively unjust distribution. So, even if the objection were to be granted, it is difficult to see how it could have redistributive implications.

But should the objection be granted? The argument is that the natural endowments of the least well-off among us are so very meager that a world including such people cannot (from the point of view of justice) be the best of all possible worlds. To be fair, my imaginary interlocutor is not claiming that the mere existence of disabilities suffices to show that the distribution of natural advantage in our world does not satisfy the Cosmic Difference Principle: he recognizes that a disability is merely one constituent part of an individual's overall bundle of natural assets (a blind man might be Milton), and that disabled people are capable of leading extremely fulfilling lives. He is arguing, rather, that there are individuals in the world (say, people with Tay-Sachs disease) whose overall bundles of natural assets are so wretched as to make it absurd to suppose that their situation could not have been improved under any conceivable distribution of advantage (or, more precisely, that there is no possible world such that the least advantaged person within it would be better off than the worst-off person is in this world).

This claim returns us, perhaps fittingly, to the theodicy debate itself, and in particular to the version of that debate that preoccupied European philosophers in the wake of the Lisbon earthquake of 1755.[59] Does the fact of earthquakes (i.e., natural catastrophes that cause immense suffering) suffice to show that there is no God, or that God is not just? What if one can't have a human world without earthquakes? In other words, what if the set of natural forces that jointly have the effect of producing earthquakes are also necessary conditions for the existence of a world that can generate and sustain human life? Voltaire, for one, ridiculed the thought:

> Are you certain that the eternal cause
> That does all, that knows all, and creates all for itself,
> Could not plant us in these dreary climes
> Without forming active volcanoes beneath our feet?
> Would you so restrict the supreme power?
> Would you forbid him from exercising his clemency?
> Does not the eternal artisan have at his disposal
> Infinite means for bringing about his designs?[60]

Glossing this very passage, Hegel added mischievously that "something very like" the Leibnizian claim dismissed by Voltaire "can be said in every-day life": "If I have some goods brought to me in the market at some town, and say that they are certainly not perfect, but the best that are to be got, this is quite a good 'reason' why I should content myself with them. But 'comprehension' is an entirely different thing."[61] Surely an omnipotent God ought to be able to do better than my grocer!

But is this the right way to understand the concept of "supreme power," or divine omnipotence? To be sure, an omnipotent God might be able to will into existence an infinite number of possible worlds, but it does not follow that there is an infinite number of ways in which any given world can be brought into existence. Perhaps, as Rousseau countered, "physical evils" of this kind are "inevitable in any world of which man is a part."[62] Trying to make a human world without the natural forces that produce earthquakes is, on this account, like trying to make chocolate chip cookies without chocolate chips. If so, the question becomes: how choiceworthy is a human world, particularly for the least well-off? Is the life of a human being who suffers terribly as the result of a natural catastrophe so bad that it would have been better for that person not to have existed at all? Or, at the very least, so bad that there is some possible nonhuman world in which the least well-off creature is better off than this human being is?

The objection under consideration raises precisely this question. Could there have been a human world without Tay-Sachs disease? And, if not, is the life of someone with Tay-Sachs so bad that justice would have required that a human world not be created, but rather no world at all, or some radically different world? Or should we conclude that the Cosmic Difference Principle can be satisfied by a distribution of natural assets that includes Tay-Sachs, because people with this condition are still people—and it is better to be a person with Tay-Sachs than not to be a person?[63] Note that the plausibility of this line of argument increases, rather than decreases, as we move away from the Difference Principle toward other Paretian alternatives: it is easier (although still far from easy), for example, to imagine that a distribution including Tay-Sachs might satisfy a weaker prioritarian principle, according to which the well-being of the least well-off need not be maximized, but only appropriately weighted.

This conundrum is of course similar to the wrenchingly concrete question that confronts prospective parents of children with such disorders: if one knows in advance that a child will have Tay-Sachs, does justice require that one not bring the child into the world?[64] Or should one conclude that being human is valuable enough to outweigh even the horrors of this disorder? To be sure, the hypothetical parent in this example only considers the relative merits of two options—(1) existing as a human being with Tay-Sachs and (2) not existing at all—whereas the participant in the theodicy debate must consider these two options alongside the potentially infinite array of further possibilities opened up by the set of possible worlds. It might be that 1 is better than 2, but not so good as some further option 3, which an omnipotent God could have elected. But the questions are clearly related, insofar as the conclusion that it is better not to exist at all than to be a human being with Tay-Sachs would suffice to show that the Cosmic Difference Principle is not satisfied by the actual distribution of natural advantage: there would then be at least one possible world in which the least well-off would be better-off—namely, a world in which people did not exist. The opposite conclusion would, in contrast, leave open the possibility of theodicy.

So which is it? I freely confess that I cannot answer this question, and I do not see how anybody could. The objection we are considering cannot be set aside, but neither can it be sustained. Indeed, at this stage in the dialectic we might profitably recall the voice that called out in the first great theodicy debate: "Hitherto shall thou come, but no further." Or, rather more fashionably, we might invoke Rawls's observation that, at some point, the "ethics of creation" will simply "outrun human comprehension."[65] This is certainly what the canonical theorists of the eighteenth century concluded. Kant had no doubt that "omniscience would be required to recognize in a given world (as it gives itself to cognition in experience) that perfection of which we could say with certainty that absolutely none other is possible in creation and its government."[66] And Leibniz was equally convinced that "all the disadvantages we see, all the obstacles we meet with, all the difficulties one may raise for oneself, are no hindrance to a belief founded on reason" that the world is the best possible, "even when it cannot stand on conclusive proof."[67] Theodicy, in the end, could neither be demonstrated nor refuted: "For can I know and can I present infinities to you and compare them together?"[68] If the luck egalitarian can see beyond this point, I am impressed.

CHAPTER FIVE

Justice, Equality, and Institutions

IF WHAT I HAVE CALLED the "theodicy challenge" is compelling, then we have good reason to question the coherence of the luck egalitarian project. Even if we were to grant that the existing, natural distribution of advantage or well-being among people is unequal, we cannot know that it is unjust—from which it follows that we cannot know that compensatory transfers from the more to the less advantaged are required by the principle of justice (even supposing we could reliably identify the more and less advantaged). But it might seem at first glance as if the implications of the theodicy challenge, thus understood, will prove destabilizing *only* for luck egalitarians. Why, we might ask, should an egalitarian of the more conventional, Rawlsian sort find any of this at all troubling? Surely a demonstration that the distribution of natural assets may not be unjust only impeaches an argument for distributional equality if that argument is grounded in the putative injustice of the natural distribution. That is, only if one thinks that an egalitarian distribution of social resources is just *because* it rectifies, or "redresses," the injustice of "the natural lottery" will one be disconcerted by the thought that, for all we know, the natural distribution might be just (or that, if it is unjust, its injustice might consist in its deviation from some other *unequal* distribution of natural assets, rather than from equality). But egalitarians in the more orthodox, institutionalist line clearly do not think this—so perhaps they're off the hook.

This thought returns us to a well-known debate about how to understand Rawls's theory of justice. On the account favored by luck egalitarians, Rawls's argument about the "morally arbitrary" character of human advantage grounds his commitment to equality (or to the Difference Principle): that is, the purpose of the principles of justice is to mitigate or redress the arbitrary distribution of natural and social advantage. But those I will call "institutionalists" about justice deny that Rawls's theory is (or ought to have been) structured in this way. Equality, as Samuel Scheffler puts the case, is, for Rawls, "not, in the first instance, a distributive ideal, and its aim is not to compensate for misfortune."[1] It is rather a freestanding "social and political ideal."

> It claims that human relations must be conducted on the basis of an assumption that everyone's life is equally important, and that all members of a society have equal standing. . . . Equality so understood is opposed not to luck but to oppression, to heritable hierarchies of social status, to ideas of caste, to class privilege and the rigid stratification of classes, and to the undemocratic distribution of power. In contrast to the inward-looking focus of luck egalitarianism, it emphasizes the irrelevance of individual differences for fundamental social and political purposes. As a moral ideal, it asserts that all people are of equal worth and that there are some claims that people are entitled to make on one another simply by virtue of their status as persons. As a social ideal, it holds that a human society must be conceived of as a cooperative arrangement among equals, each of whom enjoys the same social standing. As a political ideal, it highlights the claims that citizens are entitled to make on one another by virtue of their status as citizens, without any need for a moralized accounting of the details of their particular circumstances.[2]

On this view, Rawls's principles of justice are intended to specify the way in which the basic structure of society ought to be organized in order to realize an intrinsically valuable kind of civic equality. "For people who are committed to the social and political value of equality," questions of distribution matter, "not because a properly designed set of distributive institutions can help to minimize the influence of luck, but rather because certain kinds of distributive arrangements are incongruous with that social and political value."[3]

How, then, should we understand Rawls's argument about the morally arbitrary character of natural and social advantages? The institutionalist answer is straightforward: the notion of moral arbitrariness is not intended to ground Rawls's theory of justice, but rather to rebut a particular objection to the sort of distribution mandated by that theory for independent reasons. As Scheffler explains, "Rawls cites the 'moral arbitrariness' of natural attributes and social contingencies, not because his ultimate aim is to extinguish the influence of all arbitrary factors, but because he thinks the arbitrariness of the factors he cites serves to undermine both an important objection and an influential alternative to his view."[4] The objection in question is that "those who are more talented or intelligent or hardworking than others deserve greater economic rewards than his theory would permit them to secure,"[5] and the influential alternative is an economic system that does in fact allow those who produce greater value to realize such gains, namely the so-called "system of natural liberty," in which "prior distributions of natural assets— that is talents and abilities—as these have been developed or left unrealized" are permitted to influence the social distribution of resources.[6] Rawls rejects any such scheme on the grounds that "it permits distributive shares to be influenced by these factors so arbitrary from a moral point of view."[7]

Again, I take no position in this context on whether the institutionalist or the luck egalitarian reading of Rawls is more faithful to the text of *A Theory of Justice*. My question is, instead, whether those who take the institutionalist line can thereby avoid the difficulties of the theodicy challenge. And my answer to this question will be "no," for the simple reason that the alleged arbitrariness of the natural distribution of advantage gives the institutionalist his only apparent grounds for resisting the objection from preinstitutional justice or fairness. To say that it is objectionable to allow natural advantages to influence distributive shares because the former are arbitrary from a moral point of view seems to imply that, if they were not arbitrary from a moral point of view, it would not be objectionable for them to influence distributive shares.[8] (It is also, as we have seen, to adopt the controversial theological premise that no theodicy is possible, which sits very uneasily alongside the Rawlsian ambition to generate principles of justice that are neutral with respect to comprehensive conceptions of the good.) But the whole thrust of the theodicy challenge is to destabilize our conviction that the distribution of natural advantage is in fact morally arbitrary. It asks us to recognize instead that the distribution may or may not be morally arbitrary—that we simply cannot know.

To make this point more vivid, imagine a world in which an omnipotent Distributor assigned to each human being an exactly equal share of natural advantage (or elected whichever alternative distribution you take to be required by what Rawls called "the ethics of creation," rightly understood).[9] Now, to be sure, these equal parcels of natural assets are themselves no more "deserved" by those to whom they are assigned than unequal parcels would be. But the distribution they embody is certainly not "arbitrary from a moral point of view." On the contrary, it is, by hypothesis, perfectly fair. In such a world, why would it be objectionable to allow natural advantages to influence the social distribution of resources? Indeed, in this scenario, it looks as if preventing the natural distribution from influencing the social distribution would introduce, rather than mitigate unfairness. Suppose that the perfectly just Distributor assigns A greater beauty than B, but compensates B by making him healthier than A. A's beauty counts as advantageous largely because of its social consequences: the Distributor knows that human beings assign great importance to beauty, that those who are beautiful will accordingly tend to attract mates of their choice, and so on. If the social consequences of A's beauty were to be neutralized (say, by means of a compulsory scheme in which mates were distributed by lot), A's level of advantage would drop below B's—thereby creating unfairness where (again, by hypothesis) there was none before. It follows that, if we knew that the just Distributor had done his work in this way, we would have yet another good reason not to adopt a lottery system for spouses.

One could say much the same thing about social advantages, such as socioeconomic position or family background. Suppose these were arranged in such a way that everyone had a fair share, as if they fell to earth like Nozick's "manna from heaven" and were then equitably distributed. John is accordingly born into a wealthy but not particularly nurturing family, while Frank is born into a nonwealthy but loving one. Why should these different bundles of social advantage not be allowed to influence distributive shares? If John is going to end up emotionally stunted and less able to lead a satisfactory family life, on account of his cold Victorian parents, why should the wealth that he is likely to accrue be transferred to Frank? If his offsetting social advantages (his quality education and access to networks of privilege) were to be deprived of their distributive significance, the result would be an unfair level of advantage for Frank, who would then enjoy the benefits of a nurturing family, without the disadvantages of a non-wealthy upbringing. Advantages are only advantages if they are allowed to have advantageous consequences—that is, if they are allowed to influence distributive shares.[10] A fair distribution of advantage that is not allowed to influence distributive shares is a chimera.

Thus, if the distribution of natural and social advantage were in fact *not* arbitrary from a moral point view, the institutionalist could not rebut the objection that these facts about people should, after all, be allowed to influence distributive shares. Indeed, in such a world, it looks as if this kind of influence would not merely be permitted, but required. Individuals would have a claim to the social consequences of their advantages, on the grounds that these consequences are, effectively, part of their fair share of natural and social assets. They would, in that sense, "deserve" to have them, even if the advantages themselves were all undeserved (in the same way that no one deserves, or has earned, any manna from heaven in Nozick's example).

It does not follow, of course, that claims of this kind must necessarily "trump" the demands of equality as a freestanding social and political ideal. It is open to the institutionalist to argue that claims of distributive fairness should be balanced against the demands of other values. He might, in other words, say something like the following: "While I acknowledge the independent moral force of John's claim to his wealth (supposing that the distribution of social and natural advantages were perfectly fair), this claim must be weighed against the distinct moral imperative to create a society of free and equal citizens—which requires that we adopt a method of assigning distributive shares that takes no notice of the differential abilities and advantages of individuals." Such an interlocutor would then need to specify how these two competing values ought to be balanced against one another.

It seems unlikely, however, that any plausible weighing of the two could assign trumping force to the requirements of an egalitarian social ideal. That is, it would seem odd to suppose that *any* degree of distributive unfairness, no matter how great, could be justified by the freestanding value of living in a particular sort of civic community. The moral weight of the notion of fairness is greater than that. Indeed, the putative *unfairness* of the distribution of natural and social advantages is apparently sufficient, for egalitarians of all stripes, to render the "system of natural liberty" ineligible, irrespective of whatever benefits it might be taken to yield. At the very least, then, an institutionalist egalitarian would be required to assign some nontrivial amount of weight to claims of desert, in a world in which the distribution of advantage were not arbitrary.

The question then becomes: how should we proceed, if we accept that the distribution of advantage may or may not be arbitrary—that we may or may not be entitled (as a matter of "the ethics of creation") to the natural endowments we possess, and/or to the value they produce? How ought we to deal with this uncertainty? What we have here, I want to suggest, can best be understood as an idiosyncratic variant of the problem of "unjust enrichment."[11] In the standard version of the case, a bank teller mistakenly transfers some of Bob's money to Fred's account. If we know the identity of the two parties and the sum of money that has accidentally ended up in Fred's account, then the case is relatively straightforward (although there is a rich discussion in the private law literature concerning why exactly Fred ought to be under a legal obligation to return the funds). Now suppose instead that we know the identity of the two parties, and that *some* money has mistakenly ended up in Fred's account, but we do not know how much. This is quite like the version of the case that confronts egalitarians (of either stripe) who suppose that the distribution of natural and social advantage *is* arbitrary from a moral point of view, but who nonetheless believe that some facts about people that cause them to do better or worse in life are *not* arbitrary in this way (say, their level of effort or industriousness). As we have seen, Rawls himself seems to adopt this posture in one stray passage from *A Theory of Justice:*

> None of the precepts of justice aims at rewarding virtue. . . . The distributive shares that result do not correlate with moral worth, since the initial endowment of natural assets and the contingencies of their growth and nurture in early life are arbitrary from a moral point of view. The precept which seems intuitively to come closest to rewarding moral desert is that of a distribution according to effort, or perhaps better, conscientious effort. Once again, however, it seems clear that the effort a person is willing to make is influenced by his natural abilities and skills and the alternatives open to him. The

better endowed are more likely, other things equal, to strive conscientiously, and there seems to be no way to discount for their greater good fortune. The idea of rewarding virtue is impracticable.[12]

Here Rawls appears to suppose that some portion of the "effort a person is willing to make" is *not* attributable to his natural abilities and social position. The problem, as Rawls characterizes it in this context, is that one's natural abilities and social position "influence" one's character, and so contribute to the value that one produces as a result of one's efforts—and there is no practicable way of "discounting" for the morally arbitrary factors that (partly) account for one's greater success.

Rawls concludes from all of this that the basic structure ought to recognize no freestanding claims to productive value of any kind. I have already explained in Chapter 1 that I find this conclusion unpersuasive, precisely because it fails to capture our intuitions about the sort of unjust enrichment case under consideration. If we know that the bank has mistakenly transferred some of Bob's money to Fred's account, but we do not know how much—and we know that at least some of the money in Fred's account is really Fred's—then it seems quite implausible to claim that Fred should forfeit all of the money in his account. Surely, it is at least as plausible to conclude, on the contrary, that he should forfeit none of it. Indeed, if we are entirely uncertain as to the proportion of tainted and untainted funds in his account (i.e., we have as much or as little reason to suppose it to be 1 as 99 percent), then it looks as if broadly liberal views about the requirements of permissible coercion would dictate forbearance. Liberals tend to suppose that we need better reasons to coerce than to refrain from coercion; this, I take it, is the grounding intuition behind our insistence that the burden of proof ought always to be on the state or plaintiff in judicial proceedings, whether civil or criminal. If even the "preponderance of the evidence" cannot establish the proportion of tainted funds in Fred's account, we would be inclined to resolve the case by declining to confiscate any of his money.[13] If, on the other hand, we *did* have some reliable sense of the proportions, we would surely opt for a resolution of the case that left Fred with whatever share of the funds we judged to be untainted. No morally serious adjudication of the case could leave him with nothing.

It is worth pausing for a moment to preempt two possible misunderstandings of this set of arguments. First, the question of how to address unjust enrichment cases of this kind is not exclusively a matter of what is now called "non-ideal theory." That is, such cases can arise even under conditions of full compliance with the principles of justice; no wrongdoing or faulty design of basic institutions need have taken place in order to generate these morally difficult situations.[14] Indeed, the specific case of Bob and Fred is plainly not an instance of partial compliance: neither the Bank nor Fred has committed a wrongful act in this example. Rather, the problem arises due to an accident or mistake. One can and should therefore ask how cases of this kind ought to be resolved as a matter of ideal theory. Second, and relatedly, my claims about how unjust enrichment cases may and may not be resolved should be persuasive even to those who reject what I take to be Rawls's argument in the passage quoted above about preinstitutional desert claims. In other words, even if one denies that at least some portion of our social product is attributable to nonarbitrary factors, and therefore creates a desert-based entitlement which ought (in principle) to be respected by the basic structure of society, one can still accept my suggestion about how cases of unjust enrichment should be resolved. Whether we suppose that Ben and Fred are entitled to the money initially in their respective accounts for reasons of preinstitutional desert, or (as institutionalists would have it) simply because the funds are part of their legitimate expectations under a just system of rules, the structure of the case remains the same. Either way, after the bank's error, we face a situation in which Fred is entitled to some of the money in his account, but we do not know how much. My claim is that on neither understanding of entitlement would it be acceptable to resolve this case by confiscating all of Fred's money.

Applying this set of intuitions to the case of natural endowments—where the claim is that A has been given more than his fair share of advantage—we would conclude that, if we cannot establish by the preponderance of the evidence what portion of A's overall level of advantage has been arbitrarily assigned to him (and what share of the value that he produces is due to that "extra" portion), we would be inclined not to confiscate any share of his product. Indeed, the deference due to A's product in this scenario is surely even greater than the deference owed to Fred's money in the analogous version of the bank case. For when we are talking about unjust enrichment at the level of natural advantages, there is no "Bob": no one, that is, whose share of advantage has been assigned inappropriately to the more favored individual. As we saw in detail in Chapter 2, it does not follow from the (putative) fact that A has been unfairly advantaged relative to B that the former must have a claim to the latter's advantages. This will only be the case if their levels of advantage stand in a particular kind of relation to each other. Returning to our King Lear example, to the extent that we believe that Cordelia has a claim to the portions of the kingdom assigned by Lear to Regan and Goneril, it is not merely because Regan and Goneril have unjustly been made better off than Cordelia, but because that they have unjustly been made better off *at Cordelia's expense.* They have been given "her share"—their having more is (in a sense) the cause of her having less. The game is zero sum, because the kingdom is finite. But the case of natural advantages is not like this. Even if we suppose that A has been unfairly advantaged, it is not the case that others are worse off *because* he is better off; he has not been given anyone else's "share" of natural advantage, and his having less would not mean anyone else's having more.

Moreover, as we likewise saw in Chapter 2, the nonidentity problem makes it very difficult to claim that B, who (let us continue to suppose) has been given less than the fair complement of advantages required by justice, has been made worse off as a result, and accordingly ought to be able to claim compensation from A. This is because B with a very different set of natural endowments is not B at all, but someone else. To claim that the distribution of natural advantage is unjust is simply to claim that, as matter of justice, a different set of human beings should have been brought into existence, rather than the existing set. But, if this is right, it makes no sense to claim that B is entitled to compensation from A; or that some share of A's advantages ought to have gone to B. A just distribution of endowments in this case, properly understood, requires the nonexistence of B—not his enrichment.

Thus, even on the assumption that we can know that the distribution of natural and social advantages unjustly favors A, it seems unlikely that standard liberal norms of adjudication would instruct us to confiscate any part of A's product. But this version of the unjust enrichment case, while difficult for egalitarians, is in fact far easier than the one generated by the recognition that we cannot know whether the distribution of natural and social advantage is unjust *at all.* The value that A produces is now seen to be the joint result of: (1) his effort, which is not morally arbitrary (or, at least, a share of which is not morally arbitrary); and (2) his natural and social advantages, which may or may not be morally arbitrary. Returning to our bank example, the analogy would be to a case in which we do not know whether *any* tainted funds have ended up in Fred's account, and, if they have, we likewise do not know what portion of the total they represent—but we are certain that there are untainted funds in the account. It would seem to follow a fortiori that, in such a case, we would not countenance the confiscation of any of Fred's money; and, by analogy, we would not permit the coercive redistribution of A's product.

At this point, the following objection might be offered: a finding of unjust enrichment does not require that we *know* that some of Fred's money is tainted, or that we *know* what proportion of his money is tainted. As we have seen, it requires only that we are entitled to *believe,* based on the preponderance of the evidence, that Fred has been unjustly enriched by amount X. That is, we simply need to have a justified belief that there is a 50.1 percent chance that X amount of money has wrongly ended up in Fred's account. By analogy, then, we need not have *knowledge* that A has been unjustly favored by the natural and social distribution of advantage, or that he has been unjustly favored to degree X. We simply need to have a justified belief that there is at least a 50.1 percent chance of his having been unjustly favored by degree X. And that kind of belief, it might be argued, looks quite attainable. After all, isn't it likelier than not that those who have quite a lot have too much?

In fact, the answer is clearly "no." Suppose we grant for these purposes two controversial claims: (1) individuals who are wealthier than others are more likely than not to have been assigned a greater share of overall advantage than those others; and (2) if an individual is in possession of a greater share of advantage than someone else, this circumstance is more likely than not to be unjust. Each of these claims is controversial because, as we saw at length in Chapter 4, the epistemic difficulties involved in making either assertion are profound. Judging whether A has been advantaged relative to B requires knowing far more than which of the two earns more money (what if A, who is the richer of the two, has a mental illness and, unlike B, no athletic ability or sense of pitch?). And even if A's overall level of advantage is in fact greater than B's, it does not follow that A has been unjustly advantaged: that would depend on whether there is a Pareto-superior (or "maximin-ing") distribution of endowments under which A (or the individual who would then exist instead of A) would have ended up with less. The notion that it is more likely than not that someone who is more advantaged along one observable dimension is more advantaged *tout court,* or that any superior level of advantage is more likely than not to be greater than what a Pareto-optimal distribution would require, seems quite unmotivated.

But let us grant arguendo that it is just barely more likely than not that a rich person is relatively advantaged and, separately, that any relatively advantaged person has been unjustly benefited. Would these two facts allow us to say that, on the preponderance of the evidence, unjust enrichment has occurred wherever A is richer than B? Simple arithmetic demonstrates the contrary. Let us say (concessively) that there is a 50.1 percent chance that a rich individual really has been advantaged overall relative to one who is less rich, and that there is a 50.1 percent chance that a relatively advantaged individual has been unjustly advantaged. In this case, the probability of the conjunct (i.e., A, being rich, is both relatively advantaged and unjustly advantaged) is 25.1 percent ($.501 \times .501$). And if we introduce the further, crucial question of the *degree* to which A has been unjustly advantaged, the result becomes even starker. Suppose (again quite concessively) that it is just barely more likely than not that an individual who has been unjustly advantaged owes at least 50 percent of his product to his unjustly high level of advantage. Here the probability of the conjunct (that A is relatively advantaged, unjustly advantaged, and owes at least half of his product to his unjust level of advantage) is just 12.6 percent ($.501 \times .501 \times .501$). (For the record, if we were to assume, implausibly, that there were a 75 percent chance of each of these three things being the case, the probability of the conjunct would still be only 42 percent). The "preponderance of the evidence" standard therefore cannot even approximately be met in such a case—and that is before we grapple with the additional wrinkle of the non-identity problem, which demonstrates that A cannot possibly have been enriched at B's expense, and that B can therefore have no claim to compensation from A.

To see just how outlandish it would be to conclude that an individual who merely appears to be more advantaged than someone else has in fact been unjustly enriched, it should be helpful to compare this sort of case to the one at issue in a notoriously problematic passage from Nozick's *Anarchy, State, and Utopia*. Having defended at length his "entitlement theory" of justice, according to which individuals may justly appropriate parts of the world unilaterally, Nozick briefly concedes that this view is compatible with the conviction that, in fact, a great deal of property has been illicitly acquired over time—and that, in principle, these wrongful appropriations should be "rectified" by transfers. He then offers the following striking suggestion about how we might tackle this problem of rectification:

> Perhaps it is best to view some patterned principles of distributive justice as rough rules of thumb meant to approximate the general results of applying the principle of rectification of injustice. For example, lacking much historical information, and assuming 1) that victims of injustice generally do worse than they otherwise would and 2) that those from the least well-off group in the society have the highest probabilities of being the (descendants of) victims of the most serious injustice who are owed compensation by those who benefited from the injustices (assumed to be those better off, though sometimes the perpetrators will be others in the worst-off group), then a *rough* rule of thumb for rectifying injustices might seem to be the following: organize society so as to maximize the position of whatever group ends up least well-off in the society.[15]

There is quite a lot wrong with this argument, and I will be laying out my objections to it more fully a bit later on. One important and highly relevant worry is that it might be unjust to allow purely probabilistic calculations of this kind to count as sufficient evidence of wrongdoing or unjust enrichment *at all*. If, to use a familiar example, we know that all but ten spectators in a full, thousand-seat stadium have sneaked in without a ticket, then it is overwhelmingly likely that any given spectator is guilty of gatecrashing (i.e., there is only a 1 percent chance that he or she isn't).[16] But it would still seem wrong to convict an individual of gatecrashing on the basis of this evidence alone. What we want instead is some individuated piece of evidence that, if reliable, would show that the individual in question actually did sneak in (e.g., testimony from someone who saw this particular person enter the stadium without submitting a ticket). As Judith Jarvis Thomson puts the point, if a jury were to convict on the basis of a purely probabilistic calculation of this sort, it would be "just luck for the jury if what it declares true is true."[17] To punish an individual on this basis seems inconsistent with the respect owed to persons. In a civil or criminal case against a defendant of ethnic group X, would we admit as evidence the fact that individuals of that background are more likely than others to commit the crime in question? Likewise, in Nozick's example, even if it were true that the least well-off have "the highest probability" of being the descendants of victims of expropriation—and, by implication, that the best-off have the highest probability of descending from expropriators (and even if the "highest probability" is in fact quite high in absolute terms)—these facts alone would not apparently entitle us to find against the best-off and confiscate part of their property.

But despite this grave difficulty, and numerous others, Nozick's problematic conclusion remains far less objectionable than the conclusion that any person who seems to be relatively advantaged is unjustly advantaged. For Nozick only has one conditional probability to contend with: the probability that someone who is rich is in possession of ill-gotten gains. The *identity* of the rich is not (we are entitled to suppose) itself at all unclear. We know exactly who they are. It might, then, very well be the case that there is a 50.1 percent probability that any given rich person is in possession of ill-gotten gains of some kind (although the question of "how much" will, again, prove devastatingly difficult to answer). In this case, it is not the probabilistic calculation itself that is chiefly objectionable, but rather the claim that such a calculation can justly count as evidence against a defendant. In the case of the distribution of advantage, in contrast, we know neither who is relatively advantaged, nor whether any given advantaged individual is unjustly advantaged. We are, in other words, dealing with two conditional probabilities that need to be combined. The result is that the probability of an apparently advantaged person being unjustly advantaged is massively lower than the probability of a rich person being in possession of what Nozick regards as expropriated property. Again, I intend this comparison to make clear just how deeply implausible the egalitarian case against the apparently advantaged really is.

There is, however, an obvious way of making the case easier for egalitarians, and that is to take a reductive, anti-Pelagian view of effort and industriousness, according to which they are simply derived from natural and social advantages—and might therefore be just as arbitrary from a moral point of view as all the rest. To return to our bank analogy, one of the features of the case that made it particularly difficult for egalitarians was the assumption that some portion of the money in the account is undoubtedly Fred's. If we know that some of the money is his, and we don't know that any of it isn't, liberal norms plainly favor restraint. Likewise, if we know that some portion of A's product is really his (because attributable to his non-arbitrary effort and industry), and we don't know that any of it isn't (because derived from morally arbitrary advantages), then we will have good reason to refrain from coercive redistribution. But what if, instead, we

adopt the perspective on effort and industry suggested by a second famous passage from *A Theory of Justice?*

> Perhaps some will think that the person with greater natural endowments
> deserves those assets and the superior character that made their development
> possible. Because he is more worthy in this sense, he deserves the greater ad-
> vantages that he could achieve with them. This view, however, is surely in-
> correct. It seems to be one of the fixed points of our considered judgments
> that no one deserves his place in the distribution of native endowments, any
> more than one deserves one's initial starting place in society. The assertion
> that a man deserves the superior character that enables him to make the ef-
> fort to cultivate his abilities is equally problematic; for his character depends
> in large part upon fortunate family and social circumstances for which he can
> claim no credit. The notion of desert seems not to apply to these cases. Thus
> the more advantaged representative man cannot say that he deserves and
> therefore has a right to a scheme of cooperation in which he is permitted to
> acquire benefits in ways that do not contribute to the welfare of others.
> There is no basis for his making this claim.[18]

Whereas in the previous passage, Rawls seemed to accept that some share
of our effort is nonarbitrary and, in principle, gives rise to desert claims
(although, in practice, we are unable to disaggregate the arbitrary and nonarbitrary factors that yield a given result), here he appears to state that, because
our degree of industriousness is derived "in large part" from arbitrarily
"fortunate family and social circumstances," it gives rise to no such claims
whatsoever.

Now, we have already seen that Rawls's conclusion is overly hasty: in fact,
the theodicy challenge demonstrates that we cannot know whether the distribution of advantages is morally arbitrary, and, accordingly, we cannot
know whether it gives rise to legitimate claims. The relevant point is, rather,
that effort and industriousness might be assimilated to the category of natural
and / or social advantage; that they too may possibly be arbitrary. For Rawls
in this passage, effort is no different in kind from a sense of pitch; both are
determined by the "cards we are dealt." Natural endowments, social advantages, and character are all aspects of each individual's overall share of advantage, and the question simply becomes whether the distribution of
these shares across individuals is fair or not. Our bank analogy, in other
words, should be revised as follows: we now confront a case in which Fred

may or may not, for all we know, have a claim to *any* of the money in his account—and, likewise, A may or may not have a claim to any of his product.[19] Under these circumstances, would the argument for restraint collapse?

The answer, I think, is that it would not. To be sure, if effort and industriousness are recharacterized as part of the distribution of advantage, the case for restraint becomes weaker. But it nonetheless remains relatively strong. To see why, we need to reflect on a disanalogy between the bank case and the advantage case that we have already had reason to discuss. If we do not know whether Fred has a claim to any of the money in his account, then (barring additional information) it is mere possession that distinguishes his situation from that of anyone else who has deposited funds in the bank. The money, after all, could be anyone's. If it isn't Fred's, then it must be either John's or Steve's or Jane's, since we know it came from *somewhere*. It follows that if the probability of the money's being Fred's gets low enough, it will reach a point at which it is identical to (and then lower than) the probability of its being someone else's. Under these circumstances, the case for deference would indeed be badly weakened (unless we dubiously attach an independent moral significance to possession). But are natural and social advantages like money in this respect? In the case of natural advantages, the answer is clearly "no." For any given bundle of natural advantages, there is only one individual who is capable of possessing a claim of the relevant kind to it. A's level of advantage can be either nonarbitrary or arbitrary: if it is nonarbitrary, then it is justly A's; if it is arbitrary, then it is justly no one's. This result, as we have seen, is delivered by the nonidentity consideration: it cannot be the case that, if my level of endowment is unjustly great, the excess belongs rightfully to other existing persons. Rather, for such persons, their not having been given the attributes in question is a condition of their existing at all.

But if we know that no one other than A can have a claim to his advantages, and that A may or may not have one, it ceases to be obvious why we should only defer to A's claim if there is less than a 50.1 percent probability that he has been unjustly advantaged. Suppose you're walking down the street and you spy a ten dollar bill lying on the ground beside you. You're not certain whether the money came from your pocket; you put the odds that it did at about 48 percent. But everyone else on the street is absolutely certain that the money did not come from him or her. What should happen to the bill? The question is not an easy one to answer.

On the one hand, it seems clear that a 48 percent chance that an asset is justly yours should count for something in a world in which there is no probability of its belonging to any other potential claimant. Indeed, if no one besides you can conceivably be wronged in the relevant sense by being deprived of the ten dollar bill, it looks as if the best way to avoid the risk of wrongdoing is to assign the money to you. If the money is really yours, we will have vindicated a just claim; if it isn't, we will simply have given you an extra ten dollars to which no one else was entitled. On the other hand, this line of thought begins to look less plausible as the probabilities go down. Would we really want to say that *any* nonzero probability of a valid claim should trigger our deference under these circumstances? What if there was only a 1 percent chance that you dropped the money? At this point, many readers would doubtless be tempted to reply that the case for deference has been exhausted—particularly if there happened to be urgent reasons to distribute the money in some other way. But where precisely to draw the line is something about which reasonable people can differ. Suffice it to say for our purposes that, even if we choose to regard A's effort and industriousness as potentially every bit as arbitrary as a ten dollar bill one finds lying on the street, we might in some cases continue to defer to his possible claims, even if the preponderance of the evidence counted against them.

But, surely, the more important point to make at this stage is that we should be exceedingly reluctant to regard our effort and industry as potentially arbitrary in the first place. The cost of accepting this thoroughly anti-Pelagian account of human agency, as we have seen, is prohibitive. If our actions really are completely determined in this way—not just influenced by natural endowments and social advantages beyond our control, but constituted out of nothing beyond them—then it becomes very difficult to explain why we are beings whose autonomy and choices matter in the way that liberals suppose that they do. Of course, it may give me pain to be prevented from doing what I desire to do, but many things give me pain. In order to make sense of liberalism, we need to explain what is uniquely bad about being my being directed by an outside force or agency. If the alternative is simply being directed by my own DNA sequences or class consciousness (or some combination thereof), why should it matter to me that my actions are dictated by your DNA sequences instead? It seems odd to attach moral significance to the *location* of the lines of code that dictate my every action.

Indeed, if G. A. Cohen is to be believed, Rawls himself seems eventually to have reached something like the same conclusion:

> I remember with particular pleasure one lunch that we [Rawls and Cohen] took, in what was for a (too) short time, a lunchtime haunt of ours. . . . We were talking about Kant and free will, and I was delighted that, as it seemed to me, Rawls expressed the belief that if all our choices really were causally determined, then many of our customary judgments of the moral worth of people would make no sense. Since I had been inclined to think the same for about thirty years, against the grain of the compatibilist consensus, it delighted me that Jack Rawls was on our minority side. There was a satisfying sense of conspiring together against the consensus.[20]

I too am on the "minority side" in this debate. If our effort and industry are potentially every bit as arbitrary from a moral point of view as our height or sense of pitch, then we have much bigger problems than figuring out how to redistribute the value that they produce. Seen from this perspective, strongly anti-Pelagian egalitarians begin to look a bit like Butch and Sundance: jumping off a cliff and worrying that they'll drown in the river below.

I

There is, however, one line of argument open to the institutionalist that undoubtedly does have the effect of neutralizing the theodicy challenge. This view, which I will call "pure institutionalism," holds that the distribution of natural and social advantage, whatever its character, is simply orthogonal to the question of the just distribution of social resources. The pure institutionalist believes, in other words, that Rawls was wrong to argue that the distribution of natural and social advantage should not be allowed to influence the distribution of wealth within society *because* the former is arbitrary from a moral point of view. In fact, on this account, there is no possible set of facts about the distribution of advantage that would qualify it to influence the social distribution. Even if the division of natural endowments among individuals were perfectly fair, the basic structure of society should take no notice of it when allocating social goods. Rather, society should be conceived of as a "cooperative scheme for mutual benefit" that gives rise to its own distinctive and purely internal distributive requirements. More specifically, as

T. M. Scanlon puts the case, since all citizens are "participants in a cooperative scheme," each must be "given equal standing, in determining what the
norms of social cooperation should be."[21] The question, then, becomes: which
distributive norms would honor the equal standing of participants in the sort
of cooperative enterprise that society is taken to embody?

One might begin, as Scanlon does, by analogizing society to a private
business partnership. "If partners in a business enterprise have made the same
investment of money and time, then it is plausible to say that a fair mechanism for dividing the profits should give each an equal share."[22] The only
considerations relevant to the division of proceeds among partners, we might
say, are those arising out of the reciprocal character of the partnership agreement itself. If each partner has contributed an equal amount of capital, each
should receive an equal share of the product. This is what "equal standing"
amounts to in such a case. We do not ask, in determining how the proceeds
ought to be distributed, whether one partner has been unfairly advantaged
relative to another in the distribution of natural endowments. If Ben and
Jane have each invested equal amounts of money and labor in their partnership, the fact that Ben is a diabetic while Jane is a gifted triathlete has no
bearing on the case. In particular, it does not suggest that Ben should receive a greater share than Jane. The partnership agreement does not (and
should not) set itself the task of rectifying unfairness in other domains; but
nor should it allocate benefits and burdens differently because some other
distribution of goods and bads happens to be fair. It is a closed system.
Likewise, if each member of society has contributed an equally valuable
quantum of cooperation to the overall scheme, each is entitled to an equal
share of the social product—irrespective of the broader distribution of advantage and disadvantage that happens to obtain among them.

Another way of putting the point is that, for the pure institutionalist, the
problem of whether it is fair or just to allow those who are more productive
(because of their natural and social endowments) to claim a larger share of
the social product does not arise, because, in the relevant sense, no one is
taken to be more productive than anyone else. Everyone fundamentally contributes the same thing to the cooperative scheme: his or her cooperation.
And everyone's cooperation is taken to be equally valuable, because equally
necessary. To be sure, some people create more wealth than others in the
economy (if institutionalists did not believe this, they would be unable to
make sense of the Difference Principle, which requires paying unequalizing

incentives to the unusually productive if this will improve the situation of the least well-off),[23] but this is taken to be incidental. At bottom, we are equal partners who contribute the same equity to our cooperative scheme.

One might, of course, query the plausibility of the view that the overall distribution of goods and bads among people should have no bearing whatsoever on cooperative agreements of this kind. Suppose, for example, that Ben has certain knowledge that he has, on the whole, been massively and unjustly advantaged relative to Jane: he is much smarter, healthier, and more talented, and he knows that this unequal distribution of natural endowments is not Pareto-superior to an equal distribution (on whichever version of the Paretian insight we might choose to endorse). Upon entering into a cooperative venture with Jane, might he not have a moral reason to accept a larger share of the burdens and / or a smaller share of the benefits? It is, at least, not obvious that the distribution of goods within a cooperative scheme should be wholly insensitive to the broader set of facts about how the parties fare.

But if we set aside this objection, we do indeed seem to have entered a world in which the theodicy challenge has no purchase. The intuition that we cannot know whether the distribution of natural and / or social advantages is just or fair will obviously be of little consequence if even certain knowledge of its injustice or unfairness would not cause us to alter the terms of social cooperation. So to the extent that pure institutionalism commends an equal distribution of social resources, it delivers a form of egalitarianism that is robust against the objections we have been considering. The question is whether pure institutionalism, rightly understood, *does* in fact commend an equal distribution of social resources.

Scanlon himself, after all, acknowledges a serious difficulty with the analogy between society and a business partnership: the assumption that, just as business partners "have made the same investment of money and time," so too have cooperating members of society contributed equally to the social scheme, is difficult to sustain. Arguably, "participants in social cooperation make very different contributions of resources and abilities."[24] We could put this point slightly differently. When evaluating the manner in which the proceeds of a business venture ought to be distributed among partners, we do not tend to reason that, because each partner contributed *something* of value to the enterprise, each should receive an equal share of the profits. Imagine that John, Tom, and Fred decide to cooperate to raise a million dollars in capital to invest in a new enterprise. John and Fred each contribute $450,000, whereas Tom contributes the remaining $100,000. In this scenario, each has contributed something of value to the partnership, and we might even say (more controversially) that the cooperation of each was equally necessary to the success of the venture—in the sense that, had any one of them declined to cooperate, the requisite million dollars would not have been raised. But few of us would conclude as a result that Tom, John, and Fred should all be equal partners and receive an equal share of the proceeds. Likewise, the mere fact that each citizen contributes to the social enterprise, and even the supposition that each citizen's contribution is equally necessary to the success of that enterprise, does not suffice to show that each citizen should be regarded as an "equal partner" in the relevant sense. To defend this stronger conclusion, one would need to demonstrate that each citizen's contribution to the cooperative scheme is equal in value to everyone else's.

Is such a view at all plausible? It is difficult to see how it could be. There is indeed some minimum contribution that most (but certainly not all) citizens make to society: namely, their acceptance of the state's lawful authority and their corresponding disavowal of private violence, and so on. But some citizens contribute very much more than this. It seems uncontroversial to observe, for example, that Steve Jobs contributed far more to our joint social venture than my friend the ski bum has. The former's talents and industry created a company worth half a trillion dollars, which in turn has revolutionized the private and professional lives of hundreds of millions of our fellow citizens (to say nothing of billions around the world). The latter has simply, and perhaps blamelessly, elected to spend his days sliding down mountains on parabolic boards for his own amusement. Is the relationship between Steve Jobs and my friend aptly analogized to the one that obtains between two business partners who have each contributed the same equity and industry to a joint venture? How could it be? That my ski bum friend has, despite his indolence, contributed something of value to the social enterprise is plausible; that his contribution is equal in value to Steve Jobs's is not.

But there is a second, distinct form of what I am calling pure institutionalism, which does not depend for its force upon the dubious claim that all citizens contribute equally to the social enterprise. This second sort of pure institutionalism is "conventionalist," in the sense that it holds that the state and its institutions are the unique source of entitlements to property and material resources. There are, on this view, no preinstitutional or prepolitical moral facts or principles that could even potentially give citizens claims to

particular assets against the state itself. The state is therefore free to establish whichever regime of property holdings and market relations it wishes,
provided that these form part of an overall institutional scheme that is itself
justifiable (by which the pure institutionalist means that it promotes a range
of important values, including social justice). The "equal contribution" view
that we have just been discussing plainly is not a conventionalist view, since
it holds that there is a freestanding distributive principle that the state ought
to honor in allocating social resources: viz. that shares should be proportional
to contribution. The conventionalist, in contrast, will deny the existence of
any such principle. While he accepts the existence of other freestanding
moral principles that can give rise to individual claims against the state (say,
claims to freedom of religious worship, speech, and occupational choice), he
regards the state as relatively unconstrained in its prerogative to distribute
material goods. The state is therefore permitted to equalize property holdings—and might even be required to do so, if an egalitarian distribution of
wealth is taken to advance its various moral purposes. Here too the distribution of other nonpolitical goods (including natural endowments), whatever its character, is taken to be irrelevant to the distribution of social
resources.

Consider as an example the argument of Thomas Nagel and Liam Murphy.
In defense of the claim that "the conventional nature of property is both
perfectly obvious and remarkably easy to forget," they offer the following
considerations:

> There is no market without government, and no government without taxes;
> and what type of market there is depends on laws and policy decisions that
> government must make. In the absence of a legal system supported by taxes,
> there couldn't be money, banks, corporations, stock exchanges, patents, or a
> modern market economy—none of the institutions that make possible the
> existence of almost all contemporary forms of income and wealth. It is there-
> fore logically impossible that people should have any kind of entitlement to
> all their pretax income.[25]

Or again:

> The modern economy in which we earn our salaries, own our homes, bank
> accounts, retirement savings, and personal possessions, and in which we can

use our resources to consume or invest, would be impossible without the framework provided by government supported by taxes.[26]

These passages admit of at least two possible readings, one weaker and the other stronger. On the weaker reading, what is being claimed is simply that we cannot have a moral claim to "all" of our pretax income, because that income is made possible by state institutions financed by the tax regime. So it is incoherent to regard our pretax income as basic and primary—as what is "ours," before we turn to the question of what the tax structure should be. The tax regime must come first, both logically and temporally, from which it follows that the state must have a claim on our product from the very beginning. This view has its difficulties, not least one of the "chicken and egg" variety: mustn't there be income to tax before taxes can finance the government that enables the creation of income? But we need not deal with these here, since this argument, even if granted, proves too little for Murphy and Nagel. It simply establishes that at least some of our pretax income comes into the world already encumbered, owed as payment to the state for its contributions to our economic product. This view therefore leaves open the possibility that we might have a nonconventionalist moral claim to all the rest (there is nothing exotic, within the natural rights tradition, about supposing that we could not *enjoy* our natural rights absent the state; this is often said to be equally true of natural rights to free speech, religious worship, and so on).[27]

The second, stronger reading of the argument, in contrast, forecloses this possibility. It holds that because the state is the source of all our wealth, in the sense that no wealth would exist absent the institutional framework that the state provides (and in the sense that wealth only takes the contingent form that it does in virtue of that institutional scheme), it is therefore free to dispose of that wealth as it chooses. To be sure, it must do so in the context of an overall social and political order that is justifiable, but there are no entitlements that individuals preinstitutionally have to things, such that failing to honor them would render such an order unjustifiable.[28] Government "creates" or "defines" a set of property rights, which it then has an obligation to enforce and respect.[29]

The first thing to notice about this view is that it is not conventionalist "all the way down." It is conventionalist insofar as it holds that any scheme of property rights that a legitimate state chooses to institute will be legitimate—and that it is, accordingly, simply a matter of convention that what is mine is mine and what is yours is yours (there is no pre-institutional, external standard that dictates what should be mine and what should be yours). But it offers a straightforwardly nonconventionalist account of why the state has the prerogative to distribute resources as it sees fit. The argument holds, as we have seen, that the state may allocate wealth as it chooses because it is the source of that wealth; more specifically, the state provides the institutional context without which that wealth could not be produced. But this argument, read charitably, is enthymematic. It omits an implied premise, namely, that if an agent or agency is responsible for the creation of a resource (in the sense that its contribution is a necessary condition for the creation of the resource), then it has the right to dispose of that resource as it sees fit, subject to certain constraints. The state's prerogative to allocate resources as it sees fit is, therefore, not *itself* a matter of convention (as it is, say, for Hume), but is rather derived from a freestanding moral principle: to each according to what he makes possible.

The problem with this view is that economic production involves a host of necessary, but not sufficient conditions. Take the case of the corner store. Nagel and Murphy (on this reading) want to argue that, because the store could not sell food to its customers without the roads, security, and financial apparatus that the state provides, the state therefore has a claim to 100 percent of the wealth produced by the store. None of this wealth would exist, but for the state's contribution; therefore there is no share of it that can be claimed by others against the state. But the store is run by George, who works long days behind the counter. Absent his willingness to work, nothing would be sold in the store, and no wealth would be produced. The state's contribution would therefore be for naught. By the same argument, then, George has a claim to 100 percent of the wealth produced by the store. But then again, absent the refrigeration system in the store, there would be no fresh produce for George to sell his customers, so it looks as if the company that supplied the refrigerator has a claim to 100 percent of the wealth created by the store. And so on. We might call this "The *Producers* Problem," after Mel Brooks's classic film.[30] Just as Max and Leo sell 100 percent of *Springtime for Hitler* to each of about 250 little old ladies—which is to say, they sell 25,000 percent of the play—this form of pure institutionalism will end up assigning 100 percent of the economic product to a vast array of different agents. But, as Leo forlornly reminds Max, you can really "only sell 100 percent of anything."

There is an obvious solution to the problem, but it is not one that Nagel and Murphy can adopt without cost. One could hold instead that different contributions, even if equally necessary to a given enterprise, have different values, and therefore entitle their providers to different shares of the resulting product. Just because you can't build a skyscraper without nails doesn't mean that the nail supplier ought to own the skyscraper. Rather, he ought to be compensated for the value of the nails that he provides, understood in some more sensible fashion. Likewise, the state does indeed make crucial, necessary contributions to economic production, but these entitle it to a commensurate share of the resulting product, not to the entire product. But to concede this point is, of course, to leave the realm of pure institutionalism behind: it is to accept that some share of society's wealth—the share not attributable to contributions made by the state—is not rightly the state's to dispose of as it sees fit. From which it follows that, even if the state's various purposes might best be advanced by equalizing holdings, the pre-institutional claims of individual citizens to the value of their respective contributions might well stand in the way of such a program.

II

So does the theodicy challenge undermine "institutionalist" egalitarianism? In the case of ordinary institutionalism, of the kind arguably defended by Rawls and certainly defended by many of his disciples, I have suggested that the answer is "yes." By insisting that individuals cannot have freestanding, pre-institutional claims to the value that they produce *because* the distribution of natural and social advantages is "arbitrary from a moral point of view," these institutionalists concede that, if the distribution of such advantages were *not* arbitrary from a moral point of view, individuals would have such claims (since they provide no additional argument for why these claims would be ruled out). Institutionalists of this stripe implicitly accept, in other words, that the character of the distribution of natural and social advantages matters for the distribution of social goods. The question simply becomes: is the distribution of natural and social advantage in fact morally arbitrary? And the theodicy challenge instructs us to reply with a resounding: "who knows?" Not only can we not know which of two individuals is more advantaged on the whole, we cannot know whether a relatively advantaged individual has been unjustly advantaged. It follows, I have argued, that uncontroversial liberal norms require us to respect the claims of individuals to their product.

In the case of what I have called "pure institutionalism," however, the case is quite different. The pure institutionalist does not think that it is the alleged arbitrariness of the distribution of natural and social endowments that disqualifies it from justly influencing the distribution of wealth, but rather argues that the former, whatever its character, is simply orthogonal to the latter. The rules governing the distribution of social resources, on this view, derive purely from the nature of the social enterprise itself—either because society is conceived of as a "business partnership" among equally contributing members, or because the state is regarded as the unique source of claims to material goods. As a result, neither variant of pure institutionalism is vulnerable to the theodicy challenge: the recognition that we cannot know whether the distribution of natural and social endowments is just causes nothing in these arguments to come undone. The problem with pure institutionalism is, rather, that neither version of it persuasively underwrites egalitarianism. If we take the "business partnership" model seriously, we cannot conclude that citizens are entitled to equal shares of the social product, because it is implausible to argue that each citizen contributes the same "equity" to the social enterprise. On the other hand, if we take the route proposed by "conventionalists," we likewise fail to reach an egalitarian conclusion: the fact, if it is one, that the state is a necessary condition for the creation of all wealth does not give us reason to deny that individuals might have preinstitutional claims to the value that they produce. And if such claims exist, they give us reason not to equalize holdings coercively. The conclusion is straightforward: either institutionalism is vulnerable to the theodicy challenge, or it is not an egalitarian theory.

CHAPTER SIX

"God gave the world to *Adam,* and his posterity in common"

Appropriation and the Left-Libertarian Challenge

WE HAVE SEEN THAT both luck egalitarianism and institutionalism fail to deliver a satisfactory account of how egalitarian conclusions are to be derived from liberal premises. There is, however, one additional argument from within the landscape of contemporary liberal political philosophy about why the principle of justice, rightly understood, requires an egalitarian distribution of goods. This final critique comes to us from those who identify themselves as "left" libertarians. The theorists in question share with the more familiar "right" libertarians three crucial beliefs: (1) that individuals are self-owners, in the sense that they have the exclusive right to dispose of their bodies, talents, and powers (as well as the fruits of these assets) according to their own preferences, irrespective of the character of the resulting distribution of holdings, opportunity, or welfare; (2) that individuals so conceived either possess ex ante, or legitimately can come to acquire, property rights in natural resources that do not depend for their force on convention, statute, or the overall justifiability of the institutional or legal systems under which these individuals happen to live; and (3) that the coercive redistribution of assets is (in general) only justified when it rectifies previous or ongoing violations of property rights.[1]

Right libertarians reason from these premises to a defense of what Locke called "a disproportionate and unequal possession of the earth," whereas left libertarians arrive instead at a commitment to the egalitarian ownership of natural resources.[2] The cause of this divergence, both groups of theorists seem to agree, is a disagreement over the correct answer to the following question: Is there an individual right to appropriate natural resources in the state of nature? Or, in the original formulation of the question: Would a just God have bestowed such a right on individuals? Had our Maker "permitted a state of property to be everywhere introduced; that the industrious might enjoy the rewards of their diligence; and that those who would not work, might feel the punishment of their laziness," as Bishop Richard Watson suggested?[3] Or was Thomas Paine right to conclude instead that the earth must be "the free gift of the Creator in common to the human race" and that God intended no man "to *locate* as *his property* in perpetuity any part of it; neither did the Creator of the earth open a land-office, from whence the first title-deeds should issue."[4]

This diagnosis of the dispute between libertarians should surprise us for the simple reason that, from the birth of "state of nature" theory in the thirteenth century until its decrepitude in the late eighteenth, none of its practitioners seems to have supposed that the answer to this question would reveal much of interest about the legitimacy of contemporary holdings in the "civilized" world. Political and religious writers in Medieval and early-modern Europe turned to the state of nature in order to address any number of questions about property. Franciscans and their opponents wanted to know whether it was possible to go through life without owning anything[5]; Grotius and Selden wanted to determine who owned the sea[6]; Locke himself, as we now know, initially wrote the famous fifth chapter of his *Second Treatise* as a freestanding vindication of the colonial project in Carolina.[7] Yet precisely no one invoked the state of nature in order to ground a defense or rejection of contemporary holdings in those parts of the world where property had been "settled."[8] Even Rousseau, who lyrically mourned the moment at which men in the state of nature forgot that "the fruits are everyone's and the Earth no one's,"[9] took considerable pains to insist that property's allegedly invidious origins do not (by themselves) commit us to any particular view of its contemporary distribution.[10]

The contrary position seems to have first emerged among Rousseau's rather incautious readers—a fact for which we have the testimony of the least cautious of all, Pierre-Joseph Proudhon.[11] In his polemic *What is Property?* (1840), Proudhon writes that, although the learned men of his time "still disagree" about the question of property rights, "on one point only are they in agreement, which is that the validity of the right of property depends upon the authenticity of its origin."[12] If one can defend an initial right to appropriate natural resources in the state of nature, then today's private property is saved. If not (as Proudhon wants to argue), then the rights of today's proprietors are exposed as pernicious fictions, and "we live in a permanent condition of iniquity and fraud."[13] For Proudhon, if we accept Rousseau's claim that private property had its origin in unjust usurpation, then all subsequent holdings ought to be regarded as "fruit of a poisonous tree" and hence invalid. It is, after all, "a rule of jurisprudence that a fact does not produce a right"[14]—thus no alchemy can "turn the possessor into a proprietor."[15] Following Proudhon, Henry George likewise reasoned in his *Progress and Poverty* (1882) from the premise that no one in the state of nature may justly claim "exclusive possession and enjoyment" of land to the conclusion that "though his title have been acquiesced in by generation after generation after generation, to the landed estates of the Duke of Westminster the poorest child that is born in London today has as much right as his eldest son."[16] It is this understanding of the question of property rights that has come to organize the present-day debate between right and left libertarians. All apparently agree that a rights-based defense of contemporary holdings must rest on the assertion of a natural right for individuals to appropriate parts of the world.[17] If left libertarians can show that no such right can be defended, both they and their opponents seem to agree that widespread redistribution would then be required by the principle of justice (in order to return natural resources to some form of common ownership[18]). Accordingly, right libertarians have been dedicated above all to the vindication of a natural right to appropriation, while left libertarians have been dedicated above all to its rejection.

Yet all of the canonical natural law theorists seem to have recognized that this construal of the question is characterized by a glaring non sequitur—or, rather, by two of them. The first is perhaps easier to see, and has been noticed before (not least by left libertarians). If we assume, with Locke and the right libertarians, that there *is* a natural right of appropriation, it certainly does not follow from this fact that the contemporary distribution of property is legitimate. That would only be the case if one could *also* show that all current holdings can be traced back in pristine fashion to licit acts of individual appropriation[19]—a prospect which, to say the least, appears unlikely. Yet I want to argue that we encounter very similar difficulties if we assume instead (with Rousseau) that there is *no* natural right of appropriation and that, as a result, the initial division of natural resources among individuals was illicit. It simply does not follow from this fact, for any sort of libertarian, that current proprietors have no moral right to their holdings.[20] In order to defend *that* conclusion, one would likewise need to do much more work. In particular, one would have to defend a highly idiosyncratic (and, as I shall argue, unacceptable) principle of rectification, according to which *nothing* that transpires after an initial act of usurpation can be understood to generate rights to the (originally) usurped object on the part of its eventual possessors.

My argument, in short, will be that libertarians of both persuasions have been fighting their battles on the wrong terrain. It simply should not matter very much to a libertarian whether Locke or Rousseau was right about the justice of acquisition. In either case, they ought to begin their analysis from the supposition that illicit expropriation underlies the contemporary distribution of private property, either because Locke was right but his rules were not rigorously followed, or because Rousseau was right and individual appropriation was against the rules.[21] If this is so, then the question of rectification (that is, the question of how we may permissibly attempt to rectify previous violations of the principle of justice in acquisition) becomes, for libertarians, virtually *identical* to the question of distributive justice itself; it becomes the primary site at which the principle of justice must address the distribution of contemporary holdings. Yet both right and left libertarians have paid virtually no attention to the issue of rectification; and when they have discussed it at all, their remarks on the subject have tended to be perfunctory and unpersuasive.

Consider, for example, the case of Robert Nozick. Nozick famously devotes a great deal of time and energy in *Anarchy, State, and Utopia* (1974) to his defense of a Lockean right of appropriation. This argument is the centerpiece of his attempt to provide a plausible right-libertarian theory of the state. Yet it is, notoriously, only in the final paragraph of his eighty-page chapter on distributive justice that Nozick pauses to reflect on the problem with which we are concerned. He acknowledges here that his Lockean rules are extremely unlikely to have been followed scrupulously throughout the history of a given society, let alone throughout human history more generally. Given this fact, "the principle of rectification comes into play."[22] Yet, rather stunningly in light of this admission, Nozick declines to offer what he calls "a full treatment of the principle of rectification." Such a treatment, he says, would involve "very complex" issues and is best left to others. Instead, he offers the following tentative remarks, which we have already had reason to discuss:

> Perhaps it is best to view some patterned principles of distributive justice as rough rules of thumb meant to approximate the general results of applying the principle of rectification of injustice. For example, lacking much historical information, and assuming 1) that victims of injustice generally do worse than they otherwise would and 2) that those from the least well-off group in the society have the highest probabilities of being the (descendants of) victims of the most serious injustice who are owed compensation by those who benefited from the injustices (assumed to be those better off, though sometimes the perpetrators will be others in the worst-off group), then a *rough* rule of thumb for rectifying injustices might seem to be the following: organize society so as to maximize the position of whatever group ends up least well-off in the society. This particular example may well be implausible, but an important question for each society will be the following: given its particular history, what operable rule of thumb best approximates the results of a detailed application in that society of the principle of rectification?[23]

This paragraph leaves a great deal to be desired. Nozick's "rough rule of thumb" for pursuing rectification is not simply "implausible"; it is on its face unacceptable, even if we were to grant his very strong assumptions about the degree to which the sins of the fathers ought to be visited upon their children, and the degree to which descendants may justly claim compensation due to their remote ancestors. Perhaps it is true that, in societies like ours, those in the least well-off group have the "highest probabilities" of being the descendants of victims of expropriation, and that today's well-off have the highest probabilities of descending from original expropriators.[24] Even so, the probability that any given well-off individual descends from a well-off ancestor, let alone from a well-off expropriating ancestor, is simply not high—certainly not high enough to allow the presumption that his or her assets are the fruits of illicit expropriation in the past.[25] I, for example, am undoubtedly one of the "well-off" (considered in relation to the societal average), yet my grandparents were poor. And my case is hardly unusual. Even the most modest estimates of intergenerational income elasticity in the United States point to considerable flux in the economic status of families over time, and the number of well-off Americans who owe their wealth to inheritances (expropriated or otherwise) turns out to be quite small.[26] Nozick's justice here is not "rough"; it is, from a libertarian point of view, no justice at all.

Indeed, the obvious question to ask about Nozick's analysis is: why should we be seeking a "rough rule of thumb" *at all* in lieu of "a detailed application" of the principle of rectification in a given society? Libertarians do not, as a rule, tend to settle for rough rules of thumb when applying the theory of justice—that, indeed, is supposed to be the *whole point* of being a libertarian. Imagine, for example, how Nozick would react if someone proposed a similar rough rule of thumb for applying the principle of justice in punishment. New York City has five boroughs; of these Brooklyn has the highest crime rate. Relative to residents of the other boroughs, those of Brooklyn therefore have "the highest probability" of having committed a crime. Would this fact justify a rough rule of thumb according to which we are entitled to assume that Brooklyn residents are criminals, and therefore deserving of some form of punishment? Or even that Brooklyn residents, in virtue of the higher than usual likelihood that they have committed a crime, ought to be deprived of standard juridical safeguards, such as the right not to have their homes searched by police absent probable cause? When it comes to justice, libertarians do not settle for generic approximations; they require the "detailed application" of the correct principle. If the correct principle of rectification imposes burdens of proof that cannot be met in a given case, then justice will require that they refrain from disturbing the holdings in question, even if that means that some expropriators will fail to be punished, and some of their victims will fail to be made whole.[27] This is not to suggest that libertarians must be absolutists about justice: they need not deny that a just system of adjudication might occasionally penalize the innocent. It is only to insist that no libertarian (or liberal for that matter) could endorse a method of adjudication that imposes penalties on individuals simply because they happen to belong to a "class" in which a particular kind of wrongdoing is (allegedly) prevalent.[28]

But left libertarians suppose that they can avoid this particular predicament when addressing the issue of rectification. On Nozick's account, after all, virtually any object or natural resource is, in theory, capable of being justly acquired. As a result, it is impossible, absent detailed historical information, for Nozick to determine whether any particular piece of property was illicitly expropriated or not. However, if Rousseau and the left libertarians are right to deny that individuals have ever had a natural right to appropriate natural resources such as land, then we can know for certain that all privately held land has been usurped.[29] Any individual who now owns land is the possessor of what was initially stolen property. Given this conviction, when left libertarians discuss the issue of rectification at all, they usually follow Proudhon in assuming that it refers to the narrow question of how exactly those who hold "illegitimate legal rights" over natural resources ought to be treated, and "who should bear the transition cost from the unjust to the just world."[30] Yet this formulation begs the question. As we have seen, it simply does not follow from the fact that a given resource was initially expropriated that its current owner's legal right to it is "illegitimate." As a result, it does not follow that the world we are living in is (to that degree) "unjust," and that a world created by significant redistribution would be more just in comparison. We cannot rule on such questions until we identify the correct principle of rectification. And, as I shall argue below, given the shared convictions of both right and left libertarians, there simply is no defensible principle of rectification that would countenance the widespread redistribution of natural resources (or of their value) as a remedy for their initial expropriation in the remote past.

My claim, therefore, will be that libertarians of all stripes should concede that most (although certainly not all) contemporary proprietors have a moral right to the natural resources they own that must be respected even by those who deny the existence of any individual right to appropriate such resources.[31] I do not take a view in this context on how robust such rights are in the face of competing claims (for example, that of extreme privation). I do argue, however, that there is no reason for supposing that the rights to property I discuss ought to be distinguished from more traditional libertarian rights on the basis of "robustness." Whatever deference would be due to a (successfully defended) libertarian property right would equally be due to the property rights I delineate.

The argument offered here is thus strictly an internal one. If correct, it explains why libertarians should (in general) respect the contemporary distribution of private property, not why nonlibertarians should become libertarians. Nonetheless, I believe that my argument has important implications for nonlibertarian liberals. First and foremost, this is because many egalitarians have been persuaded that right-libertarianism, on closer inspection, simply collapses into left-libertarianism, which in turn fails to distinguish itself meaningfully from more familiar forms of egalitarianism.[32] That is, they have tended to suppose that the libertarian perspective on property rights is incoherent when it is not uninteresting. My argument suggests, in contrast, that libertarian premises do in fact lead to potentially inegalitarian conclusions, even if left-libertarian arguments about the illegitimacy of individual appropriation are granted. At the very least, then, egalitarian liberals will need to revise their understanding of the nature of the libertarian challenge. But I am also convinced that a number of the considerations and arguments adduced in this chapter about the moral significance of good-faith rule-following can and should be taken seriously by liberals who reject all three of the libertarian premises with which I began. These liberals too, I shall suggest, have good reason to respect existing holdings under most circumstances

I

Let us suppose that John steals a glass from Fred in 2018. Let us further suppose that John then sells the glass to Jane, who does not know (and could not reasonably have known) that the glass was stolen. What should happen to the glass and / or its value? There are three initially plausible answers to this question: (1) The glass should remain with Jane, with no compensation being offered to Fred; (2) the glass should be returned to Fred, with no compensation being offered to Jane; or (3) the glass, or its fair market value, should be divided between Fred and Jane.[33]

The argument for the first answer goes as follows. John has committed an injustice against Fred, and Fred correspondingly possesses a valid claim against John for the value of the glass (at the very least[34]). But Fred has acquired no claim of any kind against Jane. Jane had no reason to suppose that John was not the rightful owner of the glass, and therefore no reason to doubt his right to sell it (since she lives in a society in which the law allows the buying and selling of glasses). She parted with her money, to which she had an undoubted right, in good faith and formed a legitimate expectation that the glass would belong to her; if she were then deprived of the glass, she would, in effect, find herself being punished for a crime she did not commit— that is, for John's crime.[35] To inflict John's punishment on Jane would be to fail to respect what Rawls would call her "separateness," the inviolability and dignity that she possesses. That is, it would fail to respect precisely those features of her humanity that are meant to ground libertarian rights in the first place.[36] As Jan Narveson has put it, speaking about an analogous case, "culpable ignorance sometimes happens, to be sure; but very often our ignorance of things like this is altogether nonculpable. We were *had*. And when we are, it is a bit much to hold that we are guilty of the crime of theft on top of it. We aren't."[37] And if we aren't, then our title to the money we paid for the asset in question, which is now embodied in that asset, must be respected.

The argument for the second answer is more or less the same, but in reverse. If Fred had a perfect libertarian right to the glass, and in no way voluntarily transferred or alienated it, why should the fact that it was stolen from him and sold to Jane without his permission compromise his title? Libertarian rights, after all, are meant to be strong rights, and it seems peculiar to suppose that, from Fred's point of view, all bets are off as soon as the stolen object leaves John's hands and passes to a good-faith purchaser. Isn't the glass still *his*? If it is, then the fact of Jane's loss—while certainly unfortunate for her—is irrelevant to the resolution of the case.

It is precisely because there seems to be no principled reason to prefer either of these two arguments to the other that I believe we should be drawn instead to argument 3. What we confront in this case, in truth, is a pair of equally serious rights violations that give rise to potentially conflicting claims. John has actually stolen the value of the glass from two different people: Fred, from whom he expropriated the glass itself, and Jane, from whom he fraudulently extracted its value (by falsely claiming that the glass was his to sell). Both Fred and Jane therefore have a claim against John for the value of the glass. The proper libertarian adjudication of the case will depend on John's circumstances. If he has enough untainted money with which to make one of the two parties whole for the value of the glass, then a libertarian would resolve the case by assigning the object itself to one party (for our purposes it does not matter which) and payment for the value of the glass to the other. If it is not possible for both to recover their property from John in full (because he has insufficient funds with which to make Jane whole for the value of the glass if the object itself is to be returned to Fred, or because he is otherwise unable to make restitution[38]), then a libertarian would insist that the glass be "clawed back" to a compensation fund and the two victims be assigned equal shares of its value—just as if the glass had been jointly owned by the two of them at the outset.

The case is precisely analogous to the following one. A thief steals $10,000 from A and then pays it to B (who could not reasonably have known about the theft) in return for some asset worth at least that sum of money, and the thief has no assets remaining when A attempts to recover his stolen cash. If B's $10,000 is to be clawed back to a compensation fund, A and B (as possessors of equally strong rights to the $10,000) would each be entitled to a $5,000 settlement. To be sure, this resolution is suboptimal from a libertarian point of view, in that it makes neither party whole. But it is the only resolution that sufficiently honors the symmetrical rights of both parties. It would be straightforwardly unjust to award both the glass and its entire value to one of the two claimants while leaving the second wholly uncompensated,[39] for the same reason that it would be unjust to restore the entirety of a stolen, jointly owned asset, as well as its value, to only one of two joint owners (or to make whole one creditor while ignoring the claim of a second in the event that the same debtor defaults on both of them[40]).

This third answer, like the first, acknowledges and attempts to honor Jane's claim to the value of the glass. At issue between them is precisely how that claim ought to be weighed against Fred's in cases where the two directly conflict. Or to put it another way: even according to the third answer, it is only the existence of Fred's claim that prevents Jane's from being the *only* relevant claim to the value of the glass (i.e., prevents her "claim" to its entire value from being regarded uncontroversially as a "right" by libertarians). Her claim derives from the fact that she possessed just title to the money with which she purchased the glass and acquired the object in accordance with existing rules. A libertarian would only allow her claim to be vitiated if she knew (or reasonably ought to have known) that the glass itself was stolen: for in that case she would not have been defrauded of her money—indeed, she would have become an accessory to the theft after the fact.[41] Notice that good faith, on this account, does not *ground* her right to the glass and/or its value (if Jane had paid for the glass with money that she mistakenly, but innocently, believed to be her own, she would have acquired no claim to it), but the absence of good faith would suffice to defeat her claim to be compensated for its value. Good faith is thus a necessary but not sufficient condition for the sort of claim we are considering.[42]

If a proper libertarian adjudication of this case would assign Jane a claim to the glass and/or its value, then, a fortiori, she would have to be assigned at least an equally robust claim in any plausible libertarian adjudication of the following, modified version of the case. John steals a glass from Fred in 1750; Fred then sells the glass to Louise, who does not know (and could not reasonably have known) that the glass was stolen; a series of transactions occurs over the next 250 years, in which the glass changes hands forty times. It ends up in the hands of Jane in 2018, who, incidentally, paid a good deal more for it than Fred did in 1750 (even adjusting for inflation), because the glass is now an antique. Fred has a surviving descendant: Sam. This modified case should prove instructive for thinking through the issue of rectification when it comes to the private ownership of natural resources (again, we are assuming for the purposes of argument that Rousseau and the left libertarians are right to deny that individuals may justly appropriate such resources). On a Rousseauian account, all land that is now privately owned was initially usurped, expropriated from the common stock of mankind. Yet many, if not most present-day landowners count as "Janes," having purchased their parcels perhaps hundreds of transactions after the initial expropriation. What, then, would a defensible principle of rectification have to say about what should happen to the land? Applying the insights we gained from the example of the stolen glass, we would conclude that those who have purchased their land in good faith have a claim to its fair value *at the very least,* and that this claim would unambiguously take on the status of a right to the land and its entire value in the absence of a serious rival claim.[43] Moreover, since libertarians, both left and right, acknowledge the right of individuals to exchange and give away the things they justly own,[44] we would conclude further that those who have received such parcels of land from good-faith purchasers likewise have a right to the value of those parcels (even if *they* know that the object was *initially* stolen).[45]

The question is whether, in the case of initially expropriated natural resources, there are in fact any claims to those resources that a libertarian ought to acknowledge, apart from those of contemporary good-faith purchasers.

If we accept the first initially plausible adjudication of the "glass case," the answer would obviously be "no." Recall that, according to that view, even the original victim of the theft acquires no claim to rectification against the good-faith purchaser of the asset. It follows a fortiori that no descendant of the original victim could have a claim against any good-faith purchaser of natural resources (or against the descendants of those purchasers). The left-libertarian case would thus straightforwardly collapse.

But let us, for that reason, set aside the first resolution and focus on the third. If we agree that a good-faith purchaser of a stolen asset cannot wholly be insulated from the claims of its original owner—such that, if the perpetrator of the theft possesses insufficient funds with which to make the victim whole (or if he has died or disappeared), the asset in question will have to be "clawed back" and its value divided between the two injured parties—what should we think about the case of initially expropriated natural resources?

In order to address this question, let us return for a moment to our "modified glass case," where the relevant parties are (1) the good-faith purchaser of the glass (Jane) and (2) a descendant of the original victim (Sam). Is it only the original victim himself (Fred) who possesses a claim against Jane, or should such claims be regarded as heritable—as capable of passing from one generation to the next? Again, if we restrict the class of potential claimants to the original victims themselves, then Jane (as a good-faith purchaser) would remain the only possessor of a claim to the glass, and, by analogy, contemporary good-faith purchasers of anciently expropriated natural resources would possess the only valid claims to those resources. But suppose instead that we took the far more expansive (and controversial) view that claims to reparation are heritable. What then? To begin with, we usually accept that there is *some* generational threshold after which descendants may no longer claim reparations due to their ancestors, although we may disagree passionately about where exactly the line should be drawn: we might, for instance, concede my right to retrieve art stolen from my family during the Holocaust, but very few would acknowledge my right to seek damages from Spain for the expulsion of my relatives in 1492 (still less to sue Egypt for the enslavement of my ancestors by "a Pharaoh that knew not Joseph").[46] Nonetheless, let us assume for purposes of argument that no such limitations apply—that the descendants of the victims of expropriation, no matter how far removed from the crime itself, are in principle entitled to reparations.

Armed with this assumption, we will be prepared to concede that Sam might be the bearer of his ancestor's claim to the glass and / or its value, although he wouldn't *necessarily* be the bearer of such a claim, because a libertarian would acknowledge the right of Fred (or Fred's descendants) to *decline* to bequeath the claim to Sam.[47] But should this finding prompt us to identify a new class of potential claimants in the case of anciently expropriated natural resources? It seems to me that we must answer in the negative. There is, it turns out, a crucial disanalogy between the two cases. In the "modified glass case," we know who the initial thief was (John) and who the descendant of the victim is (Sam). When it comes to the primeval expropriation of land, in contrast, we lack both these pieces of information.[48] A left libertarian will dispute this claim, conceding that we do not know the identity of the "Johns," but insisting nonetheless that we know perfectly well who the "Sams" are: humanity as a whole, particularly those who have ended up without any land. Yet this cannot be right. Let us imagine an act of land expropriation in the remote past. Say that there are n people on earth when some nefarious usurper—call him John again—illicitly appropriates a parcel of land for his exclusive ownership. Since, on a Rousseauian account, the land belongs to all in common (that is, we might say, to Humanity Inc.[49]), John has illicitly expropriated all but one nth of the parcel in question (or all but one nth of its value). The victims of this theft are quite specific individuals: they are the n-1 co-owners of the land who have been robbed of their shares in it. Who are their descendents?

It surely does not follow that those who lack land today descend from initial victims; some are undoubtedly the descendants of expropriators who have come upon hard times. Likewise, it is certainly the case that some who now own land are themselves descended from initial victims. As a result, the sort of redistribution that left libertarians have in mind (not unlike the "rough rule of thumb" envisioned by Nozick) would have the perverse effect of enriching the descendants of expropriators at the expense of the descendants of their victims. Once again, in applying the principle of justice in rectification, libertarians should not settle for "rough rules of thumb"; they require the precise application of the correct principle. Expropriation in the past (to the extent that it occurred) was perpetrated by specific individuals and had specific victims. If we do not have sufficient evidence as to the identity of these individuals (or their descendants), we simply do not know who is owed compensation, and who ought to be providing it.[50] In

such a case, a libertarian reasoning from either our first or third principle of
rectification would recognize no claims to the natural resources in question
apart from those of their good-faith purchasers (just as Jane's claim to the
glass and its value would be trumping in the absence of a serious rival claim
by an identifiable Sam). He or she would not countenance the widespread
redistribution of land as a remedy for its initial expropriation.

But we can in fact say a bit more. Suppose that one is (mistakenly, in my
view) drawn instead to the *second* plausible adjudication of the glass case that
we canvassed at the outset, according to which the good-faith purchaser's
claim is simply trumped by the claim of the original title-holder. What would
follow in the case of initially expropriated natural resources? To be sure, if
we could identify the victims of expropriation or their descendants, this
principle would instruct us to return the expropriated resources to them
without offering compensation to good-faith purchasers. But if we cannot
identify the victims or their descendants, matters are quite different. For presumably even a libertarian who believes that the claims of title-holders
should trump the claims of good-faith purchasers would be inclined to defer
to the latter in cases where no title-holder can be identified. In other words,
if Fred or his descendants were nowhere to be found in our original case, we
would surely vindicate Jane's claim to the glass *no matter which* of the three
initially plausible principles of adjudication we happened to endorse. Why
wouldn't her claim be dispositive in such a situation? It is plausible (although,
I think, mistaken) to argue that Jane's claim ought to count for less than
Fred's; it is not plausible to argue that her claim ought to count for nothing.
By analogy, even a libertarian drawn to the second principle of rectification
ought to respect the claims of good-faith purchasers of natural resources (or
their descendants) in cases where the initial victims of expropriation (or their
descendants) cannot be identified.

Some left libertarians would resist this conclusion by arguing that one
need not be an original victim of expropriation (or a descendant of an original victim) in order to possess a claim against contemporary owners of
natural resources. Such an argument might proceed in one of two ways. The
more obvious strategy would be to insist that, by expropriating natural resources in an illicit manner, our villain John has wronged a class of future
persons who would otherwise have been in a position to exercise their equal
right to make use of the resources in question.[51] These future persons, once
they come into existence, would therefore have a claim to restitution. Here,

however, we encounter the usual difficulties associated with discussions of duties toward future persons: it seems odd to suppose that one can injure a nonexistent individual (since nonexistent individuals cannot be the bearers of rights), and it is an inescapable fact that, absent various expropriations in the past, many current persons would not exist in the first place (this is the nonidentity problem, as discussed in Chapter 4). As a result, a small number of theorists have opted instead for the argument that "late arrivals"—persons who come into contact with the original shareholders in Humanity Inc. due to the phenomenon of overlapping generations—have claims against the current owners of natural resources.[52] On this account, late arrivals do not possess a claim to *restitution*—by hypothesis, the initial division of the earth did them no injury, since they did not exist at the time—but, upon arrival, they automatically acquire a right to an equal share of natural resources which, in Henry George's phrase, "vests in every human being as he enters the world." If one deprives them of this right, one commits an injustice against them.

This is clearly a very different sort of argument from the ones we have been considering, in that it does not reason from a claim about the past injustice of individual appropriation to a redistributive conclusion. Indeed, it does not engage the issue of rectification at all.[53] The "late arrivals" in question are simply said to have a free-standing claim to an equal *n*th of the world arising out of the "equal concern" owed to them[54]; they would possess this claim even if all acts of appropriation before their births had been perfectly licit. While I believe that there are good reasons for rejecting this argument, it is not part of my brief to address it here.[55] Note, however, that even if one endorsed the "late arrivals" position, the result would simply be that the natural resource case becomes analogous to our "glass case," although far more complicated: we would then confront a situation in which *both* the good-faith purchaser of the natural resource and a class of late arrivals have symmetrical claims to some portion of its value[56] (just as Fred and Jane had symmetrical claims to the glass and / or its value). As in the case of the glass, the purchaser would be assigned a claim to that value, albeit one that is not wholly insulated from the rival claims of the late arrivals. (He would count as a good-faith purchaser if he acquired the resource on the understanding that its entire value would remain his in perpetuity, and not simply until the birth of an additional human being somewhere on earth.) Accordingly, if compensatory funds are unavailable—either because the individual who "fraudulently" sold the resource to the purchaser has insufficient assets, or because the seller himself was unaware that it came encumbered in this manner—the resource in question would be "clawed back" to a compensation fund and its value would be divided in some manner between the good-faith purchaser and the class. In short, even on this construal of the case, libertarians would assign quite robust, although not exclusive, claims to good-faith purchasers of natural resources.

II

Several possible objections might be offered to my argument. The first amounts to the charge of begging the question: to say that following the rules in good faith generates morally serious claims is, it might be argued, to assume that which is in dispute, namely that the rules in place are deserving of respect (either these *particular* rules or rules in general). But, goes the argument, this is precisely what left libertarians wish to deny.[57] They would, in other words, assert that there is an important disanalogy between the case of the glass and the case of expropriated natural resources that I have been considering. Our considered view about Jane in the former case, it might seem, depends in large part upon the unstated assumption that glasses *in general* are the sorts of things that one should be able to buy and sell.[58] That is, perhaps we feel that Jane's right to the value of the glass is grounded in her good-faith following of a *just* rule. There is, in this example, nothing morally suspect about glass-buying per se; it is only the fact that this *particular* glass was stolen that makes the case at all interesting. Yet, in the case of natural resources such as land, what certain left libertarians claim is that such resources are simply not the sorts of things that can legitimately be appropriated (in the full sense), and thus that they cannot legitimately be bought, sold, or exchanged by individuals. On this account, the land-purchaser has not simply mistaken a tainted object for one that a just rule would allow him to buy; he has failed to notice that a rule allowing private individuals to exchange such objects is *itself* unjust. Thus, my analogy between the glass case and the land case might appear to smuggle into the latter an important assumption about the legitimacy of the rule in question.

The first thing to point out about this objection is that it risks begging the question in the opposite direction. As we have seen, it simply does not follow from the fact that natural resources were initially usurped that a rule allowing them to be exchanged by their present owners must be unjust. Indeed, I have gone to some lengths to establish that any plausible principle of justice in rectification would allow and respect such exchanges, and I have likewise explained why we should not regard "humanity" in general as the rightful owner of natural resources *at this point in time*. But, for the sake of argument, let us concede the point: suppose we agree *both* that the initial expropriation of natural resources is unjust *and* that any rule allowing the full private ownership or exchange of such resources is likewise unjust. Does it then follow that those who live in societies in which such a rule is in place, and who acquire natural resources as a result of having followed this rule, have no moral right to their holdings? Can one claim to have been "defrauded" if one has unknowingly purchased an object in accordance with an unjust rule?

Although at first glance we might be tempted to answer this question in the negative, after more careful consideration, I believe, we would want to resist the temptation. To begin with, we should distinguish between two different senses in which someone might be said to be a "good-faith" follower of an unjust rule. If we use the term as we used it to describe Jane, we would simply mean that the agent in question believes that his actions are in accordance with the rule (even though they might not be). Yet, since on this account the rule *itself* is unjust, the mere fact that the agent believes that his actions are in accordance with it would not seem particularly relevant to our question: after all, the objection we are considering would find fault with him even if his actions *were actually* in strict accordance with the rule in question. But we could also mean something very different by the phrase "good-faith follower of an unjust rule." We might mean instead that such an agent acts according to a rule which, in good faith, he believes to be just. Should this fact matter from a moral point of view? Again, at first glance, there would appear to be something strange about supposing that it should. Ignorance of the law is (and ought to be) no legal defense, so why should ignorance of morality be a moral defense? Our suspicion that there is something strange about this view becomes even stronger when we consider that, taken to an extreme, it might seem to excuse all "good-faith" actions, no matter how objectively heinous. If the Inquisitor or the SS officer sees nothing immoral in his actions after careful consideration, is he therefore to be exculpated?

Yet it seems to me that, however perverse this view might initially appear (and however damning the reductio just sketched out would be if sustained), there is something compelling about it. A crucial difference between the law and morality is that the former is promulgated in concrete form, whereas the latter is not. Ignorance of the law is no defense because it is not unreasonable to expect individuals to be capable of familiarizing themselves with whatever aspects of it are relevant to their situation (in a case in which it *is* unreasonable to expect this, we might very well accept ignorance of the law as a defense). The law is there to be examined, and, if one fails to examine it, one is simply negligent. Morality is very different in this respect, and one can say so without being any sort of relativist. Derek Parfit famously suggested that the study of ethics is a discipline (like the study of the natural world) in which considerable progress has been made over time—and in which we should expect much further progress to be made.[59] Although some of its basic principles might be comparatively obvious, the more detailed specifications of its requirements are not at all. We have already seen that John Locke made precisely the same point in response to those who lay "blame on men's negligence, that they did not carry morality to an higher pitch; and make it out entire in every part, with that clearness of demonstration which some think it capable of" before the coming of the Gospel:

> Nothing seems hard to our understandings that is once known: and because what we see, we see with our own eyes; we are apt to overlook, or forget the help we had from others who showed it us, and first made us see it; as if we were not at all beholden to them, for those truths they opened the way to, and led us into. For knowledge being only of truths that are perceived to be so, we are favourable enough to our own faculties, to conclude, that they of their own strength would have attained those discoveries, without any foreign assistance; and that we know those truths, by the strength and native light of our own minds, as they did from whom we received them by theirs, only they had the luck to be before us. Thus the whole stock of human knowledge is claimed by every one, as his private possession, as soon as he (profiting by others discoveries) has got it into his own mind: and so it is; but not properly by his own single industry, nor of his own acquisition. . . . A great many things which we have been bred up in the belief of, from our cradles, (and are notions grown familiar, and, as it were, natural to us, under the gospel,) we take for unquestionable obvious truths, and easily demonstrable;

without considering how long we might have been in doubt or ignorance of them, had revelation been silent.[60]

From this point of view, it is not much more surprising that our remote ancestors failed to understand the precise implications of the principle of justice than it is that they failed to grasp the principle of general relativity. And if the study of ethics is still in its infancy, future generations will presumably refine our own moral convictions quite considerably. In that case, we would seem to have good reason for acknowledging at least *some* role for the notion of "good faith" in moral evaluation. When considering whether an agent has any moral claim to what he has acquired by following an unjust rule, we should be interested in determining whether that agent could reasonably have been expected to know that the rule in question was unjust.

Let us return now to the issue of land purchasing in the remote past. It was in the late eighteenth century that European theorists first asserted that rules allowing the ownership, purchase, and exchange of natural resources by individuals are to be regarded as unjust due to the illegitimacy of unilateral appropriation in the state of nature. Is it reasonable to expect a resident of the Bronze Age to have anticipated these findings (even if correct) millennia *avant la lettre*? If our bronze-age man lived in a society in which land purchase was allowed by law, and purchased a piece of land—and if it is unreasonable for us to expect him to have divined that the rule allowing the purchase was unjust—is he nonetheless to be blamed?[61] And, if we conclude that he is not blameworthy, do we not do violence to him if we deny that he has a moral claim to the value of the land that he purchased in good faith (for the same reasons that Jane had a right to the value of her glass)?[62] If we answer this last question in the affirmative, then it would seem that, even if rules allowing the exchange of land in the remote past were unjust, those of today certainly are not: for if we attribute to good-faith purchasers in the past a right to the value of the land they purchased (despite the injustice of the rules under which they purchased it), then, for any sort of libertarian, rules allowing such purchasers to exchange those rights cannot now be considered unjust.

But what of the reductio that we anticipated earlier? If good faith can ground a claim in this case, why not in cases of heinous wrongdoing? If we accept that moral ignorance ought in some sense to indemnify the land-purchaser, are we committed to excusing the committed Nazi who believed in the justice of his actions? The answer, I think, is that we are not. Recall that our standard does not concern itself with what one *believes* per se, but rather with what one could reasonably be expected to know about the requirements of justice. If Locke and Parfit are right, then the recognition of *some* of these requirements may indeed be too much to expect from our bronze-age man, but certainly not the recognition of *any* of them. It does not seem like special pleading to point out that the moral principle "it is wrong to murder" is of a different order of self-evidence than the (hypothetical) moral principle "it is illicit for individuals to appropriate natural resources in the state of nature, and, accordingly, all rules allowing the private ownership, purchase, or exchange of such resources are unjust." Expecting our bronze-age man to recognize the first seems far more reasonable than expecting him to intuit the second. And given the fact that the period stretching from the Bronze Age to 1933 witnessed significant advances in moral understanding, we would have reason to expect a good deal more from our Nazi.

Yet my left-libertarian critics might object that the Nazi case is too easy by half. The most obvious practice to contrast with land purchasing, on their account, would instead be the institution of human slavery.[63] We agree that it can never be just to own, purchase, or exchange a slave, and that rules allowing such practices are unjust.[64] Yet, for millennia, rules existed in almost every society on earth allowing slaves to be owned, purchased, and exchanged. The case is the same, goes the argument, with natural resources, although left libertarians will admit a difference of degree in the injustice of the two practices (after all, the wrong of slavery is that it treats subjects as objects, while existing practices of land purchase stand accused only of mistaking one kind of object for another). Nonetheless, they might argue, if the good faith rule-following of the land-purchaser requires (at the very least) that he be compensated for the value of his land if and when it is reclaimed by others, would not the same logic require offering compensation to the slaveholder for the value of his slaves upon emancipation? If the thought of the latter appalls us, we should concede that the good-faith following of an unjust rule cannot give rise to the sorts of moral claims I have been defending.

Yet, as we have recently been reminded,[65] the case of slavery is more difficult than it might initially seem, and its very difficulty should, I think, serve to reinforce, rather than undermine the case I have been making. Given the Lockean / Parfitian view of morality with which we have been working, our

answer to the question of whether a "good-faith" slave-purchaser has a claim
to compensation for the value of his slaves—indeed, our answer to the question of whether someone, in purchasing a slave, can even be said to be
acting in "good faith"—would seem to become more or less obvious depending on when our hypothetical slaveholder happened to live. If he were
alive today, living in a society in which the trade in human slaves continued
to be legal, we would almost certainly conclude that the answer was "no." It
is reasonable to expect a present-day human being to recognize the injustice
of slavery; if he cannot, he is not trying hard enough, and should not be
regarded as a good-faith rule-follower. If, however, our hypothetical slaveholder were instead a resident of the Bronze Age, our answer would be a good
deal less obvious. The man in question would then have lived at a time in
which slavery was an unquestioned norm, sanctioned by virtually every social and religious system on earth.[66] The authors of the Bible, living centuries later, did not for a moment dispute its legitimacy, and neither did the
philosophers of ancient Greece who lived centuries after them. To argue that
our bronze-age slaveholder would not have a claim to the value of his slaves
if we went back in time and emancipated them is to insist that he *should
have known* that the rule under which he purchased them was unjust.[67] Is
that a reasonable expectation, given who he was and when he lived? If we
are even *somewhat* hesitant about answering "yes" in this case, how much
more so in the case of the bronze-age land-purchaser?[68]

III

I have argued that, even if we concede that individuals have no right to
appropriate natural resources, libertarians cannot plausibly reason from this
premise to the conclusion that present-day owners have no moral right
to their holdings in such resources. I first defended this claim by arguing
(1) that any just principle of rectification must assign good-faith purchasers
a claim to the value of assets that they have purchased according to existing
rules; and (2) that, where we cannot identify the victims (or the descendants
of the victims) of expropriation, no sound principle of rectification would
allow present holdings to be disturbed as a remedy for that expropriation.[69]
On the grounds of Argument 1, I concluded that good-faith purchasers of
these resources have a moral claim to their value; and, on the grounds of
Argument 2, I concluded that these purchasers have a right to the natural

resources themselves, as well as to their entire value. It follows that rules allowing such purchasers to exchange the natural resources that they own cannot be regarded as unjust by libertarians. However, as I proceeded to argue, the moral rights of those who have purchased natural resources ought to be defended even by those who (mistakenly) *reject* this conclusion—that is, by those who regard rules allowing the ownership and exchange of natural resources as unjust. I suggested that those holding such a view should concede that we often have reason to attribute good faith even to those who act in accordance with unjust rules, and that such good-faith rule-following itself gives rise to claims of the same force as those defended in Argument 1. If this analysis is correct, it would appear that the sort of redistribution envisioned by left libertarians cannot be justified on libertarian grounds.

These, then, are the implications of my argument for libertarians, both right and left. But we might well wonder whether this argument *only* has implications for libertarians. In particular, it is worth pausing to consider whether it has consequences for liberals in general. The answer to this question would clearly be "no" if by "liberals in general" we meant "all liberals." Certainly my arguments do not address utilitarian liberals in the tradition of Mill (that is, those who defend liberalism on the grounds that it maximizes well-being): such liberals might indeed have reason to respect the contemporary distribution of natural resources, but their reasons would be very different from mine (indeed, they would probably resemble Hume's).[70] Yet it seems to me that my arguments should have important consequences for all dignitarian liberals—that is, for all of those who defend liberalism on the grounds that it respects the inviolability and "separateness" of persons—even if they dissent from libertarians in arguing for a "patterned," rather than an "historical" approach to the theory of justice. For *any* theory of justice will necessarily confront the question of rectification. Whether we suppose that, in the abstract, the principle of justice requires equality of resources, equality of opportunity for advantage, the delivery of basic capabilities to all persons, or the maximization of the welfare of the least well-off, we have to consider the moral significance of the fact that we inhabit a world that has been structured by an infinite number of good-faith human transactions that conflict with our chosen principle.

This is not to say that we find ourselves in the realm of "nonideal theory," at least if by that phrase we mean a world in which we are unable to do the perfectly just thing and must accordingly settle for a second-best option.[71]

It is rather to say that what justice itself requires *now* might be different from what justice would have required in a world being built "from scratch."[73] Is it really only the libertarian who ought to conclude that we do violence to persons if we assign their good-faith transactions little or no weight in our moral evaluation of a given distribution of holdings? To be sure, the *kind* of claims that libertarians deal in might be idiosyncratic, but the considerations that prompt them to assign such claims to good-faith purchasers and to deny them to those who have not acted in good faith seem quite general. Suppose you were asked to apply your favored, nonlibertarian theory of justice to two nonconforming societies: one is populated by self-servers who advance their own interests without any regard to what they take to be correct moral principles, while the other is made up of well-intentioned individuals who scrupulously adhere to what they (mistakenly but not unreasonably) believe to be the correct principles of justice in all their dealings. Suppose further that the resulting distributions of assets in the two societies are equidistant from what your favored theory of justice would require. Is the distribution of holdings in the second society really entitled to no more of your respect than the distribution in the first?

To the extent that theorists have been willing to consider endorsing a posture of limited deference toward existing, imperfectly just distributions, it has usually been on the grounds of Henry Sidgwick's principle of "conservative justice." In Joel Feinberg's formulation, the principle holds that "to change the rules in the middle of the game, even when those rules are not altogether fair, will disappoint the honest expectations of those whose prior commitments and life plans were made in genuine reliance on the continuance of the old rules."[73] But quite a lot hangs on what is meant by the words "honest" and "genuine" in this context. If we simply mean, as Feinberg evidently does, that the agents in question have acted in accordance with existing, unjust (or imperfectly just) rules under the sincere and reasonable expectation that those rules would remain in place, then it is far from clear that their transactions are entitled to our respect—for such agents might not have acted in what we have been calling "good faith." They might have known all along that the rules in question were unjust, or they might negligently have failed to scrutinize the moral status of the rules with appropriate rigor.[74] It is perfectly possible, in short, that the self-servers in our first hypothetical nonconforming society could count as "honest" rule-followers in Feinberg's sense. What distinguishes the denizens of our second nonconforming society is not simply that they have made "commitments and life plans" on the reasonable assumption that the existing, unjust rules would remain in place, but that they have done so in good faith—that is, they have acted on the mistaken, but not unreasonable belief that the rules in question were just. If their commitments are "honest" in this sense, then it seems that the very principles that dignitarian liberals take themselves to be defending require that we respect the resulting distribution of holdings. This, I take it, is the view gestured at by Edmund Burke in a well-known passage:

> When men are encouraged to go into a certain mode of life by the existing laws, and protected in that mode as in a lawful occupation; when they have accommodated all their ideas and all their habits to it; when the law had long made their adherence to its rules a ground of reputation, and their departure from them a ground of disgrace and even of penalty—I am sure it is unjust in legislature, by an arbitrary act, to offer a sudden violence to their minds and their feelings, forcibly to degrade them from their state and condition and to stigmatize with shame and infamy that character and those customs which before had been made the measure of their happiness and honor. If to this be added an expulsion from their habitations and a confiscation of all their goods, I am not sagacious enough to discover how this despotic sport, made of the feelings, consciences, prejudices, and properties of men, can be discriminated from the rankest tyranny.[75]

It is not mere reliance on existing rules that commands our respect, but rather the good-faith reliance of those whose "minds," "feelings," and "consciences" assure them (mistakenly but not unreasonably) of the justice of those rules. What the requisite sort of respect amounts to—whether it should be conceived as a trumping consideration or simply as a pro tanto reason for deference (and if the latter, how it should be weighed against other concerns)— must of course remain an open question. But it is a question that political theorists should be interested in answering.

Back to Representation

THE FOREGOING CHAPTERS HAVE suggested that the most prominent forms of contemporary liberal political philosophy, when rightly
understood, do not successfully vindicate the claim that an equal or egalitarian distribution of wealth is required by the principle of justice. I have
argued further that this fact about contemporary liberalism only comes into
clear relief when we observe that present-day liberal theorists are unwittingly taking up untenable positions in the theodicy debate—positions that
were anathema to their early-modern predecessors, who understood the
structure of that debate far better, and who self-consciously grounded their
moral and political commitments in an avowedly Pelagian understanding
of God's justice.

Does it follow, then, that a liberal society must be inegalitarian? The answer, I think, is clearly "no." The view that egalitarianism is not *required* by
the principle of justice leaves open the question of whether such a distribution is permitted by that principle. And it seems difficult to argue that one
is not. After all, even the most committed right libertarian would concede
that an egalitarian distribution of assets can be morally permissible. Owners

of property, on this account, may always decide voluntarily to assign part or all of what is rightfully theirs to others.[1] It is therefore always possible to imagine a just libertarian society in which citizens consensually equalize their holdings. But right libertarians regard this conclusion as consistent with their defense of the minimal state. That is, while they accept that individuals might consensually assign part of their wealth to others, they hold nonetheless that it is unjust for the *state* to redistribute the wealth of its citizens, apart from narrow cases in which taxation is justified to fund the public protection of rights. What it means, on a right-libertarian account, for citizens to agree to equalize their holdings is, in essence, for each individual citizen to sign a private grant transferring the wealth in question to others, or to the state. And since it is surely difficult in practice to generate and coordinate such a multitude of transfers, egalitarianism understandably plays no role in right-libertarian political theory.

We might ask, however, whether the right-libertarian conclusion actually follows from its premises. The right libertarian supposes, for instance, that if the state wishes to use my money to help finance a new park, it must elicit my explicit contractual agreement to that particular expenditure; if it then wishes to use my money to help build a new school, it must secure yet another distinct permission; and so on. But we are familiar with numerous, apparently consensual practices from everyday life that do not seem to involve such granular, iterated acts of permission. I might hire a stockbroker who is empowered to buy and sell shares on my behalf without clearing each individual purchase with me. Or I might grant someone a power-of-attorney right to enter into complex transactions and agreements in my name for a period of years, or even for my entire life, without requiring that he elicit my specific approval for each. In either case, the agent is still said to act with my consent, even if I disapprove of the transactions in question. So why should we suppose that consent works differently when it comes to the state?

To this question, the right libertarian has a clear and apparently powerful answer. The difference between the broker or lawyer and the state is that I grant the former the right to act in my name in an array of cases; but, for the right libertarian, I cannot be said to have authorized the state to act as my representative in the same sense. We are born into states and constitutional orders that we have not chosen, and it is ordinarily quite difficult for us to extricate ourselves from these. At no point in our lives are we asked to authorize the state to act for us, or to assent to its basic structure, nor have we any opportunity to refuse our permission. Right-libertarianism therefore may be seen to rest chiefly upon a rejection of what we have identified as the liberal theory of political representation. The right libertarian will agree with his or her predecessors that authorization is a necessary and sufficient condition of representation—that if, and only if, I have authorized you to speak and act in my name can you be regarded as my representative—but will deny that this condition is satisfied in the actual relationship between citizens and states.

To resist this right-libertarian perspective on the concept of political representation, we must have recourse to what is arguably the most abused and derided concept in contemporary political philosophy: that of tacit consent. Indeed, we might say that libertarians, Rawlsians, and democratic theorists are united chiefly by their conviction that tacit consent cannot do the work of grounding political authorization. For Rawlsians, the coercive authority of states gives rise to special requirements of justification precisely because this authority is taken to be wielded over those who have not consented to it. In other words, it is the putative fact that the state operates over us *without* our permission that, on this view, obliges it to ensure that its decisions are justifiable, in principle, to each citizen.[2] Rawlsians therefore famously ask, not what citizens *have* agreed to, but rather what they would have (or ought to have) agreed to in an imaginary situation of fairness. A particular kind of democratic theorist, in contrast, accepts that political authorization is possible and practicable, but insists that it can only be conveyed through voting, rather than through tacit consent.[3] A democratic people, on this view, can consent to the actions of the state if and only if they approve of these actions at the ballot box, or by way of a referendum. Here too, tacit consent—the idea that individuals might be taken to have authorized the state to act as it does without ever having given it their explicit permission—is taken to be not "worth the paper it isn't written on."[4]

But is it, in fact? Most of us would, for example, wish to say that the people of the United States and Great Britain are "self-governing" in a way that the people of North Korea and Syria are not. A democratic theorist, as we have seen, would attempt to explain this intuition by claiming that, in democracies, citizens authorize the state to act in their name by voting in favor of the course of action it will take—but this plainly cannot be right. To see why, imagine a political community in which all laws are submitted for approval or rejection to the entire citizen body (say, by means of electronic voting on smart phones). In this community, every approved law will have the endorsement of a majority of the voting public. The voting theory of authorization favored by the democratic theorist would easily explain why those on the winning side of such plebiscites could be said to have consented to the resulting laws (i.e., because they have voted for them); but what about those on the losing side who refused to vote in favor? We need a theory that explains why they too might be said to have authorized the state to act as the majority has decided it should, or else we will have to concede that, in fact, it is only the *majority* that is self-governing in democratic states. In other words, we have to explain why those who vote against a given law can nonetheless be regarded as part of a group agent called "the people," the decisions of which are determined by majority rule.

How can those in the minority have agreed to join such a corporation? Perhaps, one might reply, by voting in favor of a constitution or fundamental law that provides for such democratic procedures. But this response simply kicks the proverbial can down the road: we would then want to know why those who have not voted in favor of such a constitution (either because they were not yet of age when the constitution was ratified, or because they voted against ratification) can nonetheless be said to have agreed to become part of a group agent ("the people") which is governed according to it. One cannot give a plausible answer to this question that does not rely on the concept of tacit consent. It is not by voting in favor of particular laws, constitutional or otherwise (let alone for the representatives who in turn approve such laws), that we can be said to have authorized the state to act in our name. Such authorization must come, if it comes from anywhere, from our underlying agreement to be governed by the decision procedures and institutions under which we live. And this sort of agreement, since it *grounds* the authority of whatever voting procedures we may have in place, cannot itself be conveyed through voting. In other words, if the citizens of the United States are self-governing in a way that the citizens of North Korea are not, it cannot be because the former are governed by the outcomes of mass suffrage elections, while the latter are not.

Any plausible theory of popular self-government must therefore make use of the concept of tacit consent. But it of course does not follow from this fact that the concept is tenable. Perhaps we should simply concede, as Rawlsians do, that there are no self-governing peoples, if by a "self-governing people" we mean one that has actually consented to be governed by the basic

structure of society. I want to suggest, however, that the case for tacit consent is far from hopeless, and in order to sketch the contours of this case, I
shall turn to the somewhat surprising figure of David Hume. Hume makes
an unlikely ally for me, in that he is usually credited with having offered the
most devastating critique on record of the notion of tacit consent. In his essay
"Of the Original Contract" (1748), Hume ridicules the view that "by living
under the dominion of a prince, which one might leave, every individual
has given a *tacit* consent to his authority, and promised him obedience."[5]
The problem, as he explains, is that "such an implied consent can only have
place, where a man imagines, that the matter depends on his choice."[6] "Can
we seriously say," Hume asks, "that a poor peasant or artizan has a free choice
to leave his country, when he knows no foreign language or manners, and
lives from day to day, by the small wages which he acquires? We may as well
assert, that a man, by remaining in a vessel, freely consents to the dominion
of the master; though he was carried on board while asleep, and must leap
into the ocean, and perish, the moment he leaves her."[7]

The objection is persuasive, but it is worth pausing to note its specific character. Hume is arguing that, given certain conditions that exist in states
with which he is familiar, at least some citizens of those states cannot be said
to have tacitly consented to their governments. He is not denying the coherence of the concept of tacit consent itself; he is denying its application to
circumstances in which an individual cannot plausibly "imagine, that the
matter [in question] depends upon his choice," and then claiming that
the situation of contemporary citizens is of this kind. Indeed, Hume elsewhere offers one of the more powerful defenses of the view that "agreement"
can be expressed tacitly, without a formal "promise" or "compact"—and
here again he takes as his image of choice a boat. "Two men," he famously
observes, "who pull the oars of a boat, do it by an agreement or convention,
tho' they have never given promises to each other."[8] Cooperation, in other
words, counts as consent. If I engage in joint action with others, or partici-
pate in an overarching cooperative scheme, I have given my "agreement" to
the enterprise. It makes no moral difference that I have not declared my
agreement explicitly by means of a promise or contract. What Hume adds
to this picture in "Of the Original Contract" is, in essence, a qualification
of the primary claim: yes indeed, one who cooperates with an overarching
scheme thereby tacitly consents to it, but only in cases where noncooperation is a viable option for that individual.

Hume would, I think, regard it as obvious that those of us who are citizens of contemporary states cooperate in myriad ways with the governments under which we live. To list only a few examples: we vote in elections if and when they call them; we pay our taxes and thereby fund their projects; we bring suits in their courts and serve on their juries; we fight in their armies and send our children to their schools; we accept their loans; we visit their museums and libraries and buy tickets for their lotteries. And, of course, we also (mostly) abide by their laws and regulations. So it certainly seems as if we are rowing along with them. The Humean question is whether we are stuck on the boat against our will, such that we have no meaningful choice but to row.

One way of answering this question, following Hume, is to determine whether contemporary citizens have a viable option of exit from the states in which they live. The notion that they do is not entirely far-fetched. Hume himself, after all, seemed prepared to concede that some subjects of early-modern states did possess such an option: his claim that "a poor peasant or artizan" could not possibly have "a free choice to leave his country," and therefore could not be supposed to have consented tacitly to his government merely by remaining, strongly suggests that those who were not poor *did* have the necessary option of exit. The Humean claim is therefore not that *no one* could be said to have consented tacitly, but rather that "every individual" could not. And we should suppose that this continues to be the case: although the percentage of citizens in the developed world (and increasingly in the developing world) who have the realistic ability to leave their countries of origin—and to leave them for a wide range of alternative states—is now exponentially larger than it was in the eighteenth century, there remains a share of the population that effectively lacks this option. So it would seem that the mere possibility of exit does not suffice to transform *everyone*'s cooperation with the state into the necessary kind of authorization.

But Hume obliquely raises a much more intriguing possibility later in his essay:

> Suppose, that an usurper, after having banished his lawful prince and royal family, should establish his dominion for ten or a dozen years in any country, and should preserve so exact a discipline in his troops, and so regular a disposition in his garrisons, that no insurrection had ever been raised, or even murmur heard, against his administration: Can it be asserted, that the people,

who in their hearts abhor his treason, have tacitly consented to his authority, and promised him allegiance, merely because, from necessity, they live under his dominion?[9]

Hume wishes the reader to conclude from this thought experiment that popular acquiescence does not suffice to establish that a people has tacitly consented to a ruler or form of rulership. What he actually shows, however, is something far narrower: namely, that if a ruler has the willingness and military means to use violence to suppress dissent ("exact . . . discipline in his troops" and a regular "disposition in his garrisons"), his people must be said to live under his rule "by necessity," rather than choice, and therefore cannot be taken to have tacitly consented. In other words, in this example, the people lack a realistic option to express their refusal of consent because of certain facts about the regime in question, not certain facts about regimes in general.

But what if we tweak the example a bit? Suppose the usurper does not garrison the country and threaten (explicitly or implicitly) to use violence again those who "murmur" against him. And suppose further that, under these very different circumstances, no one murmurs; instead, the citizenry fully cooperates with the new regime in all the customary ways. What should we say about such a case? It strikes me that, here, noncooperation must be regarded as a viable option, and that a refusal to engage in it can indeed count as tacit consent to the public authority. In other words, what separates free or self-governing countries from countries in which the government cannot be said to be authorized by the people is not the presence or absence of elections, but rather the presence or absence of a realistic option of popular non-cooperation. We know very well what such noncooperation looks like in practice. We saw it, for example, during the Tahrir Square uprisings in 2010, where millions of Egyptians took to the streets peacefully and ground the economy to a halt. Where Tahrir Square is effectively possible, its nonoc-currence has normative significance. In such circumstances, citizens who row along with the state cannot claim that they are stuck on the boat.

It should go without saying that this intuition merely gets us moving in what I hope is the right direction. The philosophical challenges that remain are daunting indeed. We need to know what the relationship is between in-dividual and coordinated noncooperation, which takes us deep into tangled questions about the character of collective action. We also need to determine how the state should think about the authorization that it receives from its citizens: should it conceive of itself as a kind of trustee for each individual citizen, or as the representative of a corporate body? And what exactly is to count as cooperation (and noncooperation) for purposes of establishing whether tacit consent has been given? What if a people goes on strike but continues to pay its taxes, for example? Moreover, we need to know how the state should understand its relationship to those who have withdrawn their cooperation: if they no longer consent to the authority of the government, does it follow that the government cannot righty compel their obedience to the law?

To answer these questions and others like them would amount to offering a full theory of political authority, and I cannot pretend to do so here. My claim is simply that it is only within the context of such a theory that one can hope to offer a genuinely liberal defense of egalitarianism. It is the concept of representation—and only that concept—that promises to explain why political authorities that take seriously the autonomy and dignity of persons might legitimately undertake to mitigate inequality through the redistribution of wealth. Like individuals, such authorized agencies might decide to do so for different kinds of reasons, ranging from the prudential (extreme levels of inequality are incompatible with political stability over time) to the moral (we have obligations to prevent suffering when we can do so at no great cost to ourselves). The great mistake has been to suppose instead that an egalitarian distribution of resources is mandated by "distributive justice"—either because unearned or unchosen advantage is unjust, or because the cooperative character of the social enterprise requires an equal division of the social product, or because the earth ought to have been given to mankind in common. Recovering the theodicy debate has, I hope, allowed us to see that the principle of justice does not settle the question of distribution one way or the other. It's up to us.

Notes

PREFACE

1. Shakespeare, *King Lear,* III.4:25–30.

2. Shakespeare, III.4:30–33.

3. See, for example, Eric Nelson, *The Hebrew Republic: Jewish Sources and the Transformation of European Political Thought* (Cambridge, MA: Harvard University Press, 2010); Nelson, "From Selden to Mendelssohn: Hebraism and Religious Freedom," in *Freedom and the Construction of Europe: New Perspectives on Philosophical, Religious, and Political Controversies,* ed. Quentin Skinner and Martin van Gelderen (Cambridge: Cambridge University Press, 2013); and Nelson, "Hebraism and the Republican Turn of 1776: A Contemporary Account of the Debate over *Common Sense,*" *William and Mary Quarterly* 70 (2013): 781–812.

1. PELAGIAN ORIGINS

1. B. R. Rees, *Pelagius: Life and Letters,* 2 vols. (Woodbridge, UK: Boydell, 1998), 2:35. "[A] Domino justitiae ac majestatis nihil impossibile esse praeceptum" (J. P. Migne, *Patrologia Latina,* 30:32). This letter was written in c. 413 CE.

2. Plato, *Euthyphro* 10a. See *The Collected Dialogues of Plato,* ed. Edith Hamilton and Huntington Cairns (Princeton, NJ: Princeton University Press, 1961), 178.

3. Hugo Grotius, *The Rights of War and Peace,* ed. Richard Tuck, 3 vols. (Indianapolis: Liberty Fund, 2005), 1:89.

4. That is, if we reject a kind of radical pluralism about value, according to which it can be morally appropriate to trade some amount of justice for, say, a quantum of goodness, beauty, or efficiency. Leaving aside the obvious difficulties that the idea of a "necessary trade-off" raises for divine omnipotence, this was not a metaethical view to which Christian theorists were attracted. This sort of pluralism is discussed in Chapter 4.

5. G. W. Leibniz, *Theodicy,* trans. E. M. Huggard, ed. Austin M. Farrer (New York: Cosimo Classics, 2009), 123.

6. Leibniz, 123.

7. About Pelagius himself we know relatively little, and medieval and early-modern theorists knew even less. The "Pelagius" of subsequent theological controversy is the one excerpted and excoriated in the writings of the late Augustine. Few of Pelagius's own works are extant, and, of these, the most substantial were not attributed to him until quite recently. See, most importantly, *Pelagius's Commentary on St Paul's Epistle to the Romans,* ed. and trans. Theodore De Bruyn (Oxford: Clarendon, 1993); and Rees, *Pelagius: Life and Letters.* For a skillful reconstruction of the Pelagian movement in late antiquity, see Peter Brown, *Through the Eye of a Needle: Wealth, the Fall of Rome, and the Making of Christianity in the West, 350–550 AD* (Princeton, NJ: Princeton University Press, 2012), esp. chaps. 18–19.

8. Augustine, *On Nature and Grace,* in *St. Augustine: Four Anti-Pelagian Writings,* ed. and trans. John A. Mourant, Fathers of the Church, vol. 86 (Washington, DC: Catholic University of America Press, 1992), 29.

9. Augustine, *On Nature and Grace,* 51.

10. Augustine, *On the Gift of Perseverance,* in *St. Augustine: Four Anti-Pelagian Writings,* 302–3.

11. Augustine, *On the Predestination of the Saints,* in *St. Augustine: Four Anti-Pelagian Writings,* 238 (quoting Rom. 11:33).

12. For Catherine Beecher, "to call all this a *mystery* is a misuse of terms, for there is no mystery about it. More direct, clear, and open injustice, folly, and malevolence, can not possibly be expressed in human language than that here set forth and attributed to God." Beecher, *An Appeal to the People in Behalf of their Rights as Authorized Interpreters of the Bible* (New York: Harper and Brothers, 1860), 263. She concluded as a result that her brother, Henry Ward Beecher, "must soon perceive that it is as much his duty openly to attack the African enslavement of Anglo-Saxon *minds,* as it ever was to combat the Anglo-Saxon enslavement of African *bodies*" (380). Augustine was bishop of Hippo, in North Africa. I am grateful to Eric Gregory for calling this fascinating discussion to my attention.

13. *Paradise Lost* III:210–12. See *John Milton: A Critical Edition of the Major Works,* ed. Stephen Orgel and Jonathan Goldberg (Oxford: Oxford University Press, 1991), 407.

14. John Locke, *The Reasonableness of Christianity as Delivered in the Scriptures,* ed. John C. Higgins-Biddle, Clarendon Edition of the Works of John Locke (Oxford: Clarendon, 1999), 5, 119.

15. Locke, 119.

16. Leibniz, *Political Writings,* ed. and trans. Patrick Riley (Cambridge: Cambridge University Press, 1988), 45.

17. Leibniz, 46 (Juvenal, *Satires* VI:223).

18. Leibniz, *Theodicy,* 95.

19. Leibniz, *Political Writings,* 46.

20. "Letter from J. J. Rousseau to M. de Voltaire" (August 18, 1756), in *Rousseau: The Discourses and Other Early Political Writings,* ed. and trans. Victor Gourevitch (Cambridge: Cambridge University Press, 1997), 242.

21. "Letter from J. J. Rousseau to M. de Voltaire," 233.

22. See Michael Rosen, *The Shadow of God: History and Freedom in German Idealism* (Cambridge, MA: Harvard University Press, forthcoming).

23. Immanuel Kant, *Lectures on the Philosophical Doctrine of Religion* [Vorlesungen über die philosophische Religionslehre], in *Immanuel Kant: Religion and Rational Theology,* ed. and trans. Allen Wood and George Di Giovanni, Cambridge Edition of the Works of Immanuel Kant (Cambridge: Cambridge University Press, 1996), 349. The lectures most likely date to 1783 / 84, with some material added in 1785 / 86.

24. Kant, 442.

25. *Paradise Lost* III:97–99; *John Milton,* 404.

26. John Milton, *On Christian Doctrine,* in *Complete Prose Works of John Milton,* vol. 6, ed. Maurice Kelley, trans. John Carey (New Haven, CT: Yale University Press, 1973), 174.

27. *Paradise Lost* III:176–79; *John Milton,* 406. It is equally important to note that, for Milton, the restoration of man's moral powers was not properly a matter of divine grace. Rather, as the Son puts the case, "should man . . . Fall circumvented thus by [Satan's] fraud, though joined / With his own folly? That be from thee far, / That far be from thee, Father, who art judge / Of all things made, and judges only right" (*Paradise Lost* III:150–55). The claim is that it would be inconsistent with God's justice for him not to restore man's moral powers, because humanity fell through deceit. Note the clear allusion in this passage to Gen. 18:25–26. For a detailed account of Milton's position on original sin, see William Poole, *Milton and the Idea of the Fall* (Cambridge: Cambridge University Press, 2005), esp. 168–94.

28. Locke, *The Reasonableness of Christianity,* 5. Chapter 2 takes up this important and striking claim about how the theory of representation intersects with the theodicy debate.

29. Locke, 7. Cf. 113.

30. Locke, 112.

31. Locke, 117, 120.

32. Locke, 21. Compare Milton: "To prayer, repentance, and obedience due, / Though but endeavoured with sincere intent, / Mine ear shall not be slow, mine eye not shut" (*Paradise Lost* III:191–93; *John Milton*, 407).

33. Locke, *The Reasonableness of Christianity*, 140.

34. See, e.g., Leibniz, *Theodicy*, 104.

35. Leibniz, 123.

36. See John Locke to William Molyneux, Jan. 1693, in *The Correspondence of John Locke*, 8 vols., ed. E. S. De Beer (Oxford: Oxford University Press, 1978–), 4:1643 (Letter 1592): "If it be possible for God to make a free agent, then man is free, though I see not the way of it."

37. Leibniz, *Theodicy*, 369 (italics added). "Et comme il est juste aussi, il s'ensuit, que ses décrets & ses opérations ne déstruisent point nôtre liberté." Leibniz, *Essais de Théodicée*, 2 vols. (Amsterdam, 1725), 2:612.

38. Rousseau, *Émile*, trans. Barbara Foxley (London: Everyman, 1996), 291.

39. Kant, *Religion within the Boundaries of Mere Reason* [Die Religion innerhalb der Grenzen der blossen Vernunft], in *Immanuel Kant: Religion and Rational Theology*, 86. Ovid, *Met.* XIII:140–41: "Race and ancestors, and those things which we did not make ourselves, I scarcely consider as our own."

40. Kant, *Religion within the Boundaries of Mere Reason*, 86–87.

41. Kant, 87.

42. Kant, 93n; *Kants gesammelte Schriften*, Deutsche Akademie der Wissenschaften zu Berlin (Berlin: Georg Reimer, later Walter de Gruyter & Co., 1900–) [hereafter Ak.], 6:49.

43. This is true from the second *Critique* forward.

44. Kant, *Religion within the Boundaries of Mere Reason*, 168. Cf. *Lectures*, 441–42. On this issue, see Michael Rosen, "Kant's Anti-Determinism," *Proceedings of the Aristotelian Society* 89 (1988 / 89): 125–41.

45. Kant, *Religion within the Boundaries of Mere Reason*, 108–9.

46. "Letter from J. J. Rousseau to M. de Voltaire," 233. Compare Leibniz: "Now this very fragility [of our bodies] is a consequence of the nature of things, unless we are to will that this kind of creature, reasoning and clothed in flesh and bones, be not in the world" (Leibniz, *Theodicy*, 14).

47. Milton, *Areopagitica*, 247–48.

48. Milton, 248.

49. Milton, 252.

50. Milton, 253.

51. Rousseau, *Émile*, 464. *Areopagitica* itself was first translated (loosely) into French by Mirabeau two decades later. See *Sur la liberté de la presse, imité de l'anglois, de Milton: Par le Cte de Mirabeau* (Paris, 1788).

52. Rousseau, *Émile*, 292.

53. Rousseau, 294.

54. Kant, *Religion within the Boundaries of Mere Reason*, 103.

55. Kant, 103; Ak. 6:93.

56. Kant, 103; Ak. 6:173.

57. Kant, 193.

58. Kant, 201.

59. Kant, *Lectures,* in *Immanuel Kant: Religion and Rational Theology*, 428.

60. Kant, 409.

61. Kant, 410–11.

62. Rousseau, *Émile*, 306.

63. Kant, *Lectures,* 413.

64. Kant, 413.

65. *Samson Agonistes* 271; *John Milton*, 679. See Sanford Budick, *Kant and Milton* (Cambridge, MA: Harvard University Press, 2010), esp. 209–52.

66. Kant, *Groundwork to the Metaphysics of Morals*, Ak. 4:434–35. For a lucid discussion of this claim, see Michael Rosen, *Dignity: Its Meaning and History* (Cambridge, MA: Harvard University Press, 2012), 19–31.

67. Kant, *Groundwork to the Metaphysics of Morals*, Ak. 4:436.

68. Kant, Ak. 4:434.

69. *Paradise Lost* III:195–97; *John Milton*, 407.

70. Locke, *The Reasonableness of Christianity*, 149.

71. See, e.g., Gideon Rosen, "Culpability and Ignorance," *Proceedings of the Aristotelian Society*, n.s., 103 (2003): 61–84.

72. Locke, *The Reasonableness of Christianity*, 155–56. For an insightful discussion of this passage, see Jeremy Waldron, *God, Locke, and Equality: Christian Foundations in Locke's Political Thought* (Cambridge: Cambridge University Press, 2002), 100–104; 240–43.

73. Locke, *The Reasonableness of Christianity*, 153.

74. Locke, 151. Much the same argument had been made two decades earlier by Samuel Parker, the strongly anti-Calvinist bishop of Oxford. See Samuel Parker, *A Defence and Continuation of the Ecclesiastical Politie* (London, 1671), esp. 365–66.

75. Locke, *The Reasonableness of Christianity*, 139–40.

76. Locke, 139–40.

77. Rousseau, *Émile*, 312.

78. Rousseau, 310.

79. Rousseau, 310.

80. Kant, *Religion within the Boundaries of Mere Reason*, 178; Ak. 6:155.

81. Kant, 123.

82. Kant, 151; Ak. 6:121.

83. *Paradise Lost* III:107–11; *John Milton*, 405.

84. Locke, "A Letter concerning Toleration," in *Locke: Political Writings,* ed. David Wootton (Indianapolis: Hackett, 1993), 406.

85. Milton, *Areopagitica,* in *John Milton,* 247.

86. John Locke, "An Essay concerning Toleration," in *An Essay concerning Toleration and Other Writings on Law and Politics, 1667–1683,* ed. J. R. Milton and Philip Milton (Oxford: Clarendon, 2006), 273. Compare: "Men cannot be forced to be saved whether they will or no" (Locke, "A Letter concerning Toleration," 410).

87. Locke, *An Essay concerning Toleration,* 272.

88. Kant, *Religion within the Boundaries of Mere Reason,* 131.

89. Judith Shklar, "The Liberalism of Fear," in *Liberalism and the Moral Life,* ed. Nancy Rosenblum (Cambridge, MA: Harvard University Press, 1989), 21–38.

90. My view of Rawls in this respect is, intriguingly, the precise inverse of the one defended in Nicholas Rengger, *Dealing in Darkness: The Anti-Pelagian Imagination in Political Theory and International Relations* (Abingdon, UK: Routledge, 2017). See, for example, 3, 65.

2. REPRESENTATION AND THE FALL

1. John Locke, *The Reasonableness of Christianity as Delivered in the Scriptures,* ed. John C. Higgins-Biddle, Clarendon Edition of the Works of John Locke (Oxford: Clarendon, 1999), 5.

2. Locke, 5. An insightful discussion of this passage appears in Ian Harris, *The Mind of John Locke: A Study of Political Theory in Its Intellectual Setting* (Cambridge: Cambridge University Press, 1994), 233–40. As will become clear, I offer a very different account of how Locke's intervention should be understood in its theological and political context. In particular, I am unpersuaded that Locke meant this argument to answer Filmer, who in fact never claimed that Adam represented humanity. Locke meant, rather, to answer a range of Calvinist parliamentarian writers. On Locke's view of the Fall more generally, see Peter Shouls, *Reasoned Freedom: John Locke and the Enlightenment* (Ithaca, NY: Cornell University Press, 1992), 194–96, 202–3; and John Marshall, *John Locke: Resistance, Religion, and Responsibility* (Cambridge: Cambridge University Press, 1994), 397–98, 414–18. For an unpersuasive attempt to align Locke with a less heterodox position on the Fall, see W. M. Spellman, "The Latitudinarian Perspective on Original Sin," *Revue Internationale de Philosophie* 42 (1988): 215–28. See in particular Spellman's claim that Locke's views were quite close to those of Richard Burthogge (221). The latter, in fact, straightforwardly endorsed the Augustinian view that Locke rejected—viz. that "mankind is an *Extended Adam.*" Richard Burthogge, *Tagathon, or, Divine Goodness Explicated and Vindicated from the Exceptions of the Atheist* (London, 1672), 69.

3. Thomas Hobbes, *Leviathan,* ed. Noel Malcolm, 3 vols. (Oxford: Clarendon, 2012), 2:244.

4. Hobbes, 2:244.

5. Hobbes, 2:246.

6. Hobbes, 2:246.

7. See, importantly, Quentin Skinner, "Hobbes on Representation," *European Journal of Philosophy* 13 (2005): 155–84. See also Eric Nelson, *The Royalist Revolution: Monarchy and the American Founding* (Cambridge, MA: Harvard University Press, 2014), chap. 2.

8. The best account of this Biblical conception appears in Jon Levenson, *Resurrection and the Redemption of Israel: The Ultimate Victory of the God of Life* (New Haven, CT: Yale University Press, 2006).

9. But see Ez. 22:17–31 for a very different view.

10. Augustine, *City of God* 13:14, in Augustine, *The City of God against the Pagans,* ed. R. W. Dyson (Cambridge: Cambridge University Press, 1998), 555–56.

11. For a lucid discussion, see David A. Weir, *Origins of the Federal Theology in Sixteenth-Century Reformation Thought* (Oxford: Oxford University Press, 1990), 22–35 (esp. 32–33).

12. Jean Calvin, *Institutio Christianae Religionis* (London, 1576), 103 (2:6:1): "Quum in Adae persona perierit totum humanum genus." Translations from Calvin are my own. For Calvin's treatment of Christ as a representative, or *legatus,* of God the father, see Stephan Schaede, *Stellvertretung: Begriffsgeschichtliche Studien zur Soteriologie* (Tübingen: Mohr Siebeck, 2004), 356–59.

13. Calvin, *Institutio,* 148 (2:16): "ita certe habendum est, fuisse Adamum humanae naturae non progenitorem modo, sed quasi radicem, atque ideo in illius corruptione merito vitiatum fuisse hominum genus."

14. For the role of Ambrosius Catharinus in originating this shift, see the valuable discussion in Weir, *The Origins of the Federal Theology,* 12–15. Other important progenitors of the argument were Zacharias Ursinus, Franciscus Junius, and Johannes Cocceius. See also Charles J. Butler, "Religious Liberty and Covenant Theology," unpublished PhD dissertation, Temple University, 1979, 19–20.

15. See, classically, Heinrich Heppe, *Dogmatik des deutschen Protestantismus im sechzehnten Jahrhundert* (Gotha, Germany: Perthes, 1857); and Gottlob Schrenk, *Gottesreich und Bund im älteren Protestantismus, vornehmlich Johannes Cocceius* (Gütersloh, Germany: Bertelsmann Verlag, 1923).

16. William Perkins, *A golden Chaine: or, The Description of Theologie* (Cambridge, 1600), 16.

17. Perkins, 254.

18. Thomas Tuke, *The Highway to Heaven* (London, 1609), 56.

19. John Yates, *Gods Arraignement of Hypocrites* (London, 1615), 331.

20. Yates, 331–32.

21. Paul Baynes, *A Commentarie vpon The First Chapter of the Epistles of Saint Paul, written to the Ephesians* (London, 1618), 223.

22. Baynes, 235. For Christ as a representative, see Schaede, *Stellvertretung.* Schaede mentions the representative role of Adam only in passing (see esp. 229).

23. Pierre du Moulin, *The Anatomy of Arminianisme,* English trans. (London, 1620), 58.

24. Du Moulin, 60. For a contrasting attempt to explain the Ezekiel passage, see Grotius, *A Defence of the Catholick Faith concerning the Satisfaction of Christ,* trans. W. H. (London, 1692), 92.

25. Du Moulin, *Anatomy of Arminianisme,* 60.

26. Thomas Goodwin, *Christ Set Forth In his Death, Resurrection, Ascension, Sitting at Gods right hand, Intercession As Cause of Justification* (London, 1642), 46.

27. See, for example, Edward Reynolds, *Three Treatises* (London, 1631), 401: "There are three Offices or Parts of the Mediation of Christ. First, his *Satisfaction* as hee is *our Suretie,* whereby hee paid our debt, underwent the curse of our sinnes, bare them all in his body upon the Tree, became subject to the Law for us, in our nature, and representatively in our stead, fulfill all righteousnesse in the Law required, both *Active* and *Passive* for us." The chief scriptural authority for this claim is found in Hebrews 7:22.

28. Goodwin, *Christ Set Forth,* 46.

29. Goodwin, 46.

30. Goodwin, 56. Compare William Bridge, *The Works of William Bridge, Sometime Fellow of Emmanuel College, Cambridge: Now Preacher of the Word of God at Yarmouth,* 3 vols. (London, 1649), 2:117, 203.

31. Westminster Larger Catechism (1648), *Quaes.* 22.

32. Anthony Burgess, *Treatise of Original Sin* (London, 1658), 39.

33. Burgess, 39.

34. Burgess, 430 ("and herein did consult for our good, better then if he had taken any other way is more to be insisted on").

35. Burgess, 393.

36. Thomas Brooks, *A Golden Key to Open Hidden Treasures* (London, 1675), 365. See also William Bridge, *The Freeness of the Grace and Love of God* (London, 1671), 72.

37. For lucid remarks on this subject, see Peter Harrison, "Voluntarism and Early Modern Science," *History of Science* 40 (2002): 63–89; and Jitse M. van der Meer, "European Calvinists and the Study of Nature: Some Historical Patterns and Problems," in *Calvinism and the Making of the European Mind,* ed. Gijsbert van den Brink and Harro M. Höppel (Leiden: Brill, 2014), 103–30 (esp. 127–30).

38. John Polhill, *The Divine Will Considered in its Eternal Decrees* (London, 1695), 178.

39. Burgess, *Treatise of Original Sin,* 431. Cf. Burthogge, *Tagathon,* 69–70.

40. Gabriel Towerson, *Of the Sacraments in General* (London, 1686), 56.

41. Towerson, 56–57.

42. See, for example, Daniel Lee, *Popular Sovereignty in Early Modern Constitutional Thought* (Oxford: Oxford University Press, 2016), 133–36.

43. George Lawson, *Theo-Politica* (London, 1659), 158.

44. Lawson, 239.

45. Lawson, 246.

46. Perkins, *A golden Chaine*, 801, 962.

47. Perkins, 1040.

48. Johann Crell, *The Justification of a Sinner: Being the Maine Argument of the Epistle to the Galations* (London, 1650), 184.

49. Lancelot Andrewes, *XCVI. Sermons by the Right Honorable and Reverend Father in God, Lancelot Andrewes* (London, 1629), 816.

50. Reynolds, *Three Treatises,* 380.

51. John Owen, *Vindiciae Evangelicae, Or the Mystery of the Gospell Vindicated, and Socinianisme Examined* (Oxford, 1655), 370.

52. Perkins, *A golden Chaine,* 965.

53. Calvin, *Institutio,* 214 (2:12:3): "Prodiit ergo verus homo Dominus noster, Adae personam induit, nomen assumpsit, et eius vices subiret Patri obediendo."

54. Patrick Gillespie, *The Ark of the Covenant Opened, or, A treatise of the covenant of redemption between God and Christ* (London, 1677), 91–92.

55. Gillespie, 397.

56. Gillespie, 397–98.

57. Gillespie, 398.

58. Goodwin, *Christ Set Forth,* 58.

59. Goodwin, 72, 78.

60. Lawson, *Theo-Politica,* 101.

61. Owen, *Vindiciae Evangelicae,* 302.

62. Owen, 337.

63. Henry Parker, *Observations upon some of His Majesties late Answers and Expresses* (London, 1642), 13.

64. See, for example, Parker, *The Altar Dispute* (London, 1641), 70, 75.

65. Parker, *Ius Populi* (London, 1644), 18–19.

66. Parker, *Observations,* 23.

67. Parker, 29.

68. Parker, 5.

69. Parker, *Ius Regum* (London, 1645), 37.

70. See, for example, Parker, *The Danger to England Observ'd* (London, 1642), 3; Parker, *Observations,* 11; Parker, *Ius Populi,* 18–19; cf. anonymous, *A Soveraigne Salve to Cure the Blind* (London, 1643), 8, 19.

71. Parker, *Observations,* 15.

72. Parker, *Ius Populi,* 18–19.

73. John Herle, *An Answer to Doctor Fernes reply* (London, 1643), 30.

74. Sir John Spelman, *A View of a Printed Book Intituled Observations upon His Majesties Late Answeres and Expresses* (London, 1643), 26.

75. Spelman, 26.

76. Henry Ferne, *Conscience Satisfied* (London, 1643), 22. For Herle's response, see *An Answer to Doctor Fernes reply*, 30.

77. Ferne, *Conscience Satisfied*, 22.

78. Dudley Diggs, *An Answer to a Printed Book, Intituled, Observations upon His Majesties Late Answeres and Expresses* (1642), 37.

79. Diggs, 113.

80. Henry Hammond, *A View of Some Exceptions which have been made by a Romanist to the Ld Viscount Falkland's Discourse of the Infallibility of the Church of Rome* (1650), 13.

81. Hammond, 72.

82. Hammond, 74.

83. William Laud, *A Relation of the Conference . . . with Mr. Fisher the Jesuite* (1639), 229.

84. For a general account, see Nicholas Tyacke, *Anti-Calvinists: The Rise of English Arminianism, c. 1590–1640* (Oxford: Oxford University Press, 1987).

85. Simon Episcopius, *Institutiones Theologica in quatuor libros distinctae*, in *Opera theologica*, 2nd ed. (The Hague, 1678), 1:403. "Impossible est, ut actuale & personale peccatum Adami, originaliter nostrum sit peccatum . . . impossible est, ut quis alio peccet, nisi accedat vel imperium, vel consilium, vel consensus sive tacitus sive expressus, vel saltem (uti quidem volunt) sceleris sive peccati, quod ex lege ad judicem deferri debet, conscientia. At nihil horum potuit locum habere in peccato isto." For Episcopius's mature position, and its divergence from Arminius's own, see Mark A. Ellis, *Simon Episcopius's Doctrine of Original Sin* (New York: Peter Lang, 2006), esp. 149–66.

86. Placeus, *De imputatione primi peccati Adami* (Saumur, France, 1665 [orig. 1655]), 41. Translations from Placeus are my own.

87. Placeus, 59–60.

88. Samuel Hoard, *Gods love to Mankind, Manifested, by Disproving his Absolute Decree* (London, 1633), 63.

89. Hoard, 69.

90. Henry Hammond, *Practical Catechism* (London, 1645), 6.

91. Jeremy Taylor, *An answer to a letter written by the R.R. the Ld Bp of Rochester. Concerning the chapter of original sin, in the Vnum necessarium* (London, 1656), 46.

92. Taylor, 105–6.

93. Taylor, 106. See also Taylor, *Deus Justificatus. Two Discourses of Original Sin . . .* (London, 1656), 55–59.

94. Taylor, *An answer to a letter*, 109.

95. Taylor, *Unum Necessarium* (London, 1655), 381–82.

96. Taylor, 382.

97. For a brief but important discussion of how Covenant theologians might have influenced Hobbes's account of representation, see Quentin Skinner, "Hobbes on Persons, Authors, and Representatives," in *The Cambridge Companion to Hobbes's "Leviathan,"* ed. Patricia Spingborg (Cambridge: Cambridge University Press, 2007), 169. See also A. P. Martinich, *The Two Gods of Leviathan: Thomas Hobbes on Religion and Politics* (Cambridge: Cambridge University Press, 1992), 147–50.

98. See, for example, Noel Malcolm, *Aspects of Hobbes* (Oxford: Oxford University Press, 2002), 10–11; and Sarah Mortimer, *Reason and Religion in the English Revolution: The Challenge of Socinianism* (Cambridge: Cambridge University Press, 2010), 63–87.

99. Numerous works by Perkins, Tuke, and du Moulin appear in the manuscript library catalogue that Hobbes prepared for his patron, the Earl of Devonshire, in the 1630s—among them Tuke's *High-Way to Heaven* (Hobbes MSS [Chatsworth] MS E.1.A, no. 439). Hobbes likewise mentions Perkins by name as one of the "Doctors of the Church" whom (along with Luther, Calvin, and Melanchthon) "I never sleighted, but alwayes very much reverenced, and admired." See Hobbes, *Questions Concerning Liberty, Necessity, and Chance Cleary Stated and Debated* (London, 1656), 212.

100. H obbes, *Leviathan,* 2:246.

101. Hobbes, 2:246–47. For Hobbes's debts in this passage to the Civilian tradition, see Daniel Lee, "Hobbes and the Civil Law: The Use of Roman Law in Hobbes's Civil Science," in *Hobbes and the Law,* ed. David Dyzenhaus and Thomas Poole (Oxford: Oxford University Press, 2012), 210–335 (esp. 223–27).

102. Hobbes, *Leviathan,* 2:247.

103. Hobbes, 2:246.

104. The most important discussions appear in chapters 36 and 41 of *Leviathan.*

105. Hobbes, *Leviathan,* 3:634.

106. Hobbes, 3:700–701.

107. Hobbes, 3:698.

108. Compare Hobbes's comment in his reply to Bramhall: "nor is there here any punishment [after the Fall], but onely a reducing of *Adam* and *Eve* to their original mortality, where death was no punishment but a gift of God." Hobbes, *The Questions Concerning Liberty, Necessity, and Chance* (London, 1656), 78.

109. Hobbes, *Leviathan,* 3:700.

110. Hobbes, 2:252.

111. Hobbes, 2:252.

112. See Willem J. van Asselt, "Expromissio or Fideiussio? A Seventeenth-Century Theological Debate between Voetians and Cocceians about the Nature of Christ's Suretyship in Salvation History," *Mid-America Journal of Theology* 14 (2003): 37–57. The alternative to a *fideiussio,* in Roman law, is an *expromissio,* in which the

debtor is immediately absolved of his debt, even before the *sponsor* has paid the creditor. Late seventeenth-century Dutch attempts to cast Christ as an *expromissor* led to predictable difficulties surrounding the efficacy and centrality of the cross.

113. Hobbes, *Leviathan,* 3:646.

114. Hobbes, 3:762.

115. Hobbes, 3:762, 768.

116. Hobbes, 3:776.

117. Hobbes, 3:776. Compare Johann Crell, *The Expiation of a Sinner in a Commentary upon the Epistle to the Hebrews* (London, 1646), 3: "Christ is the character or image of Gods person; for God did as it were imprint his person upon Christ, that Christ might be his substitute upon earth to personate, represent and resemble the person of God."

118. Hobbes, *Leviathan,* 2:560.

119. Hobbes, *Liberty and Necessity,* 87. Indeed, Bramhall relied strongly on the argument that God's punishment of mankind was just because "He made the Covenant of works with mankind in *Adam,* and therefore he punisheth not man contrary to his own Covenant, but for the transgression of his duty" (101, Hobbes quoting Bramhall).

120. On Hobbes and Socinianism more broadly, see Mortimer, *Reason and Religion in the English Revolution,* esp. 149–57.

121. Thomas Pierce, *Divine Purity Defended* (London, 1659), 61. Compare Richard Burthogge, *An Argument for Infants Baptisme* (London, 1684), 98–107.

122. Phillip van Limborch, [*Theologia Christiana*] *A compleat system of Divinity,* 2 vols. (London, 1690), 1:198.

123. Stephen Nye, *A brief History of the Unitarians, called also Socinians in four letters* (London, 1687), 56.

124. Gilbert Burnet, *Exposition of the Thirty-Nine Articles of the Church of England* (London, 1700 [1699]), 115.

125. Burnet, 115.

126. Locke, *The Reasonableness of Christianity,* 5.

127. See Nelson, *The Royalist Revolution,* 80–107; 184–228.

128. John Locke, *Two Treatises of Government,* ed. Peter Laslett, rev. ed. (Cambridge: Cambridge University Press, 1967), 384, 347–48, 431. Locke in fact stated that men could not "*think themselves in Civil Society,* till the Legislature was placed in collective Bodies of Men" (347). This passage is in obvious tension with Locke's remarks in chap. 10 (see 372).

129. See, for example, Locke, *Two Treatises of Government,* 343, 388.

130. Locke, 372.

131. Locke, 343.

132. Locke, 425–26.

133. Locke, 191.

3. "THE BARGAIN BASIS"

1. For a summary of the two views, see G. A. Cohen, *Rescuing Justice and Equality* (Cambridge, MA: Harvard University Press, 2008), 166–68.

2. See, for example, *On the Predestination of the Saints* and *On the Gift of Perseverance* in *St. Augustine: Four Anti-Pelagian Writings,* ed. and trans., John A. Mourant, The Fathers of the Church, vol. 86 (Washington, DC: The Catholic University of America Press, 1992).

3. I use the term "radical Arminianism" to underscore the fact that Jacobus Arminius himself, and various of his followers, took a far less Pelagian view of justification than others who identified themselves as Arminians in the seventeenth and eighteenth centuries.

4. John Rawls, *A Brief Inquiry into the Meaning of Sin & Faith,* ed. Thomas Nagel (Cambridge, MA: Harvard University Press, 2009), 246. The phrase clearly comes to Rawls from Augustine, *De natura et gratia.* See, e.g., *Saint Augustine: Four Anti-Pelagian Writings,* 26. Augustine is in turn adapting I Cor. 1:17.

5. Rawls, *Brief Inquiry,* 227.

6. Rawls, 231.

7. Rawls, 230.

8. The release of this volume provoked a broad and welcome awakening of interest in the early development of Rawls's ideas which is set to continue in forthcoming works, such as Andrius Galisanka, *John Rawls: The Path to a Theory of Justice* (Cambridge, Mass.: Harvard University Press, 2019) and Katrina Forrester, *In the Shadow of Justice: Postwar Liberalism and the Remaking of Political Philosophy* (Princeton, NJ: Princeton University Press, 2019).

9. Philip Leon, *The Ethics of Power, or the Problem of Evil* (London, 1935), 193.

10. Leon, *The Ethics of Power,* 12.

11. Leon, 116.

12. Leon, 296.

13. Leon, 262.

14. Leon, 303–4.

15. Karl Marx, *Selected Writings,* ed. Lawrence H. Simon (Indianapolis: Hackett, 1994), 9.

16. Marx, *Selected Writings,* 10.

17. Marx, 16–17.

18. Marx, 22.

19. Marx, 22–23.

20. H. J. Stenning renders the term as "huckstering."

21. Marx, *Selected Writings,* 24, 25.

22. Marx, 22.

23. Marx, 24.

24. Marx, 321. Rawls later annotated this section of *The Critique of the Gotha Program* at least twice, first in his copy of *Karl Marx: Selected Writings in Sociology and Social Philosophy,* ed. and trans. T. B. Bottomore, ed. Maximilien Rubel (London: McGraw-Hill, 1956), and next in in *Karl Marx: Selected Writings,* ed. David McLellan (Oxford: Oxford University Press, 1977) [inscribed "JR, Aug. '78"]. See Harvard University Archive, HUM 48.1, Box 5. This central passage is heavily underlined in both copies. In the first, Rawls placed a check mark next to Marx's claim that "right can never be higher than the economic structure of society and the cultural development conditioned by it" (258). He likewise added a pair of comments about the relationship between value and marginal product.

25. Marx, *Selected Writings,* 321.

26. "On the Jewish Question" had been translated into English in 1926. See *Selected Essays, by Karl Marx,* ed. and trans. H. J. Stenning (New York: International Publishers, 1926). Rawls probably would have encountered it at Princeton in E. Harris Harbison's History S319: "History of European Thought," which he took in the summer term of 1942—although it is also possible that the essay appeared on the syllabus of David Bowers's Philosophy 401 ("Kant and the Philosophy of the Nineteenth Century"), in which Rawls was enrolled during the fall of 1941. The description of the latter includes a reference to Marx. (See Rawls's college transcript, Princeton University Archives, AC198, Box 63. I am deeply grateful to Kenzie Bok for sharing with me her partial transcription of this document.) Rawls later annotated the essay quite extensively at least twice: first in his copy of *Karl Marx: Early Writings,* ed. and trans. Bottomore, and a second time in *Marx: Selected Writings,* ed. McLellan [inscribed JR, Aug. '78]. See Harvard University Archive, HUM 48.1, Box 5. Interestingly, in the first copy, Rawls wrote "Rhet." in the margin next to each of Marx's negative comments about Jews and Judaism in the second part of the text, indicating that he found these to be merely rhetorical (in contrast, he wrote "Thesis" next to what he regarded as the key claims in the argument). In the 1977 edition, he simply stopped annotating at the end of part I.

27. Rawls, *Brief Inquiry,* 227.

28. Rawls, 193.

29. Rawls, 227, 206.

30. Rawls, 194–95.

31. Rawls, 195.

32. Rawls, 194–95.

33. Rawls, 229.

34. Rawls, 229, 227.

35. Jeremy Waldron has fascinatingly examined the manner in which this communitarian streak in the young Rawls influenced his conception of the Trinity. See Waldron, "Persons, Community, and the Image of God in Rawls's *Brief Inquiry,*" NYU School of Law, Public Law Research Paper No. 11-03 (unpublished).

36. Rawls, *Brief Inquiry*, 230.

37. Rawls, 230–31. Cf. Augustine, *De gratia et libero arbitrio*, 24.

38. Rawls, *Brief Inquiry*, 231. As this book was going to press, Kenzie Bok generously shared with me her discovery of a remarkable college essay of Rawls's, entitled "Christianity and the Modern World," dating from the spring of 1942 (less than a year before the submission of his senior thesis). The attack on Pelagianism is already a central theme in this earlier text, and in it Rawls shows himself to be strikingly familiar with the genealogy of the Pelagian tradition sketched out in Chapter 1. He is also eager, as he is in the thesis, to reconcile the rejection of merit with a conception of human freedom (and thereby to resist predestinarianism)—although his earlier argument in this respect differs from the later one in emphasis and in some particulars. The year 1942–1943 thus emerges as one of fervent theological study and exploration for Rawls (the first in which his academic focus shifted explicitly to the subject), and his views were clearly evolving and developing quite quickly. Bok is preparing an edited version of this text for publication, for which scholars will be immensely grateful.

39. Rawls, *Brief Inquiry*, 246.

40. Rawls, 231.

41. Rawls, 125. Rawls was still defending this central theological claim in his lectures on "Christian Ethics," delivered at Cornell in the early 1950s. Under the rubric of "<u>Rewards</u> ± <u>Punishments</u>," Rawls observes in his notes that "we must notice that there is a complete rejection of all human conceptions of merit" in the Christian schema. God's "reward is hardly reward, but 'grace'; for notice two further things about it: 1) One cannot <u>claim</u> it—yet one <u>can</u> claim rewards in the ordinary sense, and one is <u>expected</u> to, 2) even if one could claim them [*sic*] it isn't at all clear what we would be <u>entitled</u> to claim—the assessment of merit is different from the 'world's' picture. <u>Finally</u>, what would the reward be: surely the Visio Dei: now what <u>sense</u> does it make to claim one is <u>entitled</u> to <u>that</u>? <u>Try</u> saying to yourself and <u>meaning</u> it, 'Oh God show thyself for I deserve to see thee'" (Rawls, "Christian Ethics, Class at Cornell" (1954?) in Harvard University Archive, Hum 48, Box 8, Folder 5, 3b).

42. Rawls, 173.

43. Rawls, 191–92.

44. Rawls, 240.

45. Rawls, 241. Cf. Augustine, *De gratia et libero arbitrio* 6.15; *Ep.* 154 5:16.

46. I Cor. 4:7. See Augustine, *De gratia et libero arbitrio*, 15.

47. Rawls, *Brief Inquiry*, 252 (see also 245–48). For a fascinating account of the degree to which Rawls remained faithful to this commitment into the mid-1950s, see David A. Reidy, "Rawls's Religion and Justice as Fairness," *History of Political Thought* 31 (2010): 309–43 (see esp. 334–36).

48. Rawls, *Brief Inquiry*, 246.

49. See, for example, P. Mackenzie Bok, "To the Mountain Again: The Early Rawls and Post-Protestant Ethics in Postwar America," *Modern Intellectual History*

14 (2015): 1–33 (see esp. 5–8). I should stress, however, that I have learned a great deal from this important essay.

50. Rawls, *Brief Inquiry,* 125.

51. John Rawls, *A Theory of Justice* (Oxford: Oxford University Press, 1971), 103–4. For a very different interpretation of this passage, see T. M. Scanlon, *Why Does Inequality Matter?* (Oxford, 2018), 126–27. My hope is that readers will find my own more persuasive in light of the continuities it highlights with Rawls's religious thought.

52. It is striking that this argument is absent from the essay by Herbert Spiegelberg that Rawls cites in defense of his position (Rawls, A *Theory of Justice,* 100). See Herbert Spiegelberg, "A Defense of Human Equality," *Philosophical Review* 53 (1944): 101–24. Spiegelberg sharply distinguishes between a person's initial natural endowments and social position and "his individual merits and demerits," or what he "makes" of his "start." His position therefore resembles a version of luck egalitarianism. It is, however, noteworthy that Spiegelberg analogizes his own position to "the Christian idea of Grace" (122). Something similar might be said of the second essay that Rawls cites in this connection, D. D. Raphael, "Justice and Liberty," *Proceedings of the Aristotelian Society* 51 (1950–51): 167–96.

53. Rawls, *Brief Inquiry,* 214.

54. Shlomo Dov Rosen is surely right, however, to see a continuity between, on the one hand, Calvin's insistence that the justice of God is inaccessible to human rationality, and, on the other hand, Rawls's later claim that the distribution of advantage among human beings is arbitrary from a moral point of view. See Shlomo Dov Rosen, "Rawls's Structural Response to Arbitrariness: An Echo of Calvin" *Philosophy and Theology* 30 (2018): 123–48 (esp. 127–30).

55. Rawls, 231.

56. I am grateful to John Acton for calling this important issue to my attention.

57. Rawls, *Brief Inquiry,* 240. Indeed, Rawls's position here is not unlike that defended by Jacobus Arminius himself, as opposed to the far more Pelagian position defended by later "Arminians."

58. Rawls, *Brief Inquiry,* 246.

59. Rawls, *A Theory of Justice,* 312.

60. On the competing readings of this passage, see G. A. Cohen, "On the Currency of Egalitarian Justice," *Ethics* 99 (1989): 914–15. Cohen construes the passage as I do, and he flags the objection that I go on to develop.

61. Rawls would have had access to this essay in the English translation of Robert E. Anchor. See *Immanuel Kant: On History,* ed. and trans. Lewis White Beck, Robert E. Anchor, and Emil L. Fackenheim (New York: Bobbs-Merrill, 1963), 69–84.

62. Immanuel Kant, "The End of All Things" [*Das Ende aller Dinge*] in *Immanuel Kant: Religion and Rational Theology,* ed. and trans. Allen Wood and George Di

Giovanni, Cambridge Edition of the Works of Immanuel Kant (Cambridge: Cambridge University Press, 1996), 223.

63. Kant, "The End of All Things," 223. Ak. 8:329–30.

64. Kant, 224.

65. This claim is to be contrasted with another argument of which Rawls makes use, to the effect that market economies do not distribute goods according to desert since "surely a person's moral worth does not vary according to how many offer similar skills, or happen to want what he can produce" (Rawls, A Theory of Justice, 274). Leaving aside the merits of this position, it simply insists that marginal product is a poor way of measuring what people deserve, not that desert claims should not be honored by the basic structure. On this argument and its pedigree, see Andrew Lister, "Markets, Desert, and Reciprocity," Politics, Philosophy, and Economics 16 (2017): 47–69.

66. Rawls, Brief Inquiry, 18.

67. Rawls, A Theory of Justice, 314–15.

68. Michael Sandel, Liberalism and the Limits of Justice, 2nd ed. (Cambridge: Cambridge University Press, 1998), 90.

69. Samuel Scheffler, "Responsibility, Reactive Attitudes, and Liberalism in Philosophy and Politics," Philosophy & Public Affairs 21 (1992): 299–323; see 306.

70. Scheffler modifies his position substantially in a later essay, which I cannot discuss in this context. Scheffler, "Justice and Desert in Liberal Theory," in Boundaries and Allegiances. Problems of Justice and Responsibility in Liberal Thought (Oxford: Oxford University Press, 2001). Suffice it to say that I find his initial contribution more persuasive. For an attempt to defend the asymmetry between distributive and retributive justice on grounds different from Scheffler's, see Michael Rosen, "Liberalism, Desert, and Responsibility: A Response to Samuel Scheffler," Philosophical Books 44 (2003): 118–24.

71. Rawls, Brief Inquiry, 191–92.

72. Of course, the set of "good" acts and the set of "productive" acts are not coterminous (it is easy to imagine good acts that are not "productive" in the relevant sense and productive acts that are not good). But it would be quite difficult to explain why our good acts should be attributed to us, but not our productive acts (or vice versa).

73. Rawls, Brief Inquiry, 214.

74. Scheffler, "Responsibility, Reactive Attitudes, and Liberalism in Philosophy and Politics," 309.

75. Judith Shklar, "The Liberalism of Fear," in Liberalism and the Moral Life, ed. Nancy Rosenblum (Cambridge, MA: Harvard University Press, 1989), 21–38. See also Eric Gregory, Politics and the Order of Love: An Augustinian Ethic of Democratic Citizenship (Chicago: University of Chicago Press, 2008).

76. Rawls, Brief Inquiry, 196, 199. Rawls is here discussing the views of Kant's German Romantic successors, but he is of course aware that the phrase "noumenal selves" is Kant's own.

77. See Rawls, "Kantian Constructivism in Moral Theory," *Journal of Philosophy* 77 (1980): 515–72 (esp. 557–72). Katrina Forrester has recently demonstrated that, although Rawls famously characterized *A Theory of Justice* as "Kantian" in its essential structure (Rawls, *A Theory of Justice,* viii), he had in fact worked out most of the core ideas of the project long before he evinced any serious interest in Kantian philosophy. See Forrester, *In the Shadow of Justice.*

78. Robert Nozick, *Anarchy, State, and Utopia* (New York, 1974), 214.

79. Kant, *Religion within the Limits of Reason Alone,* ed. and trans. Theodore M. Greene and Hoyt H. Hudson, Introduction John R. Silber (New York: Harper and Row, 1960), cxi (Silber's italics). Rawls's copy; Harvard University Archive, Hum. 48.1, Box 3. Rawls inscribed the volume "John Rawls, May, 1973," so the annotations likely date to that year.

80. Kant, *Religion within the Limits of Reason Alone,* Rawls's copy, 40. The passage, as it appears in this edition, reads: "Man himself must make or have made himself into whatever in a moral sense, whether good or evil, he is to become. Either condition must be an effect of his free choice. . . . Granted that some supernatural cooperation may be necessary to his becoming good, or to his becoming better, yet, whether this cooperation consists merely in the abatement of hindrances or indeed in positive assistance, man must first make himself worthy to receive it, and must lay hold of this aid (which is no small matter) . . . for only thus can good be imputed to him and he be known as a good man."

81. Kenzie Bok has demonstrated that Rawls's memory in this respect was unreliable: he continued to write and teach as a Christian ethicist until well into the 1950s (see Bok, "To the Mountaintop Again," 163–66).

82. Rawls, *Brief Inquiry,* 264.

4. EGALITARIANISM AND THEODICY

1. "Unde patet etiam in Atheos cadere odium Dei; quicquid enim credant dictantve, modo eis rerum natura statusque displiceat, Deum ipso facto odere, Deum non appellant," G. W. Leibniz, *Confessio philosophi, Papers Concerning the Problem of Evil 1671–1678,* ed. and trans. Robert C. Sleigh Jr., Yale Leibniz (New Haven, CT: Yale University Press, 2005), 88–89.

2. See, for example, Richard Arneson, "Equality and Equal Opportunity for Welfare," *Philosophical Studies* 56 (1989): 77–93; Arneson, "Egalitarianism and the Undeserving Poor," *Journal of Political Philosophy* (1997), 327–50; Arneson, "Egalitarianism and Responsibility," *Journal of Ethics* 3 (1999): 225–47; Arneson, "Perfectionism and Politics," *Ethics* 111 (2000): 37–63; G. A. Cohen, "On the Currency of Egalitarian Justice," *Ethics* 99 (1989): 906–44; Cohen, *If You're an Egalitarian, How Come You're so Rich?* (Cambridge, MA: Harvard University Press, 2000); Cohen, *Rescuing Justice and Equality* (Cambridge, MA: Harvard University Press, 2008);

Eric Rakowski, *Equal Justice* (Oxford: Oxford University Press, 1991); Kasper Lippert-Rasmussen, "Equality, Option Luck, and Responsibility," *Ethics* 111 (2001): 548–79; John Roemer, *Equality of Opportunity* (Cambridge, MA: Harvard University Press, 1998); Larry Temkin, *Equality* (Oxford: Oxford University Press, 1993); Temkin, "Egalitarianism Defended," *Ethics* 113 (2003): 764–82; Peter Vallentyne, "Brute Luck, Option Luck, and Equality of Initial Opportunities," *Ethics* 112 (2002): 529–57; Phillipe Van Parijs, *Real Freedom for All: What (if Anything) Can Justify Capitalism?* (Oxford: Oxford University Press, 1995) ("justice, as I conceive it, requires compensation for unequal internal endowments" [59]). Much of this literature is heavily indebted to Ronald Dworkin, *Sovereign Virtue: The Theory and Practice of Equality* (Cambridge, MA: Harvard University Press, 2000), which develops material from two earlier essays, Dworkin, "What is Equality? Part 1: Equality of Welfare," *Philosophy and Public Affairs* 10 (1981): 185–246; and Dworkin, "What is Equality? Part 2: Equality of Resources," *Philosophy and Public Affairs* 10 (1981): 283–345. Dworkin, however, claimed plausibly that he ought not to be considered a luck equalitarian, insofar as his view does not require (as a matter of justice) the elimination of unchosen inequalities. See Dworkin, "Equality, Luck and Hierarchy," *Philosophy and Public Affairs* 31 (2003): 190–98. The view is also influenced by various remarks of John Rawls—although there has been considerable disagreement about the degree to which Rawls was (or ought to have been) sympathetic to the luck egalitarian project.

3. These lines of criticism may be found in Elizabeth Anderson, "What is the Point of Equality?" *Ethics* 109 (1999): 287–337; Anderson, "The Fundamental Disagreement between Luck Egalitarians and Relational Egalitarians," *Canadian Journal of Philosophy* 36 (2010): 1–23; Samuel Scheffler, "What is Egalitarianism?" *Philosophy and Public Affairs* 31 (2003): 5–39; Jonathan Wolff, "Fairness, Respects, and the Egalitarian Ethos," *Philosophy and Public Affairs* 27 (1998): 97–122; and Wolff, "Fairness, Respect, and the Egalitarianism Ethos Revisited," *Journal of Ethics* 14 (2010): 335–50.

4. For a recent summary of these objections, see Joseph Fishkin, *Bottlenecks: A New Theory of Equal Opportunity* (Oxford: Oxford University Press, 2014), 35–65. Fishkin goes further and argues that there is in fact no such thing as a "natural talent" or asset—no natural / genetic contribution to developmental outcomes that could, even in principle, be isolated from social and environmental factors. This is true, on his account, because natural and environmental forces work in concert at every stage; it is not that nature, on its own, produces 50 percent of one's ability to play the flute and then the environment comes along and supplies the remaining 50 percent. Rather, 100 percent of fluteplaying is a matter of the interaction between nature and environment (89–99). Thus, for Fishkin, "far from being two distinct causal forces that each make an independent contribution to a final result, heredity and environment, properly understood, are not even separate" (94). This argument

seems to me to involve a non sequitur. It does not follow from the fact that two or more agents or causes produce X while acting in concert (and cannot in isolation produce any part of X), that we cannot talk meaningfully about their respective contributions to the outcome, or even measure those contributions. Still less does it follow that these causes or agents are not themselves distinct. The sperm and the egg, for example, jointly produce the entire human embryo; the sperm, on its own, creates 0 percent of an embryo, and likewise with the egg. But we can nonetheless say that the sperm and the egg are each causally responsible for precisely 50 percent of the embryo's genetic material. We can even isolate their specific contributions in many cases (for example, "you have your mother's eyes"). Or again, to borrow an example offered by Richard Tuck in a different context: suppose six people pick up a boat and carry it down to the water. It's not that person A carries it 20 percent of the way, as does person B, etc. They must act jointly to carry the boat at all. But it is perfectly coherent to talk about the share of the weight that each person is responsible for bearing: see Tuck, *Free Riding* (Cambridge, MA: Harvard University Press, 2008), 40. (Note that it does not follow from the fact that causal responsibility for an outcome can be parceled out in this manner that moral responsibility can as well; we might, for example, conclude that any contribution to a collective enterprise suffices to make an agent responsible for that enterprise as a whole.) Moreover, even if one accepts Fishkin's argument, the conclusion is not that there are no natural assets, but rather that every human asset is natural—and every asset is also social / environmental.

5. G. A. Cohen, for example, is officially agnostic on the descriptive claim. See Cohen, "On the Currency of Egalitarian Justice," 934.

6. J. R. Lucas, *On Justice* (Oxford: Oxford University Press, 1980), 191. Compare Nicholas Vrousalis, *The Political Philosophy of G. A. Cohen: Back to Socialist Basics* (London: Bloomsbury Academic, 2015), 1–2, 16 (although Vrousalis's focus in these remarks is on Cohen's attempted rehabilitation of Marx's historical materialism); and Michael Rosen, "Sensible, but Is It Just?" review of G. A. Cohen, *Rescuing Justice and Equality, Times Literary Supplement*, August 21, 2009, 29–30.

7. See John Rawls, *Lectures on the History of Moral Philosophy*, ed. Barbara Herman (Cambridge, MA: Harvard University Press, 2000), 107 [discussing Leibniz]; and Rawls, *A Theory of Justice* (Oxford: Oxford University Press, 1971), 159.

8. For an intriguing, but (I think) unsuccessful attempt to resist this conclusion, see Shlomo Dov Rosen, "A Theory of Providence for Distributive Justice," *Journal of Religious Ethics* 46 (2018): 124–55.

9. Rawls, *A Theory of Justice*, 311–12.

10. Rawls, 102.

11. For an exception, see Kok-Chor Tan, "A Defense of Luck Egalitarianism," *Journal of Philosophy* 105 (2008): 665–90 (esp. 671–72).

12. Leibniz to Antonio Magliabechi (September 1697) in *Gottfried Wilhelm Leibniz: Sämtliche Schriften und Briefe: Philosophischer Briefwechsel, 1695–1700, 3*

vols. Leibniz-Forschungsstelle der Universität Münster (Berlin: Akademie Verlag, 2013), 3:378–80. "jurisprudentia vere universalis."

13. Jan Narveson, "Cohen's Rescue," *Journal of Ethics* 14 (2010): 263–334 (see esp. 292). The italics are Narveson's. See also Thomas Nagel, *Equality and Partiality* (Oxford and New York: Oxford University Press, 1991), 107.

14. I agree here with Temkin, "Inequality," *Philosophy and Public Affairs* 15 (1986): 99–121 (see esp. 101n2).

15. For a related argument, see Derek Parfit, "Equality or Priority?" in *The Ideal of Equality*, ed. Matthew Clayton and Andrew Williams (Basingstoke: Palgrave Macmillan, 2000), 81–125 (see esp. 97).

16. I shall later argue that there is in fact no such thing (if the assets in question are not identical). I accept the possibility of such a state of affairs here only arguendo.

17. Compare Parfit, "Equality or Priority?" 111. Parfit defends the view that, in such a case, it is in no way bad for James that Bob is more intelligent—from which it would follow a fortiori that Bob is under no obligation to compensate James. My point is that the converse of this argument does not hold. It does not follow from the fact that Bob is under no obligation to compensate James that the distribution of intelligence must be in no way bad for the latter. The distribution could be unjust (and bad for James to that extent at least) without it being the case that *Bob* owes anything to James. Note also that Parfit grants that, even if Bob's having more intelligence need not be bad in any way for James, the inequality could still be regarded as "naturally unfair."

18. The second clause is needed in order to deal with cases of the following kind: suppose you steal a painting from my house on Tuesday morning, and at noon sharp my house is destroyed by an earthquake. Your stealing the painting has not apparently made me worse off, since, if you hadn't stolen it, it would have been destroyed hours later (in fact, your stealing the painting saved it, perhaps allowing me to recover it). But you are nonetheless guilty of an injustice, insofar as you took what belongs to me without my permission.

19. See Derek Parfit, *Reasons and Persons* (Oxford: Oxford University Press, 1984), 351–79; Parfit, "Energy Policy and the Further Future: the Identity Problem" in *Energy and the Future*, ed. Douglas MacLean and Peter Brown (Totowa, NJ: Rowman and Littlefield, 1983). For what strikes me as an unsuccessful attempt to argue that future persons may indeed be *wronged*, even if they cannot be *harmed*, see Rahul Kumar, "Who Can Be Wronged?" *Philosophy and Public Affairs* 31 (2003): 99–118. Kumar does not, however, attempt to argue that a nonexistent person can be the bearer of rights. For a related set of reflections on how this problem renders incoherent the notion of a "natural lottery" of talents and endowments, see S. L. Hurley, *Justice, Luck, and Knowledge* (Cambridge, MA: Harvard University Press, 2003), 118–20. For a rejoinder to Hurley on this point, see Kasper Lippert-Rasmussen, "Hurley on Egalitarianism and the Luck-Neutralizing Aim," *Politics, Philosophy, and*

Economics 4 (2005): 249–65. My sense is that Lippert-Rasmussen does not give us adequate reason to reject Hurely's "bare self" argument.

20. The relationship between attributes and identity is a classic example of the *sorites* problem: adding a single IQ point would not apparently cause me to become a different person, but adding 80 points almost certainly would (to say nothing of adding 80 IQ points alongside an operatic tenor voice, Olympian speed, and a cheery disposition)—and we cannot identify the "tipping point." Suffice it to say, for our purposes, that the wider the gap between one's actual bundle of natural endowments and the one that justice is taken to require, the less coherent it becomes for one to claim compensation for the meagerness of the bundle. My thanks to Alex Friedman for discussion of this point. On this, see George Sher, *Equality for Inegalitarians* (Cambridge: Cambridge University Press, 2014), 169.

21. Nor has he been deprived of something to which he was entitled, since, prior to his conception, he did not exist—and nonexistent beings cannot possess entitlements.

22. The most compelling attempts to resist the nonidentity problem have sought to establish that future persons can be harmed, despite not being made worse-off by the harms in question. I regard these attempts as unsuccessful. See, for example, Elizabeth Harman, "Can we Harm and Benefit in Creating?" *Philosophical Perspectives* 18 (2004): 89–113. It is, however, perfectly possible to claim that one does wrong in bringing it about that future persons are less well-off than other (different) future persons would have been, had one opted for a different course of action, while still denying that the persons who are brought into existence as a result of this wrong have *themselves* been wronged or harmed (or have claims of justice to be compensated by those who committed the wrong that was responsible for bringing them into existence). At issue is the vexed question of whether there can be purely impersonal duties (i.e., duties the performance of which benefits no agent or creature).

23. I say "necessarily," because luck egalitarians regard choice as the only possible justification for inequalities, and inequalities in natural endowments are (at least for the present) unchosen.

24. The fact that Bob will also live twenty years longer is important to the example, since it entails that his superior intelligence continues to render him more advantaged than James. I am grateful to Laura Valentini for bringing this issue to my attention.

25. G. A. Cohen, *Rescuing Justice and Equality* (Cambridge, MA: Harvard University Press, 2008), 32. In this chapter of the book, Cohen reproduces the early argument, while making clear that he will go on to set it aside.

26. Cohen, *Rescuing Justice and Equality,* 32.

27. Cohen, 49. For a similar gesture in this direction, see Nagel, *Equality and Partiality,* 107–8n33.

28. It is worth noting that, while the Difference Principle is Paretian in spirit, it can require outcomes that would not satisfy the Pareto Principle itself. If, under Distribution A, John has 2 and Ted has 6, the Difference Principle instructs us to prefer Distribution B, in which John has 3 and Ted has 5. But Distribution B is not Pareto

superior to A, since it does not make at least one person better off without making anyone else worse off.

29. Cohen, *Rescuing Justice and Equality*, 159.

30. See Cohen, 320 (esp. n67).

31. Cohen, 322.

32. See the classic discussion in Parfit, "Equality or Priority?" 97–98.

33. See, e.g., Temkin, "Egalitariansm Defended," *Ethics* (2003): 781. Temkin does not elide fairness and justice.

34. This need not involve any negligence on the part of police or those administering the system of justice; it might just be a matter of physics.

35. *Locke's Two Treatises of Government*, ed. Peter Laslett, 2nd ed. (Cambridge, 1967), 308.

36. For the same thought, see Leibniz, "Meditation on the Common Concept of Justice" in *Leibniz: Political Writings*, ed. Patrick Riley (Cambridge: Cambridge University Press, 1972), 55; and Richard Arneson, "Justice is not Equality," *Ratio* 21 (2008): 371–91 (see esp. 329).

37. Cohen, *Rescuing Justice and Equality*, 315.

38. Unless we suppose that there is some metaphysical limit, such that any creature with more than a given amount of intelligence would cease to be human. But, of course, one could then simply ask, "What's so great about being human as opposed to more than human?"

39. Rawls, *A Theory of Justice*, 62.

40. Rawls, 93.

41. It is a perfectly ordinary thought that, even if wealth is good in general, having more than a certain amount of it might be bad rather than good for us— although we might disagree profoundly about where the line is to be drawn.

42. I use the term "maximally intelligent" here in a loose, nontechnical sense, to mean "as or more intelligent than any living human being." If one supposes that the supply of intelligence is unlimited (and, further, that any given creature can, in principle, be made as intelligent as the Distributor chooses), then clearly there is no such thing as "maximal" intelligence—one could always add more. Indeed, if the supply of intelligence were truly infinite in this respect, there would be no such thing as a Pareto optimal distribution of it (if, that is, we assume that having more of it always makes one "better off," no matter how much of it one already has). It would therefore, I think, be a challenge for luck egalitarians to specify which distribution of such a good a just Distributor should elect. The problem implicates Leibniz's Principle of Sufficient Reason.

43. On this subject, see Allen Buchanan, Dan W. Brock, Norman Daniels, and Daniel Winkler, *From Chance to Choice: Genetics and Justice* (Cambridge: Cambridge University Press, 2000), 82–84.

44. See, for example, the useful exchange on the subject between Michael Sandel and Frances Kamm. Michael Sandel, *The Case against Perfection: Ethics in the Age of*

Genetic Enhancement (Cambridge, MA: Harvard University Press, 2007), esp. 85–100; Frances Kamm, "Is There a Problem with Enhancement?" *American Journal of Bioethics* 5 (2005): 5–14.

45. Leibniz offers the same argument in reply to Bayle. See G. W. Leibniz, *Theodicy*, trans. E. M. Huggard, ed. Austin M. Farrer (New York: Cosimo Classics, 2009), 198. Rawls evidently approved of this passage; in his annotated copy of the text, he wrote "Yes!" in the margin next to it. See Leibniz, *Theodicy, Abridged*, ed. and trans. E. M. Huggard (Indianapolis: Bobbs-Merrill 1966), Rawls's copy, Harvard University Archives, Hum. 48.1, Box 4, 83.

46. Compare Robert M. Adams, "Must God Create the Best?" *Philosophical Review* 81 (1972): 317–32 (esp. 321).

47. Leibniz, *Theodicy*, 165. In his annotated copy of the *Theodicy*, Rawls comments interestingly on this passage that "the question is what God finds satisfaction or Glory <u>in</u>." (See Leibniz, *Theodicy, Abridged*, Rawls's copy, 66.)

48. Leibniz, *Theodicy*, 189.

49. Quoted in Isaiah Berlin, *Russian Thinkers* (London: Penguin, 1994), 105. I owe this reference to Michael Rosen. Cf. Mary Wollstonecraft, *A Vindication of the Rights of Men* and *A Vindication of the Rights of Women*, ed. Sylvana Tomaselli (Cambridge: Cambridge University Press, 1995), 55–56: "The justice of God may be vindicated by a belief in a future state; but, only by believing that evil is educing good for the individual, and not for an imaginary whole. The happiness of the whole must arise from the happiness of the constituent parts, or the essence of justice is sacrificed to a supposed grand arrangement. . . . To suppose that, during the whole or part of its existence, the happiness of any individual is sacrificed to promote the welfare of ten, or ten thousand, other beings—is impious. But to suppose that the happiness, or animal enjoyment, of one portion of existence is sacrificed to improve and ennoble the being itself, and render it capable of more perfect happiness, is not to reflect on either the goodness or wisdom of God."

50. Compare Leibniz's argument that there is no such thing as perfect equipoise of the will (Rawls, "Leibniz II," in *Lectures on the History of Moral Philosophy*, 136–37).

51. See, classically, Robert Nozick, *Anarchy, State, and Utopia* (New York: Basic Books, 1974), 42–45.

52. See Ronald Dworkin, *Sovereign Virtue: The Theory and Practice of Equality* (Cambridge, MA: Harvard University Press, 2000), 42–45.

53. Dworkin, *Sovereign Virtue*, 69.

54. Dworkin himself offers a series of arguments for why equality of resources, as he understands the project, does not require a hypothetical auction of natural endowments (Dworkin, *Sovereign Virtue*, 79–81, 89–92). But his arguments address a situation in which these assets have already been "distributed" (i.e., there already exists a particular set of human beings with finite natural assets). He does not address the claim that one might use a hypothetical auction to establish how a counter-

factual just Distributor might bring about a fair and equal distribution of natural endowments among people in the first place.

55. It should go without saying that natural assets can and do become scarce goods in a different sense once a particular set of people with finite capacities are actually in existence. There is, for example, more demand for beauty in our world than there is supply, and this fact is to the benefit of beautiful people. To be sure, your being more beautiful does not bring it about that I am less so, but my beauty (such as it is) is rendered less valuable to others by the fact of your greater beauty—and you will likely be able to command a larger share of scarce material resources as a result. We, however, are considering a different question: namely, whether natural assets should be regarded as scarce from the point of view of a counterfactual Distributor who must elect each person's bundle of those assets. It would be very odd to suppose that the levels of these endowments that happen to obtain in our world should be regarded, in principle, as constraints on such a Distributor. If this were conceded, it would of course become vastly easier to show that the current distribution might satisfy the Cosmic Difference Principle.

56. That is, if we could find a way around the metaphysical objection canvassed above.

57. Unless natural assets and advantage are to be regarded (implausibly) as "scarce"—and even in that case, we would still confront the nonidentity problem discussed on pp. 83–84.

58. See, for example, Harry Frankfurt, "Equality as a Moral Ideal," *Ethics* 98 (1987): 21–43.

59. On the eighteenth-century theodicy debate and its ramifications, see, most recently, Steven Nadler, *The Best of all Possible Worlds: A Story of Philosophers, God, and Evil in the Age of Reason* (Princeton, NJ: Princeton University Press, 2010); and Susan Neiman, *Evil in Modern Thought: An Alternative History* (Princeton, NJ: Princeton University Press, 2002; reprinted 2015).

60. "Êtes-vous assurés que la cause éternelle / Qui fait tout, qui sait tout, qui créa tout pour elle, / Ne pouvait nous jeter dans ces tristes climats / Sans former des volcans allumés sous nos pas? / Borneriez-vous ainsi la suprême puissance? / Lui défendriez-vous d'exercer sa clémence? / L'éternel artisan n'a-t-il pas dans ses mains / Des moyens infinis tout prêts pour ses desseins?" See Voltaire, *Poème sur le désastre de Lisbonne* in *Oeuvres*, ed. Louis Moland, 52 vols. (Paris: Garnier, 1877–1885), 9:471.

61. Hegel, *History of Philosophy*, 3 vols., trans. Elizabeth S. Haldane and Frances H. Simson (London: Kegan Paul, 1896), 3:340–41. "Das Resultat der leibnizischen Theodicee ist ein 'Optimismus', auf den hinkenden und langweiligen Gedanken gestützt, Gott habe, da einmal eine Welt habe werden sollen, aus den unendlich vielen möglichen Welten die möglichst beste. . . . So etwas kann man wohl in gemeinen Leben sagen. Wenn ich eine Ware auf dem Markt in einer Stadt holen lasse und sage, sie sei zwar nicht volkommen, aber die beste, die zu haben gewesen, so ist dies ein ganz guter 'Grund,' mich zufrieden zu geben. Aber 'Begreifen' ist ein ganz Anderes."

Hegel, *Vorlesungen über die Geschichte der Philosophie,* ed. G. J. P. J. Bolland (Leiden: A. H. Adriani, 1908), 932. I have altered the translation slightly.

62. "Letter from J. J. Rousseau to M. de Voltaire" (August 18, 1756) in *Rousseau: The Discourses and Other Early Political Writings,* ed. and trans. Victor Gourevitch (Cambridge: Cambridge University Press, 1997), 233.

63. Locke, for one, seems to answer "no": "that such a temporary Life as we now have, with all its Frailties and ordinary Miseries, is better than no Being, is evident by the high value we put upon it ourselves." Locke, *The Reasonableness of Christianity, as Delivered in the Scriptures* in *John Locke: Writings on Religion,* ed. Victor Nuovo (Oxford: Oxford University Press, 2002), 94. For the contrary view, see Arthur Schopenhauer, *The World as Will and Representation,* ed. and trans. E. F. J. Payne, 2 vols. (Cambridge: Cambridge University Press, 1969), 1:325–26.

64. See, e.g., Adams, "Must God Create the Best?" 325–28.

65. Rawls, *A Theory of Justice,* 159.

66. Immanuel Kant, "On the Mistrial of all philosophical trials in theodicy" in *Immanuel Kant: Religion and Rational Theology,* ed. and trans. Allen Wood and George Di Giovanni, Cambridge Edition of the Works of Immanuel Kant (Cambridge: Cambridge University Press, 1996), 25.

67. Leibniz, *Theodicy,* 105.

68. Leibniz, 130.

5. JUSTICE, EQUALITY, AND INSTITUTIONS

1. Samuel Scheffler, "What Is Egalitarianism?" *Philosophy and Public Affairs* 31 (2003): 5–39 (esp. 21).

2. Scheffler, "What Is Egalitarianism?" 22.

3. Scheffler, 23.

4. Scheffler, 25.

5. Scheffler, 25.

6. Scheffler, 25–26.

7. Rawls, *A Theory of Justice* (Oxford: Oxford University Press, 1971), 72.

8. That is, unless some other objection was offered on different grounds.

9. Chapter 4 offers an extended argument that the notion of an equal distribution of heterogeneous endowments is incoherent.

10. This is obviously so in the case of natural advantages such as physical attractiveness, but it is even true of advantages such as good health or a sturdy constitution. A person whose body is genetically primed to function well until age eighty-five is not advantaged relative to one whose body is genetically primed to function well only until seventy if both live in a warrior society in which no one lives past fifty. I am grateful to Eric Beerbohm for pressing me to think about this point.

11. This suggestion was in fact made by Herbert Spiegelberg over seventy years ago. See Herbert Spiegelberg, "A Defense of Human Equality," *Philosophical Review* 53 (1944): 101–24 (esp. 114).

12. Rawls, *A Theory of Justice,* 312.

13. Or perhaps, if we know that some money is tainted, we would be permitted to extract the smallest practicable sum.

14. There has of course been a great deal of discussion as to what constitutes "ideal" and "non-ideal" theory. I make use of here of what I take to be the most common (and plausible) way of distinguishing between them: ideal theory assumes full compliance with the principles of justice, while nonideal theory takes as its subject a world of partial compliance. On the various contemporary uses of these terms, see Laura Valentini, "Ideal vs. Non-ideal Theory: A Conceptual Map," *Philosophy Compass* 7 (2012): 654–64.

15. Nozick, *Anarchy, State, and Utopia* (New York: Basic Books, 1974), 230–31. The "rough rule of thumb" sketched out here is Rawls's Difference Principle.

16. David Kaye, "The Paradox of the Gatecrasher and Other Stories," *Arizona State Law Journal* 101, 104 (1979).

17. Judith Jarvis Thomson, "Liability and Individualized Evidence," *Law and Contemporary Problems* 49 (1986): 199–219 (see esp. 214).

18. Rawls, *A Theory of Justice,* 103–4.

19. In fact, this too is over-hasty. Even if A's entire product were determined by his allotment of natural advantages, and even if the distribution of these advantages across persons were morally arbitrary, it would not follow that A is entitled to none of his product. For presumably at least some share of A's natural advantages would be assigned to him under a just and fair distribution of such assets. That is, we are entitled to assume that a just distribution would assign him *some* natural advantages, and these would yield *some* share of his product. But let us set this issue aside for the moment to make matters simpler.

20. G. A. Cohen, *Rescuing Justice and Equality* (Cambridge, MA: Harvard University Press, 2008), 14. There is good evidence to suggest that Rawls did not believe this earlier in his career. To take just one example, in his annotated copy of Kant's *Religion within the Limits of Reason Alone,* Rawls writes "This <u>must</u> surely be asking too much. . . . But what is required?" next to John R. Silber's claim that, for Kant, "A person capable of responsible action must be free in the transcendental [circled] meaning of the term." See Kant, *Religion within the Limits of Reason Alone,* ed. and trans. Theodore M. Greeve and Hoyt H. Hudson, Introduction by John R. Silber (New York: Harper and Row, 1960), cxi. Rawls's copy; see Harvard University Archive, Hum. 48.1, Box 3. The annotations probably date to 1973.

21. T. M. Scanlon, *Why Does Inequality Matter?* (Oxford: Oxford University Press, 2018), 136.

22. T. M. Scanlon, *Why Does Inequality Matter?* 136.

23. See Liam Murphy and Thomas Nagel, *The Myth of Ownership: Taxes and Justice* (Oxford: Oxford University Press, 2002), 61. The issue was originally raised by Nozick (see *Anarchy, State, and Utopia*, 188).

24. Scanlon, *Why Does Inequality Matter?* 136.

25. Murphy and Nagel, *The Myth of Ownership*, 32.

26. Murphy and Nagel, 8.

27. See, for example, Felix Maultzsch, "Morals and Markets: The Significance of Pre-Tax Ownership," *Modern Law Review* 67 (2004): 508–23 (esp. 512). See also Jed Lewinsohn, "Conventionalism in Law, Morality, and Politics," unpublished PhD dissertation (New York University, 2015), 12–28.

28. If the second reading is correct, it is in this sense that we have to take Nagel and Murphy's concluding remark that their view should not be taken to imply that "the entire social product really belongs to the government, and that all after-tax income should be seen as a kind of dole that each of us receives from the government, if it chooses to look on us with favor" (176). What they mean, on this view, is that any distribution of resources must be part of an overall scheme that is justifiable, in the sense that it "gives due weight to individual freedom and responsibility," along with "distributive justice" (74) and other values. In other words, the distribution adopted by the state cannot be arbitrary; it must be consistent with the requirements of a society of free and equal citizens. What Nagel and Murphy emphatically do not mean by this caveat is that individuals have pre-institutional claims to things.

29. Murphy and Nagel, *The Myth of Ownership*, 34.

30. This is an instance of what in formal logic is called the "fallacy of composition."

6. "GOD GAVE THE WORLD TO *ADAM,* AND HIS POSTERITY IN COMMON"

1. Nonlibertarian liberals, in contrast, tend to reject all three of these claims. See, for example, Liam Murphy and Thomas Nagel, *The Myth of Ownership: Taxes and Justice* (Oxford: Oxford University Press, 2002). Claim 3 is taken to follow from claim 1; the precise relation between claims 1 and 2 is a matter of dispute among libertarians.

2. John Locke, *Second Treatise of Government,* ed. C. B. Macpherson (Indianapolis: Hackett, 1980), 29. Left libertarians disagree among themselves concerning what exactly is to count as a "natural resource," and they consequently take different positions on the degree to which the state may tax one's marginal product. See the useful summary in Peter Vallentyne, "Left-Libertarianism—A Primer," in *Left-Libertarianism and Its Critics: The Contemporary Debate,* ed. Peter Vallentyne and Hillel Steiner (Basingstoke: Palgrave Macmillan, 2000), 5–10.

3. Richard Watson, *The Wisdom and Goodness of* GOD, *in having made both Rich and Poor, A Sermon . . .* (London, 1793), 2–3.

4. Thomas Paine, *Agrarian Justice Opposed to Agrarian Law, and to Agrarian Monopoly* (London, [1797]), 9. Paine's pamphlet was written in answer to Bishop Watson's sermon, cited above.

5. See Annabel Brett, *Liberty, Right and Nature* (Cambridge: Cambridge University Press, 1997), esp. 10–87; and Peter Garnsey, *Thinking about Property: From Antiquity to the Age of Revolution* (Cambridge: Cambridge University Press, 2007), 84–135.

6. See Richard Tuck, *Natural Rights Theories* (Cambridge: Cambridge University Press, 1979), esp. 58–100.

7. See David Armitage, "John Locke, Carolina, and the *Two Treatises of Government*," *Political Theory* 32 (2004): 602–27.

8. It is striking that even Robert Filmer argued only that, if the world was indeed given to men in common (as Grotius had insisted), then "the Act of our forefathers, in abrogating the naturall law of Community, by introducing that of property" must be regarded as "a sinne of a high presumption." He nowhere claimed that it would follow from the fact of this original "sinne" that all contemporary proprietors lack legitimate title to their lands. See Robert Filmer, *Observations Concerning the Originall of Government* (London, 1652), 17. See also 35, 49–50.

9. Jean-Jacques Rousseau, *The Discourses and Other Early Political Writings,* ed. and trans. Victor Gourevitch (Cambridge: Cambridge University Press, 1997), 161.

10. Note, for example, Rousseau's claim, in the unpublished *Projet de constitution pour la Corse* (1765), that the Gracchi did wrong in attempting to confiscate originally expropriated lands from patricians who had possessed them for generations. *Oeuvres complètes de Jean-Jacques Rousseau,* ed. Bernard Gagnebin and Marcel Raymond, vol. 3 (Paris: Gallimard, 1964), 192.

11. See, for example, William Ogilvie, *An Essay on the Right of Property in Land, with Respect to its Foundation in the Law of Nature* (London, 1781). Thomas Paine is sometimes taken to have adopted this position in his essay on "Agrarian Justice," but Paine in fact assigned remarkably strong, continuing property rights to contemporary landowners—such that, on his account, their holdings might not be disturbed until after their deaths. See Paine, *Agrarian Justice Opposed to Agrarian Law.*

12. Pierre-Joseph Proudhon, *What Is Property?* ed. and trans. Donald R. Kelley and Bonnie G. Smith (Cambridge: Cambridge University Press, 1994), 43.

13. Proudhon, *What Is Property?* 45.

14. Proudhon, 64.

15. Proudhon, 79. Cf. Hillel Steiner, *An Essay on Rights* (Oxford: Oxford University Press, 1994), 107; and Philippe Van Parijs, *Real Freedom for All* (Oxford: Oxford University Press, 1995), 12–14.

16. See Peter Vallentyne and Hillel Steiner, eds., *The Origins of Left-Libertarianism: An Anthology of Historical Writings* (New York: St. Martin's Press, 2000), 199–200.

17. Let us say that to "appropriate" a thing is to take unencumbered ownership of it, claiming the right to remove it from the "common stock of mankind" and to dispose of it without paying others for its use. This is an important clarification: several left libertarians have argued that their theories allow individuals to "appropriate" natural resources so long as those individuals compensate the collective for the full value of the resources and / or pay taxes on the benefits derived from controlling them. But this view invests humanity at large with significant, continuing rights to the resources in question; as a result, it does not, strictly speaking, grant individuals the right to appropriate natural resources. It would be better to say that many left libertarians allow individuals unilaterally to "lease" or "possess" the resources in question (i.e., without the explicit consent of the rest of humanity) under certain highly restrictive conditions.

18. For possible constructions of common ownership, see Peter Vallentyne, Hillel Steiner, and Michael Otsuka, "Why Left-Libertarianism Is Not Incoherent, Indeterminate, or Irrelevant: A Reply to Fried," *Philosophy and Public Affairs* 33 (2005): 201–15 (esp. 202–3). See also Mathias Risse, "Does Left-Libertarianism Have Coherent Foundations?" *Politics, Philosophy, & Economics* 3 (2004): 337–64 (esp. 343–45).

19. Or that all illicit acts of appropriation have been dealt with according to the correct principle of rectification (an issue to which the rest of this paper is addressed).

20. This, I suggest, is the non sequitur we encounter in G. A. Cohen's internal critique of Nozick's "right" libertarianism—a fact for which Nozick himself is largely to blame, as I hope to make clear below. See Cohen, *Self-Ownership, Freedom, and Equality* (Cambridge: Cambridge University Press, 1995), esp. 67–91.

21. I use this formulation as a convenient shorthand. Some left libertarians would say that Locke was right to some degree, but that he misunderstood the significance of his own argument in a crucial respect. For example, Michael Otsuka claims to agree with Locke that people are entitled to appropriate resources in the state of nature if doing so will leave "enough and as good" for everyone else—but he claims that the proviso is more demanding than Locke supposed. In particular it implies a right to equal opportunities for welfare that would severely limit the range of legitimate appropriation, and requires further that our use of these resources must also leave "enough and as good" (in the same specialized sense) for future generations. Otsuka, *Libertarianism without Inequality* (Oxford: Oxford University Press, 2003), 29–39. Accordingly, we should concede that any legitimate acquisition of natural resources such as land confers only a radically circumscribed leasehold, rather than full ownership.

22. Robert Nozick, *Anarchy, State, and Utopia* (New York: Basic Books, 1974), 230.

23. Nozick, *Anarchy, State, and Utopia*, 230–31.

24. Nozick himself is vague about this second point. He states that the worst-off have the highest probability of being the descendants of victims and that the "better-off" are "assumed" to be the beneficiaries of expropriators. Given these claims, it would seem reasonable to suppose that, on his account, the "best-off" have the highest probability of being the beneficiaries of expropriators (although the probability that the best-off are beneficiaries of expropriators need not be as high as the probability that the worst-off are descendants of victims). Nozick is likewise unclear about the sense in which we should regard the better-off as (presumptively) "beneficiaries" of expropriators: is he claiming that they are most likely to have actually *inherited* originally expropriated assets (or the assets into which these have been converted over time), or merely that they are most likely to have benefitted in some indirect way from the fact of the expropriation? Given his theoretical commitments (as well as the fact that he uses the term "perpetrators" in the parenthetical remark), I assume that he means the former.

25. Likewise, the probability that a badly off individual descends from a badly off ancestor who was the victim of expropriation is not high enough to allow the presumption that he or she is entitled to compensation. See John Christman, *The Myth of Property: Toward an Egalitarian Theory of Ownership* (Oxford: Oxford University Press, 1994), 65. Christman uses this fact to argue that the claims of any putative victims will be "outweighed" by the non–rights-based claims of the "comparatively worse-off"—rather than to argue for deference to good-faith purchasers.

26. For the state of current research on intergenerational income elasticity in the United States, see Chul-In Lee and Gary Solon, "Trends in Intergenerational Income Mobility," *Review of Economics and Statistics* 91 (2009): 766–72. Lee and Solon find that IIE has remained more or less constant at .44 for the previous three decades. For inheritances in the U.S., see Edward N. Wolff and Mary Gittleman, "Inheritances and the Distribution of Wealth, or Whatever Happened to the Great Inheritance Boom?" *Journal of Economic Inequality* 12 (2014): 439–68.

27. Contrast Jan Narveson's view that the rectification problem would not often arise in a proper Nozickian theory simply because, when A wrongs B, no one other than B has any obligation to pursue rectification (such that costs associated with "the detection and imposition of rectification on the guilty parties" cannot legitimately be assigned to others). See Narveson, "Present Payments, Past Wrongs: Correcting Loose Talk about Nozick and Rectification," *Libertarian Papers* 1 (2009): 14–15.

28. For a similar argument applied to the case of criminal jurisprudence, see Ronald Dworkin, *Taking Rights Seriously* (Cambridge, MA: Harvard University Press, 1977), 13.

29. This could be either because (1) Humanity as a whole never collectively decided (in the morally relevant sense) on a division of natural resources into truly private parcels—although, counterfactually, it *could* legitimately have done so; or because (2) Humanity could never legitimately have divided up the earth into truly

private parcels (over which individuals would have complete, discretionary control) for reasons having to do with the rights of future persons. Left libertarians take different views on this question. See my discussion below.

30. Peter Vallentyne, "Left-Libertarianism—A Primer," 15. See also Steiner, *An Essay on Rights* (Oxford: Oxford University Press, 1994), pp. 266–82; and Baruch Brody, "Redistribution without Egalitarianism" *Social Philosophy and Policy* 1 (1983): 71–87.

31. My argument does not assign claims to proprietors who knowingly acquire natural resources through theft or fraud. I do not regard it as controversial to assume that such proprietors represent only a small fraction of the total number of current owners of natural resources.

32. For a lucid statement of this view, see Barbara H. Fried, "Left-Libertarianism: A Review Essay," *Philosophy and Public Affairs* 32 (2004): 66–92; and Fried, "Left-Libertarianism, Once More: A Rejoinder to Vallentyne, Steiner, and Otsuka," *Philosophy and Public Affairs* 33 (2005): 216–22. For a denial of the claim that left-libertarianism turns out to require (more or less) what is required under various forms of egalitarianism, see Cohen, *Self-Ownership, Freedom, and Equality,* 116–43, and Eric Mack, "Distributive Justice and the Tensions of Lockeanism," *Social Philosophy and Policy* 1 (1983): 132–50 (esp. 149–50).

33. These are also the views taken by virtually every contemporary legal system. See, for example, Saul Levmore, "Variety and Uniformity in the Treatment of the Good-Faith Purchaser," *Journal of Legal Studies* 16 (1987): 43–65. Roman law denied that a good-faith purchaser of stolen property could ever possess superior title to that of the owner, but it is striking that no contemporary legal system seems to have followed it faithfully in this respect. Arguably, the system most similar to the Roman one is that of U.S. law, which still in theory accords weight to the principle of *nemo dat quod non habet* (except in cases where the stolen item is currency or a bearer instrument). But this rule has been mitigated in so many different ways that it now no longer has purchase in cases such as the one under discussion.

34. Fred might well be entitled to compensation for the time and effort he has had to expend to retrieve the value of the glass.

35. The state would, in other words, be fining her for the value of the glass.

36. Narveson makes a similar argument in order to demonstrate that Nozick's theory need not, on account of the rectification issue, collapse into something like Rawls's. He does not, however, take what I regard as the crucial next step: namely, to recognize that, given these limits on permissible rectification, the question of justice in *acquisition* (to which both he and Nozick assign such overwhelming importance) becomes something of a red herring.

37. Narveson, "Present Payments, Past Wrongs," 9. A similar argument is frequently made in the legal literature on unjust enrichment: if we extract restitution from a blameless defendant, do we not treat him as "a mere means," using him "as an

instrument in the service of the plaintiff's interest?" See Dennis Klimchuk, "The Normative Foundations of Unjust Enrichment," in *Philosophical Foundations of the Law of Unjust Enrichment*, ed. Robert Chamber, Charles Mitchell, and James Penner (Oxford: Oxford University Press, 2009), 97.

38. Say, because he has died or disappeared.

39. It would seem equally arbitrary to divide its value 60 / 40 or in any other un-equal proportion.

40. Unless of course their contracts happen to specify a hierarchical relationship among the creditors.

41. For this reason, not all purchasers of land will count as "good faith pur-chasers." Just as private law draws a distinction between the purchaser who buys a television from off the back of a truck in an alley at midnight and one who buys a television from Best Buy, the principle of justice will not recognize the claims of those who purchase assets under suspicious circumstances or without having done their due diligence (e.g., a title search in the case of a house or a provenance inquiry in the case of a painting). What I deny is that we have good reason to treat all owners of natural resources as if they acquired these assets off the back of a truck at mid-night or, in Steiner's formulation, as if they had "bought the Brooklyn bridge" from a "confidence trickster" (Steiner, *An Essay on Rights,* 103).

42. This should answer Christman's objection that, unless we follow Proudhon, we must embrace a "paper-thin first occupancy theory," according to which "I could simply kill the rightful owner of a piece of property . . . and if I could guard my pos-session while paying for my crime, then I would be the owner of the property by natural right" (Christman, *The Myth of Property,* 65).

43. One might object that, just as Jane would have no claim to the glass if the money with which she purchased it was in fact not her own (even if she did not know this), those who purchased expropriated land would have no claim to the land if the funds with which they purchased it were derived from the proceeds of previous acts of expropriation (even if they did not know this)—and that, in fact, it is very likely that this is the case. By way of reply, we first need to stress that, as part of their com-mitment to self-ownership, libertarians of all stripes acknowledge that individuals have just title to their own labor. Accordingly, even the very first piece of (putatively) expropriated land might have been bought by a good-faith purchaser, viz. one who labored for some fixed term in return for it (while being under the impression that the land could legitimately be sold by its "owner"). Labor here takes the place of "money" in the glass case. As to whether any given piece of land was *actually* pur-chased with labor (or the monetized version of it)—or with funds derived from the sale of natural resources by good-faith purchasers who paid for the resources in ques-tion with their labor—or from the sale of illicitly expropriated assets by those who do not count as good-faith purchasers, the question cannot be answered by appeal to a "rough rule of thumb."

44. Some, such as Otsuka, would deny individuals testamentary rights over natural resources, but this limitation is simply part of his theory of justice in *acquisition* (i.e., it derives from his conviction that such resources cannot licitly be appropriated in the full sense of the term). He explicitly states that people *do* have the right to bequeath things that they *do* justly own in the full sense of the term (39). My argument here is that, even if Otsuka is correct about justice in acquisition, he should concede (as a matter of justice in *rectification*) that good-faith purchasers have a right to the value of the natural resources they have purchased. If this is so, it would follow on the basis of Otsuka's own argument that such purchasers should enjoy testamentary freedom over that value. Steiner, in contrast, does indeed deny that the right of bequest is one of the incidents of ownership, on the grounds that the testator (once dead) cannot be the bearer of rights or the object of duties (Steiner, *An Essay on Rights,* 249–62). But since, on this account, the testator would still be within his rights to transfer his property to whomever he wished on the day before his death—and the beneficiary would then be the acknowledged bearer of a right to that property—the restriction is not important in this context.

45. Note that, on my account, it is not the lapse of time (on its own) or the number of transactions following the initial expropriation that generates claims— although the lapse of time together with certain decisions and behaviors on the part of an owner might well do so, as in the familiar case of adverse possession. My view is therefore different from Jeremy Waldron's; see Waldron, "Superseding Historic Injustice," *Ethics* 103 (1992): 4–28 (esp. 15–20).

46. For a rich discussion of this theme, see George Sher, "Ancient Wrongs and Modern Rights," *Philosophy and Public Affairs* 10 (1981): 3–17.

47. The question would then arise whether we are entitled to adopt the "default" supposition that, absent any recoverable bequest, the original victim of expropriation intended to pass on his claim to his remote descendants. For the difficulties surrounding such an assumption, see Waldron, "Superseding Historic Injustice," 10–11.

48. Steiner suggests that a way out of this impasse would be to broaden the class of potential claimants to include all those who "would have been better off" had the initial expropriation not taken place (Steiner, *An Essay on Rights,* 267n3). But this strikes me as implausible. If I steal $100 from William, he himself undoubtedly has a claim against me for $100. But suppose that, had I not stolen the $100, William would at some later date have used that money to buy a sweater from Phil. Does Phil have a claim against *me* (or my beneficiaries) for $100? Surely not, since Phil has/had no claim to the $100 in the first place. Thus, a fortiori, Phil's descendants can have no claim against my descendants.

49. One could also argue for a "negative" account of original community—that is, in the beginning everything was *res nullius*. In this case the potential wrong would not be "expropriation" (since no one can be deprived of an ownership share that he does not possess in the first place), but rather "exclusion" (which would then

need to be compensated in a similar manner). On this distinction, see Waldron, *The Right to Private Property* (Oxford: Oxford University Press, 1988), 285–86; and Brody, "Redistribution without Egalitarianism," 76–77.

50. It should go without saying that this particular argument does not address cases in which we *do* possess such information (or could acquire it if we tried). If, for example, we know that European colonists expropriated land from a given Native American tribe, and we know that the tribe in question continues to exist (i.e., we can identify descendants of the original victims), my argument does not rule out the possibility that reparations might legitimately be claimed by these descendants. In order to determine whether reparations are appropriate in such a case, we would need to settle the far more controversial question of the "generational threshold" (and we would also want to know, of course, whether the tribe in question was *itself* guilty of expropriating the land in question at an earlier date).

51. For a gesture in this direction, see Otsuka, *Libertarianism without Inequality,* 35–40.

52. The phrase "overlapping late arrivals" is Steiner's *An Essay on Rights,* 272.

53. Except insofar as "late arrivals" who were denied their equal *n*th of the earth would *then* possess claims to restitution.

54. See Joseph Mazor, "Liberal Justice, Future People, and Natural Resource Conservation," *Philosophy and Public Affairs* 38 (2010): 380–408.

55. Proponents tend to appeal for support to the following analogy: a ship-wrecked sailor washes up on a desert island previously inhabited by only two other people, who have by this time divvied up the island between themselves. Why, we are asked, should the mere fact that the shipwrecked man arrived *later* than the other two cause us to deny his claim to an equal share of the island? But it strikes me that the analogy is poor, not least because children do not simply "wash up" on shore like shipwrecked sailors. See, for example, Steiner, *An Essay on Rights,* 271; and Mazor, "Liberal Justice," 389–91.

56. That is, to whatever share of its value is required to satisfy the claims of late arrivals to an equal *n*th of global natural resources.

57. A conventionalist about property rights would also deny this, but for different reasons. The left libertarian argues that there are "natural" rights to property that legitimate rules must protect; if the rules of a given society violate these rights, then the rules in question are unjust and are not entitled to respect (from which it is supposed to follow that transactions entered into on the basis of these rules are likewise not entitled to respect). The conventionalist argues in contrast that there are no natural rights to property and that property rights established by convention are only deserving of respect if the overall institutional scheme of which they are a part is consistent with a given principle of justice.

58. Although, since glass is made from sand (a natural resource), committed left libertarians would assert that at least some portion of the glass (or of its value) is

likewise to be regarded as stolen property. Such theorists should simply substitute a lock of hair for the glass in this example.

59. Parfit, *Reasons and Persons,* 453–54. Parfit's explanation for this fact—that for most of human history "people have believed in the existence of a God, or of several gods"—I take to be quite wrong.

60. John Locke, *The Reasonableness of Christianity as Delivered in the Scriptures,* ed. John C. Higgins-Biddle, Clarendon Edition of the Works of John Locke (Oxford: Clarendon Press, 1999), 155–56.

61. We might of course ask a different question about the situation of our bronze-age man: if, as we usually suppose, "ought" implies "can," is it really possible to defend a view of justice that requires him to "share" natural resources with all other human beings (that is, to forbear expropriating them so as not to deprive the other members of Humanity Inc. of their shares in these resources)? After all, he doesn't even know of the existence of most of his fellow human beings, and certainly would be in no position to consult with those living far away. This point seems compelling to me, but, since it would suggest that individual appropriation in the Bronze Age actually was *not* unjust, it is not germane to our discussion.

62. Note again that blamelessness alone is insufficient to generate a moral claim in this case. The point is, rather, that blameworthiness *suffices* to defeat any such claim.

63. This analogy goes back to Henry George, *Progress and Poverty* (1879), chap. 28.

64. I am considering here the case of those enslaved against their will; this discussion will not address the comparatively vexed question of voluntary slavery.

65. Gideon Rosen, "Culpability and Ignorance," *Proceedings of the Aristotelian Society* (2002): 61–84.

66. Rosen likewise invokes the example of "an ordinary Hittite lord" (64–66).

67. Rosen does not consider the question of whether his Hittite slaveholder has a claim to the value of his slaves; he simply wishes to argue that, on account of the man's "blameless moral ignorance," he should not be "blamed" for committing the unjust act of enslavement. But, since we have established that only blameworthiness for the theft of an object is capable of defeating the moral claim of one who has purchased that object according to the rules laid down, my position is a natural extension of Rosen's.

68. This comparison, however, raises a further question: if we are prepared to conclude that a present-day slave-purchaser cannot be said to act in good faith because it is not unreasonable to expect him to recognize the injustice of slavery, why should we not conclude something similar in the case of the present-day land-purchaser? After all, such a purchaser is living 200 years after European theorists announced the (hypothetically) correct, relevant moral principle. Why at this point is it unreasonable to expect him to recognize the injustice of rules allowing individuals to purchase land? One possible reply would stress that, while the recognition of

the injustice of slavery is deeply embedded in our civilization, awareness of the Proudhonian principle is not. It might, then, seem not at all unreasonable to attribute "good faith" to present-day purchasers of land.

69. That is, assuming that current owners have acquired their natural resources through good-faith rule-following. If this is *not* the case, and if we cannot identify the victims of expropriation, then, on my account, *no one* has a moral right to the resources in question. My argument is silent about how natural resources should be disposed of in such cases.

70. See, for example, David Hume, *An Enquiry concerning the Principles of Morals,* ed. Tom L. Beauchamp, Clarendon Edition of the Works of David Hume (Oxford: Clarendon Press, 1998), 101. Cf. Jeremy Bentham, "Principles of the Civil Code," in *Jeremy Bentham: The Theory of Legislation,* ed. C. K. Ogden (London: Routledge and Kegan Paul, 1931), esp. 113–14.

71. If we mean instead a condition of "partial" (as opposed to "strict") compliance with the principles of justice, then of course *all* theories of rectification (and punishment) will count as non-ideal. See A. John Simmons, "Ideal and Nonideal Theory," *Philosophy and Public Affairs* 38 (2010): 5–35.

72. See Waldron, *The Right to Private Property,* 443.

73. Joel Feinberg, "Duty and Obligation in the Non-Ideal World," *Journal of Philosophy* 70 (1973): 263–75 (this passage appears on p. 268). Cf. Sidgwick, *The Methods of Ethics,* III.5.3.

74. There might well be cases in which we would assign moral claims to agents who have acquired "sincere" expectations in the course of following rules that they knew to be unjust—but surely our default supposition ought to be that those who knowingly commit injustice do not thereby acquire claims to our respect or deference.

75. Edmund Burke, *Reflections on the Revolution in France,* ed. L. G. Mitchell (Oxford: Oxford University Press, 1993), 156–57.

CONCLUSION

1. See, classically, Robert Nozick, *Anarchy, State, and Utopia* (New York: Basic Books, 1974), esp. 265–68.

2. See, for example, Ronald Dworkin, *Sovereign Virtue: The Theory and Practice of Equality* (Cambridge, MA: Harvard University Press, 2000), 6; and Thomas Nagel, "The Problem of Global Justice," *Philosophy and Public Affairs* 33 (2005): 113–47 (esp. 128–30).

3. See, for example, Richard Tuck, *The Sleeping Sovereign: The Invention of Modern Democracy* (Cambridge: Cambridge University Press, 2015). For a theorist of this kind, the central question becomes whether voting on constitutional structures alone is sufficient for democratic control, or whether the latter must extend to other kinds of political decisions as well.

4. Nozick, *Anarchy, State, and Utopia,* 287. I am grateful to Arthur Applbaum for reminding me of this wonderful turn of phrase.

5. *Hume: Political Essays,* ed. Knud Haakonssen (Cambridge: Cambridge University Press, 1994), 193.

6. *Hume: Political Essays,* 193.

7. *Hume: Political Essays,* 193.

8. David Hume, *A Treatise of Human Nature,* ed. David Fate Norton and Mary Norton, 2 vols. (Oxford: Clarendon Press, 2007), 1:315.

9. *Hume: Political Essays,* 194.

Acknowledgments

This book had its beginnings in 2010, when my colleague Michael Rosen suggested that he, Jeremy Waldron, Tamsin Shaw, Sam Moyn, and I should meet for an afternoon in New York to discuss the place of religion in contemporary political philosophy. Jeremy had the idea that we should all do some common reading in advance of the event, and he accordingly assigned us John Rawls's undergraduate senior thesis. I recall at the time being rather annoyed at having to engage with this piece of Rawlsian juvenalia. But as I read the text, I became transfixed. I had always joked with my students that Rawls's political theory was secularized Augustinianism. I now began to consider for the first time the possibility that this might not be a joke.

I had the opportunity to explore my intuition in a more sustained way as I prepared to co-teach a graduate seminar on "Foundations of Justice" with Amartya Sen in the fall of 2013. I am, as always, deeply grateful to Amartya for his guidance and intellectual companionship, as well as to the members of the seminar for many illuminating exchanges. In the spring of 2015, my friend and colleague Patrick Riley passed away quite suddenly and I stepped in to teach the remainder of his graduate seminar on "Justice as Love and Benevolence." The endeavor forced me to deepen my engagement with the theodicy problem, and I am eager to thank Patrick's superb students for helping me to do so. I was then fortunate to be able to present my ideas at a more advanced stage in a graduate seminar on "Liberalism and Theodicy" in the spring of 2017, and I am equally indebted to the students in that class for helping me to clarify and refine a number of important claims.

The Center for American Political Studies at Harvard generously sponsored a day-long workshop on the manuscript in December 2018, when it was in the final stages of preparation. I am deeply grateful to Steve Ansolabahere, the director of the Center, for his enthusiastic support of the program, and to Laura Donaldson for coordinating the logistics so efficiently. But my chief thanks must go to the extraordinary scholars who served as commentators on the various chapters: Eric Beerbohm, Katrina Forrester, Barbara Fried, Eric Gregory, Lucas Stanczyk, Richard Tuck, and Laura Valentini. Their criticisms and suggestions, along with remarkable contributions by members of the audience, have immeasurably improved the final product.

Chapter 2 was first published as "Representation and the Fall" in *Modern Intellectual History* 15 (2018) and is reprinted with minor edits. I am grateful to Cambridge University Press for permission to include the essay here. Material from this study was also presented to audiences at Cambridge, Columbia, Harvard, Princeton, Stanford, Toronto, and Yale Universities, as well as at the CUNY Graduate Center, the University of London, and the University of Wisconsin, Madison. I am deeply indebted to all who attended my talks for their advice and encouragement.

Much of the writing was accomplished during a year's sabbatical in 2015–2016, which I spent in part as a Visiting Fellow Commoner at Trinity College, Cambridge. I am deeply grateful to the Master and Fellows of my old college for hosting me so graciously, as well as to my dear friend Simon Goldhill for arranging a concurrent International Visiting Fellowship at the Centre for Research in the Arts, Social Sciences and Humanities.

For counsel and suggestions on particular aspects of the project, I am eager to thank the late Daniel Aaron, Bernard Bailyn, Teresa Bejan, Kenzie Bok, Chris Brooke, Greg Conti, Noah Feldman, Benjamin Friedman, Duncan Kelly, Tae Yeoun Keum, Adam Lebovitz, Jed Lewinsohn, Jeff McDonough, Sarah Mortimer, John Patty, Michael Sandel, James Simpson, Michael Sonenscher, Dennis Thompson, Michael Walzer, and Matt Weinzierl. A small group of friends read the entire manuscript, in some cases in multiple drafts, and served as crucial interlocutors throughout its composition. I am more grateful than I can say to Eric Beerbohm, Eric Gregory, James Hankins, Shirley Sarna, Quentin Skinner, Lucas Stanczyk, and Richard Tuck. Their influence can be felt on almost every page of this book.

Harvard University Press has once again treated me exceedingly well. My editor, Ian Malcolm, not only shepherded the manuscript through the publication process with characteristic skill and enthusiasm, but also offered crucial substantive suggestions along the way. I owe the title of the book to George Andreou, the director of the Press, who came up with it over Scotch one evening in Cambridge. My deepest thanks go to both of them, and to two anonymous referees, for their incredibly rich and constructive engagement with my argument. I am also grateful to Tweedy Flanigan for expert assistance with the proofs.

I must not close, however, without acknowledging the special contributions of two individuals. The late Patrick Riley was a valued colleague of mine during the final decade of his life, and I benefited enormously from the steady stream of handwritten notes about eighteenth-century philosophy and theology that he left in my mailbox over the years. It was Patrick, perhaps the greatest Leibniz scholar of the last half-century, who pushed me to think more seriously about this brilliant and misunderstood figure, and it pains me greatly that I was never able to show him the fruit of our exchanges. I like to think he would have approved.

Lastly, I owe an immense debt to my friend and colleague Michael Rosen. Michael walked into my office about ten years ago and asked me whether Milton was a Pelagian; this first exchange led to hundreds, and virtually every aspect of this book has been worked out in dialogue with him. Those familiar with the thrillingly revisionist reading of Kant's moral philosophy that Michael defends in his forthcoming monograph, *The Shadow of God,* will easily recognize the degree to which his ideas have stimulated my own reflections, particularly in Chapter 1. For all this, and much more, he has my deepest gratitude.

This book is dedicated to Andrew Stern, father of my two goddaughters, with whom I have been arguing about distributive justice since the ninth grade. His friendship makes theodicy seem more plausible.

Index